4HL, UK

ch Centre
3H9

tre 2002

ion data

velopment services in

K).

studies.

d Latin Ame
-8

gy Dev
elopi
to

PUBLISHING

RNATIONAL DEVELOPMENT RES
aro • Dakar • Montevideo • Nairobi

Published by ITDG Publishing
103–105 Southampton Row, London WC1B
www.itdgpublishing.org.uk

and the International Development Resear
PO Box 8500, Ottawa, ON, Canada K1G
www.idrc.ca

© International Development Research Cen

First published in 2002

ISBN 1 85339 494 7
ISBN 0 88936 986 0 (North America)

National Library of Canada cataloguing in publica

Kapila, Sunita

Building businesses with small producers: successful business de
Africa, Asia and Latin America

Co-published by ITDG Publishing (London, U
ISBN 0-88936-986-0

1.   Small business – Developing countries – Case studies.
2.   Small business – Developing countries – Management – Case
3.   Informal sector (Economics) – Developing countries.
4.   Non-governmental organizations – Developing countries.
5.   Economic development projects – Developing countries.
6.   Technical assistance – Developing countries.
7.   Developing countries – Economic conditions.
I.   Mead, Donald C., 1935–
II.   International Development Research Centre (Canada)
III. Title.
IV.   Title: Successful business development services in Africa, Asia an

HD2386.5K36 2002   338.6'42'091724   C2002-98002

ITDG Publishing is the publishing arm of the Intermediate Technolo
Group. Our mission is to build the skills and capacity of people in dev
through the dissemination of information in all forms, enabling them
quality of their lives and that of future generations.

The International Development Research Centre is a public corpora
the Parliament of Canada in 1970 to help developing countries use
technology to find practical, long-term solutions to the social, eco
environmental problems they face. Support is directed toward dev
indigenous research capacity to sustain policies and technologies devel
need to build healthier, more equitable, and more prosperous so

Typeset by Dorwyn Ltd, Rowlands Castle, Hants
Printed in Great Britain by Cambrian Printers Limited, Aberystwyth

Contents

Preface

THIS BOOK PRESENTS the findings and comparative analysis of seven case studies that were carried out under the research project 'Methodologies for the design and delivery of business development services for small producers'. The purpose of this project was to carry out an analysis of approaches to the design and delivery of various business development services (BDS) in developing countries and gain insight into how this can be done cost effectively, with high impact and sustainability.

The term 'business development services' refers to a range of non-financial services provided to micro- and small enterprises (MSEs) at various stages in their development, including before start-up. BDS focus on reducing poverty by raising the productivity and the incomes of small and microproducers and entrepreneurs. Contained within the broad concept of BDS are such activities as group training, individual counselling and advice, the development of new commercial entities, technology development and transfer, information provision, business links and policy advocacy. BDS are aimed at assisting MSEs to overcome internal and external constraints to their start-up, development and performance.

The International Development Research Centre (IDRC) supported research on seven BDS projects considered to be successful by their implementing agencies, five non-governmental organizations (NGOs): Intermediate Technology Development Group (UK), EnterpriseWorks Worldwide (USA), TechnoServe Inc. (USA), Mennonite Economic Development Associates (Canada) and Sarvodaya Sharmadana Sanamaya (Sri Lanka). These NGOs were IDRC's partners in this project and contributed significant in-kind support to the researchers. Representatives of IDRC, the partner NGOs and a resource person formed the project steering committee that guided the work of the researchers and engaged in the analysis presented in this book.

Three services were given particular attention in the case studies: marketing, access to technology, and acquisition of business and management skills. The researchers conducted the seven case studies guided by detailed terms of reference. The cases looked at the strategies and principal practices employed by the five NGOs in providing the BDS through a set of indicators to assess 'good practice' in terms of impact, cost effectiveness and sustainability. Some of the projects reviewed included private sector collaboration, or they began as NGO projects and evolved into private companies.

This IDRC research project addressed BDS delivery questions within a comparative framework. The comparative analysis of research findings focuses on eight key variables:

1. Specialization or diversification of services offered: do the projects examined in the case studies offer a range of services, or only one? If a project focuses on only particular services, are the others that are needed provided by the private sector or through other assistance programmes?
2. Specialization or diversification in sector(s) of activity: do the projects work with a particular product (for example, beans, or furniture), or with enterprises engaged in a diverse set of activities (for example, all MSEs in a particular locality)?
3. The roles that development NGOs and private providers play in service delivery: do these case studies show them to be changing over time? What are the reasons?
4. Nature of the BDS client – groups or individuals? How does client type affect service design and performance?
5. Poverty alleviation versus growth orientation: to what extent do the services address the challenge of poverty alleviation and to what extent does the intervention focus on the potential for growth? How are enterprises with growth potential identified?
6. Issues of scaling up: how did the seven projects studied in this project seek to optimize and broaden their impact?
7. Approaches to needs assessment: how were client needs factored into NGO programme design and service selection?
8. Flexibility of service response: how did the project change over its lifetime? In what ways did the project managers find it necessary to change their approach in response to evolving circumstances or to improved understanding of the needs of their clients?

The research findings that are presented in this book are intended to contribute to the ongoing BDS debate. It is a debate that has been prompted by the success to date in standardizing and commercializing microcredit programmes and by donors' interest in focusing their assistance on priority sectors not readily 'privatized'. Donor agencies have been considering the possibility of standardizing and commercializing the provision of non-financial BDS to existing and potential micro- and small entrepreneurs and businesses.

We hope the case studies that follow and the discourse on each will throw light on issues such as the development and implementation of BDS performance assessment; alternatives in BDS design and delivery; BDS and credit relationships; and subsidized and commercial provision of BDS.

This research project, the analysis of its findings and their presentation in this book would not have been possible without the unstinting work and support over four years of the project steering committee. Members of this committee were Anura Atapattu, Brent Herbert-Copley, Eric Hyman, Steve Londner, Donald Mead, Julie Redfern and Andrew Scott. Special thanks go to Mike Albu, Jonathan Dawson, Pam Fehr, Eric Hyman, Steve Londner, Donald Mead and Sandra Yu, all of whom stuck it out through the various case study redrafts, providing fresh, valuable insights every time. I am also extremely grateful to the field staff of the five partner NGOs who made their offices, projects and data so readily available to the researchers. The first two years (1998 and 1999) of this study were coordinated by Kenneth Loucks of Dev-21 Consulting Ltd and the last two (2000 and 2001) by myself. Thanks to Bill Carman of IDRC and Helen Marsden and Ginny Gilmore of ITDG Publishing for actually bringing this book to print. Helen van Houten did the technical editing of this work with great patience and good humour. To each and every one of you, sincere thanks.

Sunita Kapila
Nairobi, Kenya
October 2001

Contributors

Sunita Kapila has worked in international development for over two decades, especially in small enterprise development in South Asia and Africa. She has worked in the areas of women's informal income generation, the acquisition of employable and entrepreneurial skills, strengthening of micro- and small entrepreneurs' associations, and urban governance. She has worked both as a staff member and as a consultant with non-governmental organizations and donor agencies.

Donald Mead has over 40 years of experience as a development economist, including several long-term assignments in eastern and southern Africa. For the past 22 years, as professor of agricultural economics at Michigan State University, he has concentrated on prospects and problems of small enterprises and the design of effective interventions for the support of such enterprises.

Jonathan Dawson has been a consultant for 15 years, specializing in the design and delivery of business development services for small-scale producers in Africa and Asia. He is also involved as a teacher and consultant in the promotion of sustainable community development in the industrialized world and is an adviser to the Global Ecovillage Network (GEN) – Europe.

Pamela Fehr is technical adviser and consultant in microenterprise development at Mennonite Economic Development Associates (MEDA). She has worked in design and delivery of BDS marketing programmes in Bolivia, Haiti, Nicaragua and Peru. She is currently based in Port-au-Prince, Haiti, where she is focusing on institutional strengthening for MEDA's rural credit programme, which targets small producers.

Eric L. Hyman, currently with the African Development Foundation, was previously chief of program evaluation at EnterpriseWorks Worldwide. Dr Hyman has 22 years of experience in microenterprise development, economic appraisal, monitoring and evaluation, appropriate technologies and environmental impact assessment. He has worked in 23 developing countries and published two books and 73 journal articles.

Heather Rawlinson worked as an intern with the Mennonite Economic Development Associates (MEDA) in Bolivia in 1998 and 1999, and later worked in the Canadian Red Cross as the International Program Associate on the Americas Program (2000 to 2001). She recently returned to Bolivia to work with a local organization on projects for homeless children.

Lisa Stosch is the senior adviser for the Evaluation Unit at EnterpriseWorks Worldwide in Washington, D.C. Ms Stosch has worked with microenterprise development for over 14 years, specializing in monitoring and evaluation, and financial and programme management. She currently manages the Impact Tracking System, which gauges the effects of 28 projects in 17 countries. She has co-written and published several annual reports and program brochures for EnterpriseWorks.

Sandra O. Yu specializes in small enterprise and informal sector support, with focus on business and institutional development. She has been involved in research, community development and training and has worked in Asia, Africa and the Caribbean. Her work has been published by the ILO, in the *Labour Education* Journal, UN Economic and Social Affairs, International Institute of Rural Reconstruction, and as editorial columns in Philippine newspapers.

Acronyms and abbreviations

ADB	Agricultural Development Bank of Ghana
ADRA	Adventist Development and Relief Agency
AFC	Agricultural Finance Corporation (Zimbabwe)
AgENT	USAID-funded agency in Sri Lanka
AGRITEX	Agricultural Technical and Extension Services (Zimbabwe)
ANACAFE	Asociación Nacional del Café (National Coffee Association of Guatemala)
ASOFAM	Asociación Nacional de Fabricantes Artesanos de Muebles (National Association of Artisan Furniture Makers) (Bolivia)
ASOHABA	Asociación de Productores de Haba (Association of Broad Bean Producers) (Bolivia)
ASOMEX	ASOPROF/MEDA Export Company (Bolivia)
ASOPROF	Asociación Nacional de Productores de Frijol (National Association of Bean Producers) (Bolivia)
ASPECAGUA	Asociación de Pequeños Caficultores de Guatemala (Association of Small-Scale Coffee Producers of Guatemala)
ATDP	Agro-based Industries and Technology Development Project (Bangladesh)
ATI	Appropriate Technology International (former name of EnterpriseWorks Worldwide)
ATZ	Appropriate Technology Zimbabwe
BA	business adviser
BDS	business development services
BDT	Bangladesh taka
BODC	Bangladesh Organization for Development Cooperation
BRDB	Bangladesh Rural Development Board
CCCH	Central de Cooperativas Cafetaleras de Honduras (Coffee Cooperative Center of Honduras)
CEFE	Competency-based Economies through Formation of Entrepreneurs (GTZ programme)
CENCAFES	Central de Cooperativas de Caficultores de El Salvador (Coffee Cooperative Center of El Salvador)
CIDA	Canadian International Development Agency
COMERCAFE	Comercializadora Regional de Café (Regional Coffee Marketing Company) (El Salvador)
CSC	Consejo Salvadoreño de Café (Salvadorean Coffee Council)
DFID	Department for International Development (UK)
DTC	Development Technology Centre of the University of Zimbabwe
FACN	Fédération des Associations des Caféières Natives (Federation of Native Coffee Farmer Associations in Haiti)
FAO	Food and Agriculture Organization of the United Nations
FASCOM	Farmers' Service Company (Ghana)
FASCU	Farmers' Service Multipurpose Co-operative Union (Ghana)
FEDEAGRO	Federación de Asociaciones Agropecuarias (Federation of Associations of Agricultural Producers) (Bolivia)
FFPED	Forum for Food Processing Enterprise Development
GECLOF	Ghana Ecumenical Church Loan Fund
GHC	Ghanaian cedi

GIF	Global Investment Fund (a division of MEDA)
GTZ	Deutsche Gesellschaft für Zusammenarbeit (German Technical Cooperation)
IAE	Institute of Agricultural Engineering (Zimbabwe)
ICP	Inventory Credit Programme
IDB	Inter-American Development Bank
IDRC	International Development Research Centre
ITDG	Intermediate Technology Development Group
ITDG-B	Intermediate Technology Development Group–Bangladesh
LJSSS	Lanka Jathika Sarvodaya Shramadana Sanamaya
LKR	Sri Lanka rupee
MEDA	Mennonite Economic Development Associates
MIDAS	Microenterprise Development Assistance Service (Ghana)
MIP	Microenterprise Innovation Project (USAID-funded global programme)
MoFA	Ministry of Food and Agriculture (Ghana)
MSE	micro- and small enterprise
MTI	Management Training Institute (Sri Lanka)
MUS	Mouchas Unnayan Sangstha (organization involved in bee culture)
NARA	National Aquarium Research Agency (Sri Lanka)
NGO	non-governmental organization
PEP	Productive Employment Project (Bangladesh)
PRISMA	El Programa de Incentivos y Soportes a las Microempresas (Microenterprise Incentives and Support Programme – former MEDA programme)
PROCAFE	Fundación Salvadoreña para Investigaciones del Café (Salvadorean Foundation for Coffee Research)
PROCOR	Proyecto de Comercialización Rural (Rural Marketing Project – a CIDA-funded project MEDA is carrying out)
PRODECOOP	Promotora de Desarrollo Cooperativo (Promoter of Cooperative Development in Nicaragua)
RAM	Rural Associated Manufacturers Pvt. Ltd (Zimbabwe)
REDS	Rural Enterprise Development Services (a division of SEEDS)
REP	Rural Enterprises Programme (a division of SEEDS)
RESP	Rural Employment Sector Programme (Bangladesh)
SECID	South-East Consortium for International Development
SEEDS	Sarvodaya Economic Enterprises Development Services
SEM	Sistemas Empresariales de Mesoamérica (Business Systems of Central America)
TCC	Technology Consultancy Centre, Kumasi, Ghana
UCAFES	Unión de Cooperativas de Cafetaleros de El Salvador (Union of El Salvador Coffee Farmer Cooperatives)
UCRAPROBEX	Unión de Cooperativas de la Reforma Agraria de Productores, Beneficiadores y Exportadores del Café (Union of Cooperatives of Agrarian Reform Producers, Processors and Exporters in El Salvador)
USAID	United States Agency for International Development
VERC	Village Education Resource Centre (Bangladesh)
VIP	Village Infrastructure Project (World Bank project)
WUSC	World University Service of Canada
ZOPP	ZOPP Pvt. Ltd

1 Introduction

JONATHAN DAWSON, SUNITA KAPILA, DONALD MEAD[1]

Research context: The business development services debate

IN RECENT YEARS, increasing attention has been devoted to business development services (BDS) for micro- and small enterprises (MSEs), recognizing that credit alone is not enough to result in sustainable increases in productivity and income. 'Business development services' refers to support other than credit. Non-financial services include training; giving technical and managerial assistance; developing, adapting and promoting new technology; assessing markets and giving marketing support; providing a physical infrastructure; and advocating policy.

Many early business development services were in the form of training provided with microcredit by a microfinance entity. This training was driven by supply rather than demand and was often required as a condition for a loan. These early BDS projects were often characterized by high cost per client, limited outreach and impact, and low cost recovery, needing continued donor subsidy.

The past decade has seen important developments and innovations in the design and delivery of business development services in an attempt to make them more cost effective and sustainable. Some of these innovations drew on the experience of the microcredit pioneers. Three aspects of the microcredit experience have proved especially valuable. First, microcredit schemes built on existing informal credit and savings practices among the poor. They strengthened, rather than replaced, traditional systems. Second, they demonstrated that low-income people could pay commercial interest rates on loans. Good practice could prompt repayment rates of 95 per cent or more. The best microfinance programmes showed they could be sustainable. Third, the minimalist credit model was demand driven because it left decisions on loan use to the entrepreneurs. All three principles have affected recent developments in business development service design and delivery.

Systems theory has also been important in forming new ideas for the design and delivery of BDS initiatives. Subsector analysis or value chain analysis has been a core tool in new BDS approaches. These approaches help to identify 1) sectors in which large numbers of entrepreneurs are active, 2) bottlenecks or constraints on the economic development of these entrepreneurs, and 3) measures to remove these constraints.

Evidence is growing that recent BDS innovations have in fact improved impact and outreach, improved cost effectiveness and enhanced

1

sustainability. However, a clear picture has yet to emerge about the precise nature of these achievements and the key factors underlying them. Several recent initiatives have sought to throw light on these questions.

In 1995, the Committee of Donor Agencies for Small Enterprise Development agreed on a framework for donor support of microfinance. The framework proved influential in encouraging donors to support microfinance programmes that were moving toward more businesslike approaches and greater cost recovery. In 1997, this committee turned its attention to the more complex task of reaching agreement on good practices for providing non-financial services to small enterprises.

The committee sponsored regional conferences in Harare (1998), Rio de Janeiro (1999) and Hanoi (2000) to discuss ways to achieve greater outreach, cost effectiveness, impact and sustainability of business development services. In late 2000, it released a set of guidelines called 'Business development services for small enterprises: guidelines for donor intervention'. These guidelines emphasized developing vibrant private sector markets for BDS and urged donors to offer subsidies for activities that help to develop the capacity of private providers of BDS.

In response to questions being raised in the donor and practitioner debate on BDS for small enterprises, the International Development Research Centre (IDRC) of Canada developed a collaborative research initiative with five major NGOs in early 1998. The research focused on methodologies for the design and delivery of high-impact, cost-effective business development services for small producers. This global project drew on experience from Africa, Latin America and Asia and described factors that appear important in good BDS design and delivery. This book presents the findings of this research initiative.

Research partners

IDRC provided funding to bring together representatives of five major NGOs engaged in providing business development services to small producers, and covered the research expenses. The NGOs provided substantial in-kind support for the studies. Each NGO identified projects that they felt represented 'good practice' in providing BDS to small producers. Case studies were commissioned, examining seven projects in detail. Independent consultants hired by IDRC did most of the studies.

The case studies were reviewed by a steering committee, which included a resource person and representatives from IDRC and the five partner NGOs. Since the steering committee included BDS practitioners, considerable attention was given to project design and management, as mistakes can often occur at the design stage. On the other hand, one main finding of the case studies is that good business development support is evolutionary in nature, modifying in response to changing circumstances as well as a changing understanding of the needs and opportunities for the clients.

Five NGOs participated in the project:

- EnterpriseWorks Worldwide, a not-for-profit development assistance organization whose mission is to generate economic growth and alleviate poverty through business development programmes. Its headquarters are in Washington, D.C., with field offices in Africa, Asia and Latin America. EnterpriseWorks supports local partners and small-scale producers of agricultural and other commodities to build more competitive enterprises.
- Intermediate Technology Development Group (ITDG), an agency that works to provide practical answers to poverty. Founded in 1966 by economist Dr E.F. Schumacher (author of *Small Is Beautiful*), its vision is of a more equitable and just world in which technology enriches and benefits the lives of poor people in a sustainable way. ITDG, through its offices in seven countries in Africa, Asia and South America, concentrates its efforts on research and facilitating technical change and on building knowledge and skills, particularly among small-scale producers.
- Mennonite Economic Development Associates (MEDA), an association of Christians committed to applying biblical teachings in the marketplace. It promotes developing business for the benefit of the disadvantaged of low-income countries and in partnership with them. MEDA works in Latin America, the Caribbean, Africa and Asia, developing pilot projects and programmes that establish businesses by providing credit, business training and interventions addressing production and marketing barriers.
- Sarvodaya Shramadana Sanamaya, a Buddhist voluntary organization in Sri Lanka. Its programme of economic support is implemented by Sarvodaya Economic Enterprise Development Services (SEEDS). This comprises three specialist units: the Rural Enterprises Programme, the Management Training Institute, and the Rural Enterprise Development Services (REDS).
- TechnoServe, which focuses on low-income rural people, helping them to build commercial skills and create and strengthen local businesses and commercial activities. TechnoServe works in Africa, Latin America and Poland. Its current business development services focus on private sector market links, business planning and operations, and entrepreneurial development.

Case study characteristics

Much recent donor debate has focused on the need to develop vibrant BDS markets. This discussion has assumed the existence of discrete small enterprises, often urban, making decisions on the services they wish to purchase.

Services are seen as being delivered separately and not as a diversified package.

That model is unquestionably valuable. But the case studies in this book suggest there are small enterprises (or prospective small enterprises) where that approach, for several reasons, does not apply. First of these reasons is that in several of the case studies, the 'enterprise' is not clearly defined. It is one among many livelihood strategies used by poor households. The ornamental fish farmers of Sri Lanka, the oil press entrepreneurs in Zimbabwe and the grain farmers of Ghana, for example, all had various sources of income. The unit of analysis for identifying opportunities and constraints was not the individual enterprise but the subsector. The BDS were aimed at changing systems and institutions to benefit subsector participants rather than individual enterprises. Second, many implementing agencies delivered a package of assistance, involving several different BDS and also in several cases included credit. Third, in these case studies, an NGO played a key role in identifying and initiating the project. Moreover, even in those cases where independent and financially self-sustaining institutions were created by the project, the NGO had a long-term supporting role. Recent discussions on small enterprise development assume that NGOs should have only a short-term, facilitative role. Fourth, a primary concern of all these projects was promoting entrepreneurial activity among the rural poor, in many cases including groups and clusters of microentrepreneurs.

It is from these enterprises that the current case studies were drawn. They focus on the opportunity for many microentrepreneurs, or for farmers still limited to primary production, to move into higher-value processing or manufacturing. However, they also recognize the inability of many of these microentrepreneurs to pay for the services that add value.

Case study projects

The projects reviewed in the case studies started from identified market opportunities. In most cases, these opportunities were tied to subsectors perceived to offer good prospects for small enterprise income and employment, and the assistance was carefully designed such that client enterprises could take advantage of these particular market opportunities. The support services offered were not all-purpose business development services. Seven case studies were chosen for analysis:

EnterpriseWorks Worldwide's *El Salvador Small-scale Coffee Producers Project*. This initiative was to help smallholder coffee farmers in El Salvador increase the volume and value of the coffee they grew. The project did this by helping farmer cooperatives to provide extension services, upgrade or build processing facilities, improve quality control, and access more profitable markets. The project also operated a revolving credit fund for small farmers.

EnterpriseWorks Worldwide's *Zimbabwe oil press project* sought to build a new industry – small, rural oilseed processing in Zimbabwe. Project activities included developing and disseminating five oil press models; producing and distributing improved planting seed; training manufacturers, repair artisans and new oil-processing enterprise managers; establishing commercial systems to distribute oil presses and peanut butter mills; and, in the early stages, providing credit to promote purchasing the new processing equipment.

ITDG's *food processing project in Bangladesh* aimed to help very poor people, mainly women, establish small enterprises to process foods for sale in local markets. The Bangladesh project provided training in production technology and simple business management and transferred training capacity to other indigenous NGOs.

ITDG's *light-engineering project in Zimbabwe* sought to increase the availability of tools and equipment for small manufacturing enterprises. In addition to working with small-scale engineers to increase domestic capacity to manufacture new and appropriate machines, the project helped to establish marketing systems through which these capital goods could be bought or hired by small enterprises.

MEDA's *ASOMEX project in Bolivia* provided marketing services to link small farmers with export markets for their products, with a focus on edible beans.

SEEDS's *ornamental fish project in Sri Lanka* helped small-scale producers to establish and operate ponds to raise ornamental fish and linked these small producers with traders who purchased the fish for export, with smaller amounts for sale in the local market.

TechnoServe's cereal storage, processing and marketing project in Ghana helped small-scale farmers to increase the benefits they received from their crops by improving grain marketing. It permitted participating farmers to store grain, either for later consumption or later sale, when prices were more favourable than at harvest.

Case study terms of reference

The terms of reference for the case studies included the following:

- a description of the business development services delivered; although the projects had diverse services, the case studies focused on three: marketing, acquisition of business and management skills and access to technology
- management of the project, with attention to its planning, organization, supervision, monitoring and evaluation
- the approach of the project in measuring cost effectiveness, impact, and sustainability

- an analysis of relationships between the design and delivery of the business development services and the performance
- lessons to be learned from the case study, with observations on aspects of design and delivery worthy of emulation.

A principal goal was to identify success factors for the projects under review – the characteristics that contributed to favourable results of the projects. Eight major issues were addressed in the analysis of the design and implementation of the projects:

- specialization versus diversification of services offered
- specialization versus diversification in products or sectors
- roles that NGOs and private providers played in service delivery
- groups or individual business service clients
- poverty alleviation versus growth orientation
- scaling-up issues
- approaches to needs assessment
- evolution and flexibility of service response.

Lack of a common method among the different participating NGOs for assessing impact made comparisons across projects extremely difficult. Indeed, in several cases the lack of rigorous data collection and analysis made even simple benefit/cost calculations impossible. Nonetheless, the case studies were able to identify and quantify the key achievements resulting from the business development services and describe how these services worked.

Note

1 Although the authors jointly wrote this chapter, they drew on discussions with and contributions by Anura Atapattu, Pamela Fehr, Eric Hyman, Steve Londner, Julie Redfern, Andrew Scott and Sandra Yu.

2 Food processing to promote sustainable livelihoods in Bangladesh

SANDRA O. YU

Introduction

THE INTERMEDIATE TECHNOLOGY DEVELOPMENT GROUP (ITDG) promotes food processing to help the rural poor in developing countries to secure sustainable livelihoods. This is part of ITDG's goal to build the technical skills of poor people in developing countries to improve their lives.

In Africa, Asia and Latin America, ITDG has provided support in food production, energy, building materials, transport, manufacturing and food processing using the principles of appropriate technology. ITDG provides technical assistance to small-scale producers and non-governmental and government organizations through training, information dissemination, research, market identification, policy advocacy and networking.

ITDG began operating in Bangladesh in the early 1980s, but the ITDG–Bangladesh (ITDG-B) programme was not formally established until 1990. ITDG-B provides technical assistance to small producers and local organizations, including training, product research and development, disseminating information, networking and policy advocacy.

It focuses its work on the poorest and most marginalized people, which in Bangladesh includes the following:

- the functionally landless
- peasants with less than 0.02 acre landholdings[1]
- divorced or widowed women, the most vulnerable in Bangladesh society
- those having a very low income (less than BDT 200 or US$4 per month)[2].

As part of its commitment to reach the poorest of the poor, ITDG-B has focused much of its activity in the Greater Faridpur District, one of the least developed districts. Here it works in food processing, food production, manufacturing and small-enterprise development.

ITDG-B has a staff of 35. The food processing unit has four staff: manager, project officer, food technologist and programme assistant. The programme's average annual budget is £78 000 (for 1999 to 2002). It is funded by DFID (50 per cent), the national lottery (40 per cent) and ITDG-B's own revenues (10 per cent). The food processing programme itself accounts for nearly 35 per cent of the ITDG-B total programme budget, or, if food production is included, 68 to 70 per cent. ITDG-B works with 80 development organizations all over the country.

After a 1989 study looked at the different subsectors within food processing, local organizations and ITDG-B selected three subsectors on which to focus: rice processing, *gur* (brown sugar) manufacturing and food processing. ITDG-B introduced its food processing programme in 1990. Over time, it specifically promoted processing snack foods, fruits and vegetables, and phased out rice and *gur* processing.[3]

Food processing to promote sustainable livelihoods

Food processing benefits

ITDG believes that food processing could help the rural poor in Bangladesh, especially women, who are among the most disadvantaged. Food processing often requires only a little capital and can use local produce. It is an activity in which women, who may be culturally restricted to their homes, can engage.

Many Bangladeshi women, ITDG-B found, were already processing rice and making snack foods. Building on their own know-how, women could increase their household income by using local resources to process foodstuff. The Food and Agriculture Organization (FAO) has pointed out that the value realized from processing and marketing farm products can surpass primary production (FAO 1995). Preserving food stretches the utility and productivity of farm produce, which is often wasted during peak seasons but scarce during lean seasons. Food processing helps to make food available during lean seasons and helps to stabilize household income.

Food processing can serve several development objectives for households: increased income, greater savings, food security and better nutrition (ITDG 1999). Agro processing in the broad sense is important to the national economy, having shown a purported 32 per cent annual growth in past years (*Bangladesh Economic Review* 1995). While large companies have now entered the snack food market, small producers serve local markets and boost local economies.

Constraints

While small-scale food processing offers numerous opportunities for improving livelihoods, several constraints that hamper development need to be addressed. A major one is that large companies have begun producing myriad processed foods, including snacks, pickles, jelly and jam. While 20 years ago no large companies produced *channa chur* (a traditional product made of fried noodles, nuts and spices, similar to 'Bombay mix'), the Bangladesh Rural Development Board (BRDB) reported that by April 2000 approximately ten large companies were manufacturing it.

Another problem is that small producers have limited know-how in the technology of preparing food products. When ITDG-B started its programme in 1989, few Bangladeshi organizations had researched and documented food technology. Furthermore, what documentation and recipes existed were written in English and were therefore inaccessible even to NGO workers.

A number of other concerns that inhibit small-scale food processing in Bangladesh (ITDG 1998) need to be addressed by the project:

- There is a significant difference between having the ability to produce for home consumption and establishing a small business based on this product. A range of skills (both technical and business) is needed to make the transition from home production to the running of a small-scale enterprise.
- Linked to this is the ability to locate and target markets. This is a dynamic sector. Rural producers need to learn how to monitor change, develop markets and sell their products. Know-how in selling and locating wider markets was a common limitation.
- Consumer perception is an important issue faced by small-scale processors. There is a common perception that foods produced by small-scale operators are unhygienic and unsafe. This may be somewhat true but is commonly exaggerated. Nonetheless, processors need to be more conscious of hygiene, quality and consistency in food handling, including dangers of adulteration.
- Lack of access to raw materials, appropriate equipment and packaging materials are obstacles that small-scale processors frequently face.
- Access to credit is lacking. Many of the small-scale processors belong to the most marginalized sector of the population and do not have disposable income. To enable them to put their skills into practice, most need access to credit to purchase equipment and raw materials.
- They also lack access to appropriate and timely information on a range of topics. To compete effectively, small-scale food processors need reliable technological information and information on suppliers and prices of materials, equipment and packaging, and marketing information.
- Recording transactions is a problem because of low literacy. In the 1990s, only 34.4 per cent of Bangladesh's population was literate. Literacy among women was 25.5 per cent. In rural areas it was as low as 13 per cent (BBS 1999).

Development organizations in Bangladesh involved in food processing often focused more on products and inputs and less on markets. In 1996, ITDG-B asked these organizations about the difficulties their beneficiaries encountered. Most problems were market related: competition with large companies, inconsistent quality, inferior packaging and labelling, marketing and selling, insufficient access to quality raw materials, and lack of confidence among consumers in products of small-scale producers (Azami et al. 1996; Chowdhury and Azami 1996).

Market and beneficiary needs

A study was commissioned at the programme's outset to review food processing in Bangladesh. It also assessed the market and the potential of each activity (Chowdhury and Sarker 1989).[4] The following crops were found to have good processing prospects: paddy, jute, wheat, sugar cane, pulses, oilseeds, cotton, tobacco, fruits, vegetables, potatoes, spices, tea, rubber and silk. Snack foods were considered secondary food processing. Some interesting findings included the following:

- Many crops were produced throughout the year. Yet because the farms and production were small, the volume of crops that could be processed was smaller than the capacity of even the smallest machines. In 1996, for example, 52.85 per cent of holdings were small, 0.05 to 2.49 acres. Medium-sized farm holdings, 2.5 to 7.49 acres, made up 11.65 per cent, and large holdings were only 1.67 per cent (BBS 1999).
- Most crops, except jute and tea, were produced for the local market, but production was still less than the country's total demand. Some crops, therefore, were imported.
- Crop processing could provide employment for women and the rural poor. However, without appropriate equipment, modern capital-intensive production could overrun the industry and displace women and landless workers.

ITDG-B organized a national workshop where it presented the study results. Over 30 development organizations attended. It was determined that while some development organizations were involved in food processing, they were not proficient in handling the commercial aspects of their work. This often resulted in unviable products and continued dependency on subsidies.

During this meeting, snack foods were identified as a focus, along with rice and sugar cane products. This meeting also determined that there was a need to train fieldworkers on how to make snack foods so that they could guide beneficiaries in running food processing businesses. Post-workshop consultations with development organizations emphasized the need to train fieldworkers further in establishing sustainable small-scale food processing businesses, particularly since the business orientation of these organizations and their staff was inadequate. When ITDG-B looked at existing suppliers of technology and training, it found that the existing training courses were oriented towards large-scale operations.

Programme components

ITDG-B's food processing programme provides training, technology research and development, networking, policy advocacy and information dissemination.

Training

The main type of training is in food processing, conducted as a 15-day field-worker training course and as short courses on specific food products. The 15-day training course is now held annually, although from 1990 to 1996 it was held twice a year. It includes ten days of technology training in food products and five days of business management training (see topics listed in Table 2.1). Trainees learn how to process *channa chur*, *murally* (a sweetened dry bread stick), doughnuts, pickles (made from green chilli, garlic, *brinjal*), chutney, pulses, *muri* (puffed rice), jams and jellies, banana chips, vermicelli, milk toffee, tomato ketchup, cheese, coconut balls and dried fish. Food topics chosen depend on what the participants request.

Table 2.1 Topics in the ITDG-B 15-day fieldworker training course

Food technology topics	Business topics
Food and nutrition	Sales, cost, profit
Food processing techniques (jam, jelly, *channa chur*, pickles)	Stocks, accounts
	Depreciation costs
Causes of food spoilage	Balance sheet: liabilities, assets
Food preservation	Break-even analysis
Hygiene	Cash-flow forecasting
Quality control	Costing and pricing
Raw material preparation	Bookkeeping
Packaging	Market survey
	Business plan writing and finalization

These training courses are usually held near a participating organization. This has increased the ITDG-B outreach and its understanding of local conditions. Partner organizations initiate short courses, to which ITDG-B staff are invited as speakers. These courses span three to ten days and cover mainly food technology training.

Twelve training courses for fieldworkers have been completed (Table 2.2). Around 145 fieldworkers from approximately 80 organizations have been trained. Each fieldworker has trained from 20 to 125 beneficiaries (60 beneficiaries average per trainer). Approximately 21 per cent of those trained have set up food processing businesses (Azami et al. 1996).

In 1997, ITDG-B began charging the sponsoring organization BDT 3000 per participant for the annual training. It estimates that each annual training course costs BDT 60 000. From a class of 15 to 17 people, ITDG-B receives around BDT 45 000 to BDT 50 000. The requesting NGO sponsors the short courses, and ITDG-B does not charge the NGO for its experts, treating its technical input as a grant.

11

Table 2.2 Annual food processing training (1990–99)

Date	Venue	Participating fieldworkers (no.)	Organizations represented (no.)
November 1990	VERC, Savar	14	9
August 1991	FIVDB, Sylhet	10	5
February 1992	FIVDB, Sylhet	12	6
August 1992	Proshika Central Training Centre, Manikganj	10	7
May 1993	ITDG-B Office, Dhaka	7	3
October 1993	VERC, Savar	11	5
May 1994	Uttaran, Satkhira	16	10
November 1994	Barisal Development Society, Barisal	10	8
June 1995	Comilla Proshika, Comilla	13	7
September 1997	VERC, Savar	10	7
November 1998	Prayas, Dinajpur	15	9
November 1999	Gono Unnayan Kendra, Gaibandha	17	13
	Total	145	

Food product technology

ITDG-B identifies and tests the food products that it plans to promote. It has a small laboratory for testing and improving recipes and has some 50 to 60 recipes on hand. Since 1997, the laboratory has developed some 10 to 12 products. New technology and recipes are sought, and consultants are at times hired to supply recipes for specific products. Some products have been discovered in the field, since traditional foods in Bangladesh have rarely been documented. Food items that can be produced in Bangladesh are further developed in the ITDG-B laboratory.

The food processing unit spends approximately one week each month researching and improving recipes. Its laboratory has a micrometer, refractrometer, oven, micro-oven, and protein-content tester – all valued at around BDT 24 000. It may also occasionally test food made by the beneficiaries. Food is tested for moisture, acid and protein. Achieving a standard on these counts is desirable when tapping city markets, and is crucial when venturing into the international market. After the testing, the unit elicits feedback from the NGOs, fieldworkers and trainees on what further improvements are needed to the products.

ITDG-B also designs packaging materials and contracts out their production. In special cases it designs and produces equipment; it has produced a tomato and fruit crushing machine and three sets of *channa chur* equipment, which were all given to partner organizations. The *channa chur* equipment makes a product of a size different from that normally found – possibly for differentiation in the market. The small fruit-crushing machine is the only one in Bangladesh, created after an ITDG-B partner organization saw a similar one in Sri Lanka.

Although the *channa chur* equipment is available in public markets, ITDG-B manufactured several units to save the partner organizations the trouble of finding them and to save on cost. The cost of producing them, according to ITDG-B, is half the market price. Since glass containers for food products are not readily available, ITDG-B helps to produce glass bottles by manufacturing the moulds. The bottles bear the ITDG-B name, and ITDG-B hopes that its name will attract buyers to the beneficiary products. However, as it does not match this intent with quality control, it runs the risk of besmirching its name if substandard or spoiled foods are bottled. The bottles are sold at cost to some of the ITDG-B partner organizations. Table 2.3 shows the cost of producing the equipment and the glass containers.

Table 2.3   Cost of equipment and glass containers for packaging produced by ITDG-B

Equipment		Glass containers			
Fruit-crushing equipment = BDT	73 500	BOTTLE – cost of dies		PLASTIC CAP – cost of dies	
Materials and labour =	72 000	small =	BDT 3500	small =	BDT 850
ITDG-B staff time for design =	1500	medium =	4000	medium/large =	1500
		large =	4000		
Channa chur equipment =	2000	Cost of bottle manufactured by contractor			
Materials and labour =	2000	(in BDT per bottle, including plastic cap, excluding			
		depreciation cost of dies)			
		small =	BDT 5.25		
		medium =	7.50		
		large =	8.50		

Networking

ITDG-B has helped to form a network of partner organizations, called the Forum for Food Processing Enterprise Development (FFPED), to facilitate communication among the many development organizations involved in small-scale food processing. FFPED is a venue for participants to meet and exchange experiences, determine the needs of the industry, and lobby for policies beneficial to small food processors. ITDG-B intends to reduce its role as local organizations become more active.

FFPED has 40 NGO members, represented by their fieldworkers. The network is headed by a central executive committee that meets once a month. To be more effective, FFPED has divided its membership into two regional chapters and plans to establish two more. The two regional networks are in Netrokona and Gaibandha; the two additional regional networks will be in Barisal and Dinajpur.

FFPED has held workshops and plans to link with large companies and arrange regular visits among fieldworkers. It has organized two workshops in which the participants, who were fieldworkers and small-scale producers, identified the needs of the small-scale food industry and determined a plan of action. To ensure small-producer representation and to prevent NGO field-workers from dominating in the workshops, FFPED made a point of having twice as many small food processors participate as fieldworkers.

Forum members plan jointly to obtain low-cost equipment for packaging, link with credit organizations, compile laws and policies that affect the sector, and facilitate the application of members for government approval of food products. Members realize that a network can achieve more than they could on their own.

Policy advocacy

Since small producers need to know the applicable laws and standards, ITDG-B plans to study current policies on food certification, marketing and tariffs. It hopes it can also identify key local and international policies that affect small food processors. Already, ITDG-B has educated small food processors on product safety. By the end of the project, ITDG-B and local stakeholders hope to articulate policy alternatives and to take well-informed positions. Public attitudes need to change as well, mainly the common perception that products made by small food processors are unhygienic and unsafe.

Information dissemination

ITDG-B has produced illustrated booklets for fieldworkers and beneficiaries, written in Bangla and detailing how to prepare a specific product. These booklets are sold at cost to NGOs. Eighteen booklets have been published on different processed foods, each with a 3000-copy run. Approximately 60 per cent of the copies have been sold. The sale price of BDT 15 per copy covers only the printing cost, which is about BDT 12. The 18 booklets cover making the following products:

- *amra* (hog-plum chutney)
- banana chips
- *channa chur* (Bombay mix)
- cheese
- coconut balls
- garlic pickle
- green chilli pickle
- green mango chutney
- guava jelly
- *kashundi* (mustard)
- *mango morrabba* (sweetened mango preserve)
- milk toffee

- olive chutney
- olive pickle (sour-hot-sweet)
- pineapple jelly
- shiny-coloured coconut balls
- tamarind chutney
- tomato ketchup.

ITDG-B's small enterprise unit has published a business start-up booklet called 'Income-generating activity profiles', written in Bangla. It is a step-by-step guide on how to start a business and contains tips on costing, marketing, and calculating profit and loss. It also contains testimonials about the advantages and disadvantages of the business. Similar 'IGA profiles' have been written on how to start a *channa chur* business and a *chatpoti* (vegetable salad) business.

ITDG-B has also published articles in a Bangla journal, *Falak*, and in international journals such as the UK-based *Food Chain* and *Appropriate Technology*. Through such articles, ITDG-B shares its technology and discusses policies locally and internationally.

Monitoring and evaluation

ITDG-B mainly monitors and evaluates its training programme. It realizes, however, the need to evaluate its information dissemination and networking activities as well.

Partner organizations are monitored first through the fieldworkers during the annual training session. Participant experience is evaluated during and after the training. Participants are asked what they learned most in each day and which teaching techniques worked best and which least well.

Three ITDG-B staff visit partner organizations about four times a year. During these 12 to 14 visits, which reach about 40 to 50 per cent of the 80 partner organizations, they discuss technical and business concerns and beneficiaries' progress. Expenses incurred during each field visit are approximately BDT 5000, including transport and allowances.

Beneficiaries are also visited. ITDG-B recently began administering a baseline questionnaire enquiring into beneficiary operations, including raw material sources, equipment owned, packaging, hygiene, market information, financing, record-keeping, revenue and profit.

In-depth reviews are done mid-term and at the end of a project by an external consultant and ITDG staff, including the programme manager. During the programme's first phase, 1990–96, evaluations were conducted in 1993 and 1996. The second phase of the programme, 1998 to 2002, underwent a mid-term evaluation in 2000. Surveys are conducted for trainers and for beneficiaries. The survey for trainers covers the usefulness of the training course, suggestions to improve the course, teaching quality, support needed, problems that beneficiaries face, suitability of food products, support received by trainers, number of people trained or advised, and businesses established.

The beneficiary survey establishes beneficiaries and non-beneficiaries in food and non-food businesses and enquires into demographics, years in operation, food products, raw material sources, equipment, packaging, health and safety, marketing and profitability. Results are compared between beneficiaries and non-beneficiaries. The survey analyses the programme's impact and benefit/cost performance, covering mainly the annual training.

Partner organizations and programme approaches

Three active partners among the 80 local development organizations with which ITDG-B works were visited and interviewed in depth for this study. These organizations illustrate different approaches in promoting food processing activities. The first provided integrated support to individual enterprises, the second established NGO-owned common facilities for individual food processors, and the third supported group enterprises.

Integrated support to individual enterprises

The Productive Employment Project (PEP) that BRDB runs is part of a broader programme – the Rural Employment Sector Programme (RESP), which covers four projects: one for infrastructure development, two for institution building and one for poverty alleviation. PEP, established in 1986, runs RESP's poverty alleviation component.

PEP aims to provide the rural poor (defined as households having less than half an acre of land and relying mainly on manual labour for sustenance) with sustainable livelihoods. It is working in 27 subdistricts of five districts within Greater Faridpur – Madaripur, Faridpur, Shariatpur, Rajbari and Gopalganj. PEP reaches approximately 160000 beneficiaries. It supports its target groups through savings and credit facilities, training, marketing assistance, legal aid, and health and nutrition. It supports and monitors about 15 livelihood sectors, categorized broadly into production, service and processing, as shown in Table 2.4.

PEP's beneficiaries are organized into 15- to 20-member groups, regularly visited by fieldworkers. PEP has 430 fieldworkers, 16 to 18 per subdistrict, each handling about 20 groups. Fieldworkers collect loan payments from beneficiaries and obtain feedback on the beneficiaries' progress. They respond to the members' livelihood problems insofar as they can. Fieldworkers are supported by district extension officers, who provide more specialized technical

Table 2.4   Livelihood sectors supported and monitored by BRDB

Production	Service	Processing, transformational
Paddy cultivation	Shopkeeping	Carpentry and masonry
Other cultivation	Other small trade	Weaving and tailoring
Fish culture	Rickshaw van pulling	Artisan cottage industries
Dairy cow rearing	Paddy and pulse husking*	Food processing
Other cattle rearing	Boat pulling	
Poultry and duck culture		

*PEP has reduced its support to paddy husking since it found that it benefits mostly middlemen who buy parboiled rice from farmers and have it husked.

input to the fieldworkers and beneficiaries. A typical district office has four extension officers, a fisheries officer, a livestock and veterinary officer, an agricultural officer and a microenterprise officer, who is responsible for food processing.

PEP started work with ITDG-B in 1992 when five PEP fieldworkers attended the food processing training course. Since then, PEP has annually sent fieldworkers for training. To date, 16 to 20 fieldworkers have attended and they have trained their beneficiaries and other staff.

PEP realized that many women beneficiaries process food, or could easily do so. While homestead cultivation and livestock rearing sustain many households, food processing is the most common supplementary income-generating activity. In Shariatpur, more women PEP beneficiaries engaged in food processing than in other non-traditional business, as is shown in Table 2.5.

Table 2.5   Distribution of enterprise activities supported by PEP in Shariatpur District (as of April 2000)

Type of enterprise	Female	Male
Food processing	108	40
Jute craft	37	3
Tailoring	30	–
Cane work	23	7
Dressmaking	20	–
Decorative pottery	10	10
Soap making and various other activities	4	6

Source: Mohammed Aminul Islam, Microenterprise Extension Officer, Shariatpur District, RESP-PEP

Food processing was profitable and a good job generator. A PEP survey showed food processing as third in profitability, next to fisheries (no. 1) and jute products (no. 2). It provided better jobs than fisheries and farming partly because, unlike those activities, food processing and selling did not stop during the rainy season and thus provided more workdays.

17

Another study showed food processing had good growth potential. BRDB examined the impact of the project after ten years, asking its fieldworkers to select five to seven most successful beneficiaries. They deemed that a successful enterprise was one that had at least three permanent workers and earned BDT 25000 annual net income. Each fieldworker, who covered a fairly wide range of beneficiaries, made a subjective selection. Thirty per cent of those selected were engaged in food processing.

PEP supported food processing by providing training and financial services, including savings and loans, to its beneficiaries. PEP also sold polyethylene bags for packaging.

Food processing training spanned three to ten days using ITDG-B and PEP experts. For a ten-day programme, PEP handled eight days while ITDG-B had the remaining two. The training taught food product technology, hygiene and business management. Food products covered were those that were desired locally. For instance, in Shariatpur, *channa chur*, milk toffee, doughnuts, *murally*, pickles (green chilli, garlic, and *brinjal*), solid pickles or chutney, pulses, fried nuts and chips were preferred.

From 1995 to 1999, PEP's fieldworkers trained 844 beneficiaries. This did not include the beneficiaries who were informally trained. In Shariatpur, only 60 of the 148 beneficiaries received formal training. The other 88 were informally trained and advised.

Beneficiaries received loans from the programme. They also deposited savings of at least BDT 4 per week. The loans had three tiers:

First loan = BDT 8000
Second loan = BDT 12000
Third loan = BDT 15000

The loans matured in one year. Nominal interest rate was 20 per cent charged on a diminishing balance. (Nominal bank interest rate was around 14 per cent per year.)

By early 2000, PEP had disbursed BDT 580 million in loans to 82000 borrowers, with an average amount of BDT 7000. The plan was for the disbursed amount to increase to BDT 650 million. In 2000, the estimated repayment rate was around 99 per cent.

Few borrowers were into food processing. In 1996/7, food processors constituted only 1.4 per cent of the borrowers and 1.3 per cent of the loans. Out of 48000 borrowers in 1996/7, only 661 processed food; out of BDT 280 million disbursed, food processing accounted for only BDT 3.74 million. It ranked a low 12th of the 15 activities that the credit programme supported. Activities were ranked according to the number of borrowers, and loan disbursement rank followed closely:

18

- other small trade
- paddy and pulse husking
- other cultivation
- shopkeeping
- dairy cow rearing
- other cattle rearing
- paddy cultivation
- rickshaw van pulling
- artisan and cottage industries
- fish culture
- poultry and duck culture
- food processing
- weaving and tailoring
- carpentry and masonry
- boat pulling.

Apparently, food processing required minimal investment. One could begin with equipment costing as low as BDT 1000, plus some regular household utensils. With BDT 2000 weekly capital, or BDT 350 daily capital, a processor could earn about BDT 650 per week or BDT 120 per day. This can double household incomes which, according to surveys conducted in rural Faridpur and Rajbari by ITDG-B, averaged BDT 21390 annually for Faridpur and BDT 29410 for Rajbari (or BDT 446 and BDT 613 per week, respectively) (ITDG 2000).

A sample case (Box 2.1) from ITDG-B's 'IGA profiles' on *channa chur* shows revenue and income that could be earned. Although interviewed beneficiaries could not provide detailed calculations, income and capital investment were similar.

Most of those interviewed took loans to build and improve homes and to buy land. While they may have used part of their loan to purchase raw materials and equipment to begin processing food, most used their loans for larger investments to improve their living conditions. Undoubtedly, food processing income helped beneficiaries repay their loans, which otherwise would not have been affordable. Pre-project income was generally sufficient only for daily sustenance.

Other benefits from food processing support included the following:

- PEP introduced new products. For instance, those who had produced only *channa chur* added pickles after learning how to make them from PEP's training course.
- PEP introduced packaging, including polyethylene bags and glass and plastic bottles. Traditionally foods were stocked in large containers, brought to the streets, scooped out in small quantities, and served on small sheets of

Box 2.1   Snack food processing, case example

Noor decides to make *channa chur* to earn extra income. She buys equipment totalling BDT 1700. She also buys raw materials from which she can produce 180 kg of *channa chur*. She sells these in small packets costing BDT 5 each. From the 180 kg of *channa chur*, she can make about 900 packets.

She spends approximately four hours per day making *channa chur*, and her son goes around the neighbourhood and to the market to sell them. Below are the estimated costs of equipment and working capital as well as the computation of Noor's earnings.

Estimated cost of equipment for making *channa chur*			Estimated working capital for making *channa chur*			
Equipment	Qty.	Cost (BDT)	Items	Qty.	Price per unit (BDT)	Total cost (BDT)
Saucepan	2 pc	500	Flour	100 kg	22/kg	2200
Bowl	2 pc	500	*Suhaga*[a]	1 kg	50/kg	50
Frying pan	1 pc	200	Salt	10 kg	8/kg	80
Dies	1 pc	100	Dye	250 g	–	50
Place mat	20 pc	400	Soda	1.5 kg	24/kg	36
Total		1700	Polyethylene	4 bundles	150/bundle	600
			Firewood	100 kg	3/kg	300
			Transport	–	–	70
			Total			3386

Source: IGA Profile: Channa Chur, ITDG Bangladesh

For 900 packets, Noor receives a total revenue of BDT 4500. Subtracting the cost of raw materials, which amounted to BDT 3386, Noor's profit comes up to BDT 1115. This represents 12 days' earnings and thus Noor earned an average of BDT 92 per day or approximately BDT 2230 per month. Noor's income can be considered typical of many beneficiaries of ITDG-B. See income comparisons in Table 2.8.

[a]borax, used as a preservative

paper. Proper packaging improved hygiene since food was no longer exposed to the elements. Storage life of the product also improved, resulting in higher income. In April 2000, the Shariatpur District RESP-PEP microenterprise extension officer[5] said that sales increased almost ten times for some beneficiaries who began packaging their food, even though they increased their price to cover the packaging cost.

• PEP discouraged using harmful ingredients, most commonly orange textile dye, often added to colour food such as *channa chur*. As natural food dyes are expensive and generally unavailable except in Dhaka, processors have turned to marketing their snack foods in their natural colour, and customers have gradually accepted them.

Common facilities for individual food processors

The Bangladesh Organization for Development Cooperation (BODC) focuses on the subdistrict of Zanjira, Shariatpur, to support mainly the landless poor. It carries out child education, adult education, water and sanitation, primary health care, and credit and savings programmes. It provides training courses in awareness building, moral education, legal education, afforestation, women's development and training for couples. It has been implementing these programmes under a five-year funding commitment from the South Asia Partnership, Bangladesh. With a staff of 25, it has been training about 250 people a year.

BODC started its food processing programme in 1999 when it sent three staff to the ITDG-B training course. Shortly afterwards, it invited ITDG-B to conduct a five-day training course for 20 beneficiaries in two batches of ten participants. ITDG-B then assisted BODC in setting up a training centre and provided tools and equipment. It also provided continuous technical guidance. A food processing unit was created. ITDG-B provided equipment worth BDT 40 000 and BODC provided equipment, land, building and workforce, worth BDT 60 000. Food processing was the only economic activity BODC was promoting, but it hoped to diversify.

Part of the BODC training was a six-month period in which 15 women beneficiaries learned all the steps involved in producing different foods at the centre. They also got accustomed to hygienic practices at the centre, such as wearing aprons and masks when preparing food. After that they were expected to produce on their own. Ten of the women work in the training centre regularly and the other five occasionally. BODC purchases the raw materials and packaging and the women take equal shares of these materials. They produce and package the food and sell it on their own.

Most of these women spend six to eight hours a day, six days a week in the centre, from 7 am to 1 pm or 9 am to 3 pm. Each produces around 5 kilograms of *channa chur* and some pickles and *murally* a day. Afterwards, they sell these in their shops or from house to house. Out of the earnings, they pay the raw material cost back to BODC weekly. The women depend on the raw materials that BODC provides. BODC tries to rotate products, providing for two to three each time: *channa chur, murally*, milk toffee, pickles and doughnuts.

Table 2.6 shows the cost and prices of products produced and sold by BODC beneficiaries.

BODC now hopes to phase out the first batch of 15 trainees and take on another batch. Planning to evolve into a marketing and sales centre, it might also continue as a common production facility for those who wish to produce and package there.

BODC lent up to BDT 4000 or BDT 5000 in one-year loans to 2000 beneficiaries. It charged 15 per cent interest. Payments were weekly, monthly or

21

Table 2.6   Prices and cost of common food products produced and sold by BODC trainees

Item	Cost (BDT)	Price (BDT)
Channa chur	30/kg	40/kg
Murally	30/kg	40/kg
Pickles	20/250 g	25/250 g
Milk toffee	0.50/pc	1/pc

Source: Jagadish Chandra Das, Director, BODC, 4 April 2000

quarterly, depending on beneficiary preference and cash flow. Food processing beneficiaries had little need to invest direct, since raw materials and equipment were at the centre and the women paid for them after they sold the food. Those who did not go to the centre regularly worked at home at minimal cost, as low as BDT 70 per day for raw materials, mitigating the need for loans. Rather, as with PEP, they used their loans to improve their homes, buy cattle and acquire land.

Among those interviewed, the food processing income ranged from BDT 70 to BDT 100 per day. For those who previously earned BDT 40 to BDT 100 per day, the addition of this amount doubled their household income. (See the profit calculation in Table 2.7.)

Table 2.7   Profit calculation of a 60-year-old beneficiary who produced and sold all her products in one day

Item (price per unit based on Table 2.6)	Profit as stated by beneficiary (BDT)	Revenue (BDT)	Total cost, based on Table 2.6 (BDT)
Pickles (4 bottles @ BDT 25/bottle)	20	100	80
Murally (1.5 kg @ BDT 40/kg)	15	60	45
Channa chur (5 kg @ BDT 40/kg)	50	200	150
Total	85	360	275

The beneficiary quoted in Table 2.7 normally earned BDT 20 from pickles, BDT 15 from *murally* and BDT 50 from *channa chur* for a BDT 85 profit. She added that summer was a peak season for snack foods and her income could double. She had previously worked as a housemaid for BDT 100 per day and had lived with relatives, but since she started her food processing business she has been able to buy her own land, build a house and raise some cattle.

Food processing thus helped some of the poorest in Bangladesh to acquire their own land. The income that they earned from food processing enabled them to take out loans to purchase land, and repay them.

Promoting group enterprises – BRDB

Other food products such as jam and jelly cannot practicably be processed by one person because they require expensive equipment, such as crushing machines. Also, very small farm holdings produce a crop volume smaller than the capacity of even the smallest machines (Chowdhury and Sarker 1989). Yet farmers periodically experience an over-supply of crops during harvest, resulting in lower prices and substantial spoilage. Some of ITDG-B's partners, concerned with the resulting low income and crop wastage, began promoting processed fruits and vegetables.

They set up small processing plants, grouped the beneficiaries into an enterprise, and tried to make processing available to microproducers and the poor. These enterprises are owned either by the beneficiaries or by the NGO, which pays its beneficiaries wages. The beneficiary-owned plant was implemented by PEP in Zanjira, Shariatpur, while the NGO-owned plant was established by MUS in Madhupur, Tangail.

Zanjira is a tomato-producing subdistrict. About 15 000 farmers produce approximately 40 000 tonnes of tomatoes annually, which was almost half the 93 000 tonnes reported for all Bangladesh in 1996/7. Because tomatoes are important to Zanjira, PEP, the Ministry of Agriculture and ITDG-B commissioned a study from 1996 to 1998 to assess the industry. It was found that during harvest the tomato oversupply would drop the price by as much as 50 per cent. PEP then sought the assistance of ITDG-B to process tomatoes in Zanjira.

PEP and ITDG-B signed an agreement that between 1998 and 2001, three batches of women (50 women in all) would be trained in food processing. In 1998, the first batch of 15 women was trained, and they subsequently formed an association to pioneer a tomato processing enterprise.

The enterprise was established with ITDG-B assistance. It committed BDT 450 000 to cover land (BDT 50 000), building (BDT 300 000), and working capital (BDT 100 000). The 15 women also contributed BDT 50 000 (BDT 3000 to BDT 4000 each) for working capital. ITDG-B fabricated and provided fruit-crushing equipment worth BDT 73 500 (Table 2.3).

Since tomatoes are seasonal, the food processing association produces and sells other food as well: *channa chur*, pulses, milk toffee, *murally*, fried nuts, doughnuts, pickles, *ber* chutney, tomato chutney, tomato ketchup and tomato sauce for making tomato ketchup. It also uses the tomato-crushing machine to crush pineapple and guava.

The typical production timetable of the association was as follows:

Feb Mar	Apr May Jun	Jul Aug Sep	Oct Nov Dec Jan
tomato crushing	processing of tomato into ketchup or sauce	pineapple and guava crushing and processing	production of *channa chur*, milk toffee, doughnuts, *murally*, fried nuts, pickles, chutney, pulses

23

The 15 association members meet formally once or twice a month. The fieldworkers and extension officers present production and marketing plans and options to the women for their views and approval, since members are not honed in these processes and their literacy is low. Because the women cannot go to market themselves, their sons and PEP officers help them. To improve sales and increase production volume, the association has agreed to hire a male marketing officer who is to receive a sales commission.

Half the association's BDT 50000 working capital represents the cost of finished products, the other half is for raw materials. From sales worth BDT 25000, they realize BDT 35000 in monthly revenue and earn BDT 10000 net income. During the summer, when pickles are much in demand, they can net up to BDT 20000.

The turnover from tomato products is relatively small. The association sells 60 per cent of its tomato products to the wholesale market and 40 per cent to the retail market. It costs BDT 20 to produce a 300-g bottle of tomato ketchup – about BDT 5 for the bottle and label, BDT 12 for raw materials, and BDT 3 for labour and utilities. The wholesale price for a 300-g bottle is BDT 24 and the retail price BDT 30. The association's average profit is BDT 6.40 per bottle, taking into account the proportions sold to both wholesale and retail markets.

The association produces two to three metric tons of tomato products during the three-month season, which can mean a BDT 50000 profit. The estimated monthly net income from all products hovers around BDT 27000, which is expected to increase gradually to BDT 40000 within three years.

Only 30 per cent of the equipment and labour capacity is now being used, since each person works for only two to three hours daily. According to the extension officer, at maximum capacity the association could have two shifts a day. Under the agreement between PEP and ITDG, the number of association women will increase from 15 to 50 within three years.

The income earned from processing food, about BDT 27000, is distributed equally among the 15 association members, about BDT 1850 each per month. Many members had been homemakers whose families earned about BDT 1600 a month. The income from the food processing association has doubled their household income.

The women speak of sending their children to school and improving their homes after joining the project. Some say they now earn more than their husbands and that they have bought land and built homes for their grown children. Some land purchases were funded out of loans, but the loans were paid back from the income from the food businesses.

Other costs, however, have not been considered. These include utilities, the service of the extension officer who functioned as manager or consultant, depreciation of the equipment, land and building, and amortization of assets that had been sold to the association rather than donated. If these were deducted from the net income, then the women's share would be eroded. Table 2.8 compares sample incomes.

Although the women earn substantial income, the comparison supports the extension officer's view that their time is underused. The income they earn from what they have invested is less than that of those who operate individually. It would be even less if other costs were included. Also, their capital turnover is monthly compared with that of individual operators, who can turn over their capital every week or two – thus their return to working capital investment is higher.

The association's operation may be part of the learning curve to develop markets and organize work. Accordingly, expansion is planned to increase production value by BDT 50000 to BDT 80000. It is hoped that the recruitment of a marketing officer will support higher production.

Table 2.8 Summary of incomes, working capital and work hours

Organization/ approach	Amount of working capital (BDT)	Hours worked (no.)[a]	Income earned per month (BDT)[b]	Income per work hour (BDT)[a]	Monthly income per working capital (%)
PEP-1[c]/ individual	2000[d]	4–5	2880	27	140
PEP-2[e]/ individual	3386[d]	4	2230	23	66
BODC[f]/ individual w/commis'n	1700[g]	6	2400	14	120
PEP-group	3000[h]	2–3	1850	17.5	61

PEP – Productive Employment Project, BODC – Bangladesh Organization for Development Cooperation
[a]production work only   [e]case example (from Box 2.1)   [h]one month turnover based
[b]calculated at 6 days of work per week   [f]from Table 2.7   on fieldworkers' estimation
[c]actual beneficiary   [g]weekly turnover
[d]two-week turnover

Promoting group enterprises – MUS

MUS was founded in 1986 to help the landless poor in Madhupur (Tangail District) and Muktagachha (Mymensingh District). It covers 51 villages in the two districts and reaches 10 000 beneficiaries.

MUS's support strategy comprises group formation, water and sanitation, child and adult education, motivational family planning, beekeeping, food processing, credit, and a trickle-up programme. MUS has 56 staff: two involved in food processing, five in beekeeping, six in credit and 43 in education.

The food processing programme began in 1996 to assist the pineapple industry in Madhupur. Pineapples were spoiling in the fields because the market was glutted. MUS sought ITDG and ATDP (Agro-based Industries and Technology Development Project, a USAID-funded project) assistance to process pineapple juice, jam and jelly.

ITDG-B provided funds to MUS to purchase equipment, including a crushing machine and a sealing machine. ITDG-B also provided training in making jam, jelly, pickles, juice, *channa chur* and *murally*, through a five-day training course that 20 beneficiaries and one staff member attended. ATDP trained 150 beneficiaries in making jam and jelly.

MUS owns and manages the factory, which for four years was in the house of the executive director. The factory produces mango pickles, jam and kashmiri *achar* (pickles made of fermented mango); pineapple juice, jelly and jam; garlic pickles; green chilli pickles; *jhal moori* (snack made of rice husk) and *channa chur*.

The production cycle of MUS is as follows:

Jan	Feb	Mar	Apr	May	Jun	Jul	Aug	Sep	Oct	Nov	Dec
channa chur olive and garlic pickles	olive pickles	mango		pineapple juice (in season)					pineapple jelly, jam (out of season)		

The factory runs on BDT 50000 working capital. Over BDT 100000 has been invested for the equipment, and the executive director is not paid rent for his own home space.

MUS uses two salesmen and three agencies to market its products. The factory earns BDT 19000 in a fair month, 20 per cent of which is profit. Sixty women beneficiaries, five at a time, work at the factory. Each works two to three days a week and earns a BDT 20 daily wage.

Their involvement in food processing gives them a minimal wage of BDT 20 per day or around BDT 240 per month, which is a small addition to their income. Most beneficiary households earn BDT 100 to BDT 200 per day from pulling rickshaw or sewing *kampa* (embroidered blankets). Others have only their tiny homestead to work on and occasionally sew *kampa* to earn about BDT 100 per month.

MUS hopes to expand its jam production, but it was using a specially shaped bottle for the jam, and the manufacturer's supply ran out. MUS has proposed that ITDG-B assist it in making moulds and equipment for glass bottles.

Programme assessment

The programme was assessed through interviews and findings from a 1996 ITDG report.

Outreach

Programme outreach is moderately successful. The 1996 ITDG-B evaluation of the food training course indicated that the 103 fieldworkers trained from 1990 to 1996 reached over 6000 beneficiaries, 21 per cent of whom have established businesses. The average reach per fieldworker was therefore 60 beneficiaries. Extrapolating these figures to the 145 trained as of November 1999, it may be assumed that 8700 beneficiaries were trained and advised and 1830 started businesses. This extrapolation, however, is based on only 22 trainers out of 103, a 15 per cent sampling.

The programme's outreach has been good mainly because of the favourable supply and demand condition for snack foods. Food processing requires minimal investment, little working capital and indigenous skills, making it easy for landless poor and women to do. Good local demand for snack food and processed fruit (though to a lesser degree since jam and jelly are more expensive) allows processors to sell right in their own neighborhoods. As women cannot go to the market to sell because they are constrained by cultural norms, their sons help them to sell the food.

Still, it is not uncommon to find only 5 per cent of an organization's members engaged in food processing. This should not be surprising since the population prefers the traditional activities of cultivation and livestock rearing. Commercial food processing, even on a small scale, requires more daily responsibility and risk (for example buying raw materials, producing, selling), a pace many rural people are not used to. Compared with other non-traditional trades, however, food processing ranks high (Table 2.5).

Food processing helps the poorest of the poor. Some beneficiaries reported a pre-project BDT 1600 monthly household income, well below the poverty threshold. Many beneficiaries are landless. In remote areas where markets are far away, development organizations may take a stronger role in supplying raw materials, packaging and marketing to reach the poorest. By having services closer to them, women who traditionally are confined to their homes, without any previous business experience, have easily engaged in this new trade and have doubled their household income.

Impact

Those interviewed averaged BDT 2240 monthly from food processing (Table 2.8). The 1996 evaluation found the average income was BDT 880 per week or BDT 3520 per month, an 82 to 140 per cent addition to the BDT 2500 monthly average rural household income for those owning small pieces of land (ITDG 2000).

Food processing brought in more money than the traditionally preferred livestock rearing (BDT 7364 annually) or chicken and duck raising (BDT 2000 annually) (Box 2.2).

Box 2.2   Impact assessment based on the 1996 evaluation

The 1996 evaluation study based its findings on data applying to 1993–96. It estimates that the 57 fieldworkers trained during this period have each trained around 60 persons and that 21 per cent of those trained have set up their enterprises. Given a total of 57 trained fieldworkers, the study assumes that 3420 beneficiaries have been trained or advised during the period 1993–96 and that 718 have set up their food processing activity.

Looking at the net income generated by the programme, it was calculated that each successful operation earns an average profit of BDT 872 per week or BDT 151 per day (calculated based on a 300-day work year) or a total of BDT 45 344 per year or £756 (using the exchange rate applicable to the period evaluation was made: BDT 60 = £1).

Considering that the 57 trained during this three-year period have in turn trained or advised 3420 beneficiaries, 719 (or 21 per cent) of whom set up a business, the project was able to generate a total income of BDT 31 million or £515 611 in one year as shown in the table below. (Note that incomes were computed for only one year, thus underestimating possible income generated by businesses running for more than one year.)

Year	No. trained	Beneficiaries (no. at 60/trainer)	Enterprises created (21%)	Net income generated (£)	Inflation rate (%) [a]	Income generated (£)[b]
1993/4	18	1080	227	171 600	–	159 184
1994/5	26	1560	328	248 000	8.9	232 427
1995/6	13	780	164	124 000	6.7	124 000
Total	57	3420	719	543 600		515 611

Source: Azami et al. 1996 and additional calculations
[a]The average inflation rate of 7.8 is applied (average of the 1994/5 and 1995/6 rates) since the beneficiaries may have been trained or they may have set up their enterprises any time during the two years following the 1993/4 training.
[b]adjusted to inflation rate

Beneficiaries reported that they could send their children to school, improve their homes and buy land. This is significant, since the projects seek to improve the lives of landless poor. Women also reported feeling more dignified, with increased income and better homes. Land and houses were directly funded from loans rather than from income earned from processing food. However, it was the income from food processing that repaid the loan. The loan therefore represented advanced income from food processing, 'withdrawn' to finance larger investments.

Food processing training has improved food preparation practices to benefit all consumers. As mentioned, ITDG-B has convinced beneficiaries to stop using textile dyes, and now *channa chur* is often marketed in its natural colour.

At the BODC training centre and the food processing association in Zanjira, women wear aprons and masks and handle food properly. The introduction of polyethylene bags and glass bottles has improved hygiene since food is no longer exposed to the elements.

Impact can be improved in group enterprises, however. While the Zanjira women have realized a 100 per cent increase in income, they do not earn as much as individual food producers. Their facilities are also underutilized. At MUS, the volume of production is too little for its 60 beneficiaries, who can work only two to three days a week and have to look elsewhere for additional work. This reflects a need for improved business development skills from the partner organization. ITDG-B might provide such assistance through its small enterprise unit, as they set out to address this lack of business know-how at the programme's outset.

Cost effectiveness

The 1996 evaluation calculated the cost effectiveness of the training from 1993 to 1996. Cost was calculated assuming all staff spent 80 per cent of their time conducting training, except for the project coordinator and the small enterprise unit, who contributed 10 per cent of their time. Indirect costs, such as rent, utilities, communication and stationery, were 80 per cent of the total. Direct costs, such as equipment and meetings, were charged in full. International travel was omitted since it was not related to the training. From these assumptions, the calculations shown in Table 2.9 were made:

Table 2.9   Food processing training cost and benefit/cost ratios, 1993–96

	1993/4	1994/5	1995/6	Total
Number trained	18	26	13	57
Total budget (in £)	11379	16801	13110	41290
Cost per trainer (in £)	632	646	1008	–
Cost per beneficiary (in £)	10.5	10.8	16.8	–
Cost per enterprise (in £)	50	51	80	–
Income generated 1993–96 (in £)	–	–	–	515611
Benefit/cost ratio	–	–	–	12.5 to 1

Source: Azami et al. 1996; benefit/cost ratio recalculated

The cost per trainer ranged from £632 to £1000. Assuming each trainer trained an average of 60 beneficiaries, the cost per beneficiary was £10.50 to £16.80. If 21 per cent of the trained beneficiaries established businesses, then the cost of training one business was £50 to £80. The programme generated BDT 31 million or £515600 total income from 1993 to 1996. Against the £41290 total training cost, the benefit/cost ratio during this period was 12.5 to 1. This demonstrates a positive rate of return for a training programme, although it should be noted that it excludes certain costs such as technology development and monitoring.

The annexe shows the cost of running the food processing programme, using data from 1998/9, the first year of the programme's second phase and the only year in the phase with complete data. Costs were estimated for each activity: technology research and product development, training, monitoring and evaluation, networking, information dissemination and administration. Some costs are directly related – for example, as technology research and product development are inputs to training and information dissemination, the cost of the research can be divided equally between these two activities. Monitoring followed up training and can be added to training costs. Only in the area of training are benefits readily identified. Information dissemination and networking improved people's knowledge of food processing, but this cannot be readily measured. The benefit/cost analysis therefore focuses on training. In 1998 to 1999, 15 fieldworkers were trained (Table 2.2). Using the same assumptions as in the 1996 evaluation, that is, that fieldworkers each trained 60 beneficiaries, the total number reached was 900 people, of whom 21 per cent or 190 set up their own successful operations (Table 2.10).

Table 2.10 Food processing training cost (including research and monitoring) and benefit/cost ratios, 1998/9

	1998/9
Number trained	15
Total training expenses (in £)	17374
Cost per trainer (in £)	1158
Cost per beneficiary trained or advised (in £)	19
Cost per enterprise (in £)	92
Total income generated in 1 year (in £)	125668
Benefit/cost ratio	7:1

Given an estimated BDT 49785 per successful producer annual income (from BDT 45 344 with 1997 inflation rate at 2.63 per cent and 1998 rate at 6.98 per cent), the year 1998/9 generated a total income of BDT 9.4 million or approximately £125000, based on the 1998 exchange rate of BDT 74.875 to £1 (BBS 1999).[6]

With the adjusted cost of training at £17 374, the training benefit/cost ratio was 7:1. The figures were less favourable than those computed for 1993 to 1996 because the training costs included the technology development and monitoring costs.

Sustainability

Sustainability can be viewed in terms of the improved capability of local organizations to run the programmes, the financial viability of the programmes, and the growth prospects of the industry being promoted. When the programme began, few organizations provided training and technical assistance in food processing, especially secondary food processing. Since then, more organizations have developed short training sessions for their beneficiaries, and two have begun conducting the trainers' training course (BRDB-PEP and the Centre for Mass Education and Sciences). Importantly, one of these is a government organization with a mandate for rural development, with a wide reach and some institutional security and sustainability. It could replicate the promotive work that ITDG-B now does.

In addition, ITDG-B has facilitated an institution to represent small-scale food processor interests. It is hoped the FFPED will continue ITDG-B's work of convening stakeholders, disseminating information and technology, and advocating for policies.

From 1997 until June 2000, ITDG-B collected fees from partner organizations at BDT 3000 per participant. For 15 to 18 people, ITDG-B could collect BDT 45 000, recovering 75 per cent of the cost (see the annexe). Development organizations trained their beneficiaries for free. However, as mentioned, some organizations do not favour charging fees to beneficiaries who are the poorest of the poor.

They argue that training produces long-term payoffs in the form of marginal income spread over time. Therefore, an organization cannot expect to cover all its training costs up front. Since the food processing beneficiaries in Bangladesh were the poorest of the poor, even if they were able to double their income, they might still be below the poverty line. In April 2000, the ITDG-B small enterprise unit manager argued that because of the dire poverty of their beneficiaries, most did not yet have the capability to pay. It is this capability the enterprise unit hopes to develop.

Food processing seems promising, its purported growth rate being 32 per cent yearly. Urban eating habits are changing in favour of traditional products such as *channa chur*. Many express doubt, however, about the extent to which small producers can sell their product in the market, given the lack of competitive packaging and the public notion that their products are not hygienic.

Still, there seems to be a niche for small-scale producers. Their snack foods are important in the local economy and markets. The small operator serves rural consumers who are not willing or able to buy the big packs that the large companies produce and sell at BDT 16, but they will buy small quantities at BDT 8. Children buy even smaller packets, at BDT 2.

Lessons learned

Specialization versus diversification of assistance

ITDG-B provides training, mainly in food processing and some in business management. It supplements training with field visits where a food technologist or project staff member discusses with the partner organizations any concerns with the product, packaging or marketing. Other business development services, such as financial assistance, marketing assistance and raw materials acquisition, are provided mainly by the partner organizations.

ITDG-B mostly focuses on food technology, but considers markets as well. Marketing is not a problem with the individual operators, who can sell in the neighborhood or public markets; rather, it is a concern for group enterprises, which produce and sell in bigger volumes.

ITDG-B could play a bigger role in strengthening partner organizations' group enterprises. For example, the women with MUS were not earning as much as they wished. Taking in fewer women to increase the income per person could be considered. In Zanjira, association members received the same income share despite different management roles. Also, several cost components seem to have been overlooked before income is distributed. These considerations are part of a business analysis, which partner organizations and their beneficiaries may learn and apply more rigorously.

The small enterprise unit of ITDG-B could play a larger role in improving business development services of the partner organizations. It now runs a capability-building programme for NGOs in which it regularly monitors business support services and advises on how to improve them. This approach could be extended to the food processing programme. The small enterprise unit was assisting 21 NGOs, and only two overlapped with the food processing programme. ITDG-B could use the small enterprise unit to complement the technical expertise of the food processing, food production and manufacturing programmes.

Specialization versus diversification of products

The food processing unit of ITDG-B focuses on snack foods. Each of the many products developed, however, has its own technology to learn and pass on. ITDG-B and its partner organizations concluded that a fieldworker can master many products, since they learn by doing and the technology is not difficult.

Fieldworkers monitored many livelihoods in addition to making snack foods (Table 2.5). PEP's approach is notable in that it supported fieldworkers with district technical experts covering fisheries, livestock, agriculture, veterinary and microenterprise development. Some workers have in fact gained enough experience to establish their own food processing businesses, or hoped to do so. These constituted perhaps an overlooked middle-class entrepreneurial sector emerging from among NGO professionals.

Institutional and market development approach

ITDG-B seeks to develop partner organizations as effective providers of food processing training. It has identified two organizations that could conduct the trainers' training courses. It has also helped to form a network of food processor enterprises and NGOs to carry on its networking, advocacy and information dissemination.

Individual versus group approaches

Group approaches were promoted when large investments were required to manufacture food products. Processing fruit into jam, jelly and juice was too expensive to carry out individually. In some communities raw materials were wasted. Efficiency therefore dictates whether a business will be operated by an individual or a group. However, group enterprises require stronger business support since they have more complex business and organizational needs.

Poverty alleviation versus growth orientation

ITDG-B aims to lift out of poverty the poorest of the poor – peasants having no or very small landholdings, divorced and widowed women, and those having very low income – by bringing technology within their reach.

A product with a large local market, snack food, suited the objective of reaching more people. By introducing mainly the technology and finding raw materials and packaging, the beneficiaries could run their own operations and find their own markets. Because of this, the programme reached many beneficiaries, increased their income, and achieved a reasonably high benefit/cost ratio.

Some difficult situations required stronger support. Those living in remote areas had little access to raw materials. Widows with no male helpers did not have access to markets. Some products, such as jam and jelly, were less suitable for individual operations. ITDG-B and its partner organizations have assisted in purchasing raw materials, setting up common facilities or establishing group enterprises so that operating costs could be borne by a group of beneficiaries. Group enterprises have had to achieve a certain scale to be viable and effectively raise the income of the beneficiaries. Therefore, growth orientation is essential. ITDG-B and its partners must upgrade their skills for the more sophisticated requirements of these larger business enterprises.

Notes

1 In 1996 statistics, those with no cultivated area (or functionally landless) and those cultivating 0.01–0.04 acres of land made up 33.8 per cent of rural households (BBS 1999).
2 The official poverty threshold for Bangladesh was 2122 calories per person per day or approximately BDT 4790 (£63) per person per year, or BDT 400 (£5) per month. The food threshold was 1805 calories per day or BDT 2810 (£37) per person per

year or BDT 234 (£3) per month. For a family of six, the poverty threshold was BDT 2400 (£30) per month while the food threshold was BDT 1404 (£18) per month.

3 These two subsectors have been completely turned over to partner organizations (based on interviews with Shaheda Azami, 2 April 2000 and S.A. Wahab, 8 April 2000).

4 Other notable studies done under the project were the 1996 evaluation of the programme (Azami et al. 1996), the field survey of NGOs enquiring into training needs and preferred training methods (Chowdhury and Azami 1996) – the preparatory research done for the 1998 project document (ITDG 1998).

5 Mohammed Aminul Islam.

6 Exchange rates for Bangladesh taka (BDT):

	Per US dollar	Per pound sterling
1996	41.86	60.00
1998	45.50	74.88
2000	51.00	76.36

References

Azami, S., S. Brough and M. Battcock (1996) *Training for livelihood security: a report on the evaluation of impact of the IT Bangladesh Food Processing Training Course*, Intermediate Technology Bangladesh.

Bangladesh Economic Review (1995) as cited in ITDG, 1998.

[BBS] Bangladesh Bureau of Statistics (1999) *Statistical Pocketbook: Bangladesh 1998*, Bureau of Statistics, Bangladesh.

Chowdhury, S.A., and S. Azami (1996) *Small-scale snack food production and distribution in Bangladesh: field findings on training programmes*, ITDG–Bangladesh.

Chowdhury, S.A., and N. Sarker (1989) *An investigation into the food processing sector of Bangladesh with case studies on paddy milling and oil extraction*, ITDG–Bangladesh.

[FAO] Food and Agriculture Organization (1995) *Food for Consumers*, FAO, Rome, Italy, as cited in ITDG, 1999.

[ITDG] Intermediate Technology Development Group (1998) 'Food processing for income generation: project document', ITDG–Bangladesh.

ITDG (1999) *Sustainable livelihoods through food processing: international food processing strategy*, ITDG, London.

ITDG (2000) 'Producer-driven production strategies in Bangladesh project, ITDG–Bangladesh: baseline information and needs assessment survey', ITDG–Bangladesh, draft.

Annexe: Programme expenses by component

Bangladesh food processing for income generation Fiscal year 1998/9	Expenses (£)	Techn. research & product develop. (%)	(£)	Skills training (%)	(£)	Monitoring & evaluation (%)	(£)	Networking (%)	(£)	Information dissemination (%)	(£)	Management (%)	(£)	Total (%)
Personnel[a]														
Programme Manager (PM)	5514	10.0	551.4	10.0	551.4	10.0	551.4	20.0	1102.8	30.0	1654.2	20.0	1102.8	100.0
including 40% of staff development	36		3.6		3.6		3.6		7.3		10.9		7.3	
Food Technologist (FT)	2975	20.0	595.0	30.0	892.5	20.0	595.0	15.0	446.3	15.0	446.3	–	–	100.0
including 30% of staff development	27		5.5		8.2		5.5		4.1		4.1			
Project Officer (PO)	1765	10.0	176.6	10.0	176.5	30.0	529.5	30.0	529.5	20.0	353.0	–	–	100.0
including 30% of staff development	27		2.7		2.7		8.2		8.2		5.5			
Driver	1353	–	–	25.0	338.3	25.0	338.3	25.0	338.3	25.0	338.3	–	–	100.0
Secretary	729	16.7	121.5	16.7	121.5	16.7	121.5	16.7	121.5	16.7	121.5	16.7	121.5	100.0
Project Assistant	1572	20.0	314.4	25.0	393.0	25.0	393.0	15.0	235.8	15.0	235.8	–	–	100.0
Communications Officer	614	–	–	10.0	61.4	10.0	61.4	10.0	61.4	70.0	429.8	–	–	100.0
Country Director	1767	10.0	176.7	10.0	176.7	10.0	176.7	10.0	176.7	10.0	176.7	50.0	883.5	100.0
Staff development added above: 40% to PM, 30% to each FT & PO	91													
Subtotal	6470													
Consultants	4183	40.0	1673.2	30.0	1254.9	–	–	20.0	836.6	10.0	418.3	–	–	100.0
Training courses	3347	–	–	100.0	3347.0	–	–	–	–	–	–	–	–	100.0
Meetings, seminars and workshop	967	10.0	96.7	10.0	96.7	20.0	193.4	30.0	290.1	30.0	290.1	–	–	100.0
Printing and publication	6020	–	–	–	–	–	–	–	–	60.0	3612.0	–	–	60.0
Vehicle running cost	528	–	–	25.0	132.0	25.0	132.0	25.0	132.0	25.0	132.0	–	–	100.0
Local travel	513	5.0	25.7	20.0	102.6	30.0	153.9	15.0	77.0	30.0	153.9	–	–	100.0
International travel, including subsistence	3278	33.3	1091.6	–	–	–	–	33.3	1091.6	33.3	1091.6	–	–	100.0
Monitoring and evaluations	156	–	–	–	–	70.0	109.2	15.0	23.4	15.0	23.4	–	–	100.0
Communications	438	20.0	87.6	20.0	87.6	20.0	87.6	20.0	87.6	20.0	87.6	–	–	100.0
Technical enquiries	33	–	–	–	–	–	–	–	–	100.0	33.0	–	–	100.0
ITDG-B administration	4128	20.0	825.6	20.0	825.6	20.0	825.6	20.0	825.6	20.0	825.6	–	–	100.0
Income from training courses	(539)													
Subtotal	39522													
ITDG-UK administrative costs	3943	16.7	657.3	16.7	657.3	16.7	657.3	16.7	657.3	16.7	657.3	16.7	658.5	100.0
GRAND TOTAL	43465	14.8	6405.0	21.3	9299.5	11.4	4943.1	16.3	7052.9	25.6	11100.8	6.4	2773.6	100.0
TOTAL COST PER COMPONENT		RES		TRAIN		M & E		NET		INFO		MGT		

Percentage of distribution of inputs based on Programme Manager's estimates

[a] no expenses for Technology/Policy Adviser and International Programme Manager

3 Creating export markets for Bolivia's dry beans

HEATHER RAWLINSON and PAMELA FEHR

Introduction – the history of ASOMEX

THE STORY OF HOW the commercial marketing company ASOMEX came about begins several years before the company was established. In 1986 MEDA helped to develop a new crop among smallholder colonizer farmers in the eastern Bolivian lowland province of Santa Cruz.[1]

Edible beans were previously barely known in the Santa Cruz region. By adopting bean cultivation as a winter crop, smallholder farmers found an excellent complement to their existing crops grown in the summer. They were able to nearly double their incomes. Part of MEDA's work with the bean project was to take the lead in opening a first-time export market for Bolivian beans in Brazil. This new market resulted in a great deal of interest on the part of small-scale rural producers in the region. In 1990, various producer groups who came together to build economies of scale formed the National Association of Bean Producers, ASOPROF.

ASOPROF is made up of 17 farmer cooperatives and the National Women's Federation; it represents 1800 members, all engaged in bean production.[2] ASOPROF became an important body for agricultural marketing in the Santa Cruz region. However, under Bolivian law its status as an association soon brought it into conflict with legal limitations that prevented it from exporting for profit. Facing this predicament, the plan arose to create an independent for-profit marketing company that could service all of ASOPROF's export orders and eventually diversify into other products.

At the same time as this need for a marketing company arose in ASOPROF, MEDA was deepening its understanding of and interest in the marketing needs of small-scale producers. MEDA has a long history in Bolivia of offering credit, technical assistance and marketing services to rural and urban small-scale entrepreneurs. Through examining this history, it became clear that marketing was an important element for assistance programmes. Limited market access was preventing small entrepreneurs from reaching their potential. MEDA saw the need to create a marketing service for small producers – a service that would help them find new markets, particularly export markets, provide them with crucial market information, and assist them with the logistics involved in marketing and exporting.

In 1993, ASOPROF and MEDA came together to form a company that could respond to both sets of needs. ASOMEX was legally incorporated in Santa Cruz, Bolivia, on 3 May 1993.

ASOMEX began with two primary objectives: 1) to export everything ASOPROF produced, and 2) to search out markets for new products and provide marketing services for other small-scale producers.

MEDA's goal for ASOMEX was to increase the income of small-scale urban and rural producers by offering competitive and profitable marketing and exporting services.

The start-up funds for ASOMEX were raised entirely by selling company shares. ASOMEX was approved for the sale of US$40000 worth of shares. ASOPROF purchased 58.09 per cent of the shares, MEDA held 17.45 per cent and individual shareholders owned the remaining 24.46 per cent. From day one, ASOMEX has been financed entirely by equity and debt as a private sector company. Fees for marketing services are set to include a profit margin.

As the primary shareholders in ASOMEX, MEDA and ASOPROF worked together in designing the structure of the new company and developing a business plan. With its wealth of experience in business development, MEDA provided vital guidance in structuring the company, designing its internal statutes and sparking the initial planning. ASOPROF, having already worked in export marketing, provided practical experience that got the company off the ground (Table 3.1).

Table 3.1 Getting started: ASOMEX activities in the first three years

1993	1994	1995
ASOMEX formed	Continued bean exports to Brazil and Japan	Continued bean exports to Brazil, Japan and Colombia
Beans exported to Brazil and Japan	New bean variety exported to Colombia	Continued work with PRISMA
Acted as marketing agent for certified corn seed	Marketed local rice	Continued work marketing broad beans
	Began work with MEDA's Microenterprise Incentives and Support Programme (PRISMA) – furniture, clothing marketed	
	Began marketing broad beans	

In 1993 ASOMEX began by exporting ASOPROF edible beans to Brazil and Japan – an activity that has continued each year since. In its first year ASOMEX also acted as a marketing agent for certified corn seed, another operation it took over from ASOPROF. In 1994 ASOMEX began exporting *haba* beans (broad beans) for new producer clients and sent new red bean varieties to Colombia for ASOPROF. That year also marked the beginning of

ASOMEX's work in local rice marketing when it assisted a group of rice producers in supplying rice to a major supermarket outlet in Santa Cruz.

MEDA's PRISMA programme (Microenterprise Incentives and Support Programme) launched a marketing project through ASOMEX in 1994–96, focusing on small furniture and textile producers.[3] Currently MEDA is involved in a project called PROCOR (Rural Marketing Project), which works with a number of small producer associations around Bolivia. ASOMEX is helping these associations to identify markets for their target products and is bringing market information to the producers. This work has opened up many possibilities for ASOMEX to develop new producer-client relationships for the future.

ASOPROF remains the largest client, but ASOMEX is actively seeking to diversify through new producer clients in new product lines. ASOMEX has developed strength in marketing agricultural products, but it remains open to working in other product lines as well. Past experience with other products has been somewhat profitable; however, not all of the variables have existed to make these products as lucrative for ASOMEX as beans have been (lack of market knowledge on ASOMEX's part, insufficient supply and economies of scale, and inability or unwillingness of the producer to pay for service, for example). Through experience, ASOMEX has learned that one strategy contributing to its success is to work primarily with associations of small producers rather than with individuals. Nonetheless, working with goods and services of small producers remains a challenge.[4]

The business development services package

Package content

ASOMEX provides specialized business development services, with the goal of increasing incomes of small-scale urban and rural producers by offering competitive marketing and export services. In responding to the needs of its producer clients, ASOMEX has designed three different types of customized marketing services:

- *Export processing service.* ASOMEX currently serves its client ASOPROF by handling all the details of transferring the sale-ready product to its final destination. ASOMEX completes the necessary steps required for successful exporting, including documentation, logistics, transport arrangements and financial arrangements with the buyer. The sale occurs between the client and the buyer, with ASOMEX providing the export processing service. Depending on the need of the client, ASOMEX may or may not be involved in identifying foreign buyers.
- *Intermediary service.* ASOMEX aims to bring a fair price to producers. Acting as an intermediary, ASOMEX buys the producers' product and in

turn sells it (usually exports it) for a higher price. ASOMEX has this type of relationship with ASOHABA, the Asociación de Productores de Haba (a Bolivian association of broad bean producers, completely unrelated to ASOPROF). The intermediary service was adopted in response to the demands of clients who wanted a lower risk option and freedom from responsibility in the export process.

- *Brokering service.* The service facilitates the process of buying and selling by doing market research and developing contacts to bring buyers and sellers together. In this situation, ASOMEX does not buy the products but simply facilitates the process, collecting a commission on sales that result from its work. This is the latest of the three services to be adopted, responding to the demand of new clients who want research and contact information while maintaining complete autonomy and control over the sale of their product.

The above three services are moderately flexible, and ASOMEX negotiates appropriate services to meet the unique needs of each new client.

It is important that ASOMEX continues to develop and strengthen its service package. To reduce the risk that depending on one client (ASOPROF) created, to stabilize cash flows, and to provide a better return to shareholders, ASOMEX has devoted considerable effort to diversification. Clients, product lines and forms of marketing services have all been examined and various modifications made, such as adding intermediary and brokering services, taking a more active role in market research, identifying buyers, providing market information and assisting in the formation of new distribution and operations systems.

All ASOMEX stakeholders agree that it is far more difficult and costly to work with small producers than with large producers. Many problems can arise with small-scale producers, including unpredictable quantities of production, poor product quality, product storage problems, non-standardized products and poor administration. To cope with these costly challenges, ASOMEX works primarily with producer groups and associations.

Specialization versus diversification

Much thought has gone into the service package that ASOMEX offers. Over the years, the company has learned that diversification of product lines is essential to meet buyer-client demands (that is, offering intermediary services as well as brokering and export processing). ASOMEX also has plans to diversify its producer-client base and is looking into marketing some new agricultural products. These are all important strategies towards developing good service, although ASOMEX has in fact remained focused or specialized primarily in agricultural commodity trading and marketing. It consistently provides services in one area of the production and marketing process – exporting. It expects to remain specialized in this area, wherein lies its knowledge and expertise and where it feels it has the most to offer.

The local development context

ASOMEX is playing an important development role in several ways. In the past decade, there has been a boom in the number of programmes and companies in Bolivia serving urban micro- and small enterprises. In fact, microcredit has become so prevalent that competition is stiff among the providers. Technical and business management assistance has also become common, yet marketing services remain an area nearly void of intervention.

ASOMEX plays another role in local economic development by bringing fair prices to small producers. It is common for other intermediaries to collaborate in setting the producer prices very low. Though operating on a for-profit basis, ASOMEX maintains a concern for the welfare of the producers and works to offer them the best possible price for their products while still maintaining a profit margin.[5] Providing the best possible price helps generate demand for the service and promotes longer-term producer-client loyalty towards ASOMEX. It can also introduce competition into the intermediary market, often forcing up producer prices.

ASOMEX is contributing towards reducing rural poverty by focusing its efforts on agricultural marketing activities – the rural poor are primarily small agricultural producers.[6]

Marketing and delivering the business development services package

Competitive and complementary services

Various export companies existed at the time that ASOMEX started, and they are still operating. However, none specialized in serving small producers. ASOPROF's experiences with these competitors motivated it to form its own marketing company. The new company, ASOMEX, would be guaranteed to have at least the business of its shareholder-client ASOPROF, providing ASOMEX with a competitive advantage.

Pricing strategy alone is often not sufficient to win the business of rural clients in the face of competition from other intermediaries. ASOMEX has found that its agricultural producers often face the dilemma of another intermediary arriving before them and offering to buy the product on the spot. In impoverished regions, the first offer of immediate cash can be very appealing. Intermediaries, however, generally buy only one bean variety, carioca, to sell to the Brazilian market. ASOPROF began working with different bean varieties that would be destined for markets other than Brazil. Intermediaries were unable to secure export channels to distant countries, and so producers sold their new varieties to ASOMEX. ASOMEX tried briefly to work with intermediaries; however, it was not a positive experience.

Currently two new companies are in direct competition with ASOMEX – Bolsemilla and Bolivian Shoji. These companies export a number of products, including beans; they have developed advanced services and maintain a strong financial base. Both companies opened after ASOMEX, with beans as their initial product. While ASOMEX has no direct relationship with this competition, it can be inferred that by demonstrating a feasible market for edible beans, ASOMEX has sparked improved system capacity. It can be further suggested that this has positive effects for producers and the industry itself.

Complementary services exist for ASOMEX and its producer clients. Credit and technical assistance are often provided to the producers through their associations and are sometimes also available through NGO projects such as MEDA's PROCOR project. Within the marketing and exporting process, complementary services are also available. ASOMEX contracts out various elements of the marketing process to other companies, including land and port transportation services and customs paperwork.

Promotion strategy

ASOMEX strives to be a demand-driven company, demand for its services coming from both buyers and producers. Buyer demand is essential, as without market interest in its products, ASOMEX would not exist. Producer clients are also important because they supply the product to meet buyer demand. The key for ASOMEX is to search continuously for new buyer clients, ensuring an end market for its products, while at the same time maintaining good relationships with its producer clients.

ASOMEX is developing a new source of clients through another MEDA project, PROCOR. MEDA is working with a number of rural associations and cooperatives of small producers to help them develop new crops with export potential. ASOMEX is helping to carry out market research for the project and is also the channel through which many of these producer groups are choosing to market their products.

Pricing strategy

ASOMEX sets the price for its services with the goal of cost recovery and profit in mind, but at the same time it tries to maintain longer-term loyalty of the producers. In the export order processing service, ASOMEX sets its price as a percentage of the sales made – 3 per cent of sales with ASOPROF.

When ASOMEX provides brokering services, it walks a fine line with the price it can charge. Once ASOMEX has brought a buyer and a seller together, the two can be tempted to cut themselves off from ASOMEX and continue their business independently. Therefore, in brokering, ASOMEX attempts to set the price low enough to maintain client loyalty but still to make money. The aim is to make a profit by turning over a high volume.

Local and international market effects

International markets affect ASOMEX in many ways. Other countries' tariffs and import regulations are important factors. For example, Venezuela has recently dropped its tariff on imported soybeans from Brazil and Argentina, which puts Bolivian soybean producers at a significant disadvantage and could cause Bolivian companies previously involved with soybeans to shift their interest and production to areas in which ASOMEX has found a niche. Exchange rate movements also affect ASOMEX. Last year, a change in the Colombian rate affected the country's level of bean imports from Bolivia, thus having a direct impact on Bolivia's export prices. These changing market conditions play a significant role in ASOMEX's profits or losses. To protect itself against major losses incurred from market shifts, ASOMEX has diversified its services and is pursuing diversified bases of client and product, to reduce the risk further.

The work of ASOMEX can also have an impact on local markets. Producer prices are affected, usually positively, by the fact that ASOMEX is exporting. Although ASOMEX offers direct competition to local intermediaries, it is furthering its goal of meeting the needs of small producers and increasing their incomes.

ASOMEX management and its stakeholders

ASOMEX and MEDA

MEDA has played an important role in starting ASOMEX and in guiding it towards meeting its objectives, becoming a stronger more stable company and achieving profitability. Here we examine the philosophy, objectives and approach of MEDA, to better see ASOMEX in the context of its NGO support.

The mandate of MEDA's International Economic Development division is 'to serve the poor through the development of businesses'. MEDA aims to work with the poorest of the economically active. A central goal of the MEDA Bolivia Country Management Unit is 'to serve the marketing, financial and economic needs of small rural and urban producers'. MEDA aims to establish sustainable businesses. While recognizing that the development agenda is much more than economic development and that businesses are not always the best vehicle for achieving development goals, MEDA believes that in many cases establishing a profitable business can be an invaluable foundation on which to build other social and economic gains.[7] This is the philosophy behind MEDA's involvement in ASOMEX.

MEDA's projects typically move through a progression of three stages. First is a *project stage*, where MEDA tests, usually for two years, the project's assumptions and potential for becoming a business. The *programme stage*, usually three to five years, develops the project to the point where it can become an independent business, testing its capacity to recover its own costs. The *business stage* works to balance the different goals of profitability and development. The company assumes financial responsibility, and MEDA terminates its role as a donor and takes on the role of a business partner.[8]

In examining the history of ASOMEX, it can be seen that the marketing work of ASOMEX underwent its transition through the project and programme stages while still a part of ASOPROF. Thus, with the birth of the company ASOMEX, MEDA moved this small-producer marketing idea into its business stage.

MEDA's initial investment in ASOMEX was carried out through MEDA's Global Investment Fund (GIF), based in North America. The fund provides investment funds to small and medium-sized businesses in developing countries that serve the needs of the poor. North American investors affiliated with MEDA provide the investment funds. Many of the businesses in which GIF invests are former MEDA programmes that have graduated to the business stage; thus ASOMEX was an obvious candidate.

MEDA has also played an important role in developing ASOMEX. Its programmes in agriculture and rural development provided a product – beans – found a market for that product, and developed a solid base of producers and production technology. In essence, MEDA contributed to the development of a successful system, which ASOMEX has taken advantage of and benefited from.[9]

At start-up, MEDA placed an equity investment in ASOMEX and provided support for the company's legal formation. Further along in its life, MEDA also extended a line of credit to the company through its revolving loan fund, in the amount of US$30 000 over two years at 12 per cent, which has already been paid back. MEDA sits on the ASOMEX board, thus assuming an important role in guiding and advising ASOMEX on how to achieve profitability. As a major shareholder, MEDA has a vested interest in ASOMEX's future as a profitable business.

In demonstrating ASOMEX's contribution to the broad development objectives of MEDA, it is best to examine data created in conjunction with ASOPROF (Table 3.2). Although the impact indicators in the table were created for ASOPROF, they describe ASOMEX's impact. See also the 'Impact' section.

MEDA's exit strategy for ASOMEX involves waiting (while continuing its guidance role as a shareholder) until the company achieves sufficient profitability and stability to attract other investors interested in buying it out. There is no specified period, and MEDA is waiting to see how ASOMEX fares over the next couple of years. MEDA's GIF will ultimately decide when MEDA sells its shares in the company.

Table 3.2   MEDA's impact indicators for ASOPROF and ASOMEX

Impact	FY 1994	FY 1995	FY 1996
Families assisted (no.)	3075	2568	2100
Full-time, year-round jobs created (no.)	506	807	350
Average client net equity increase (US$)[a]	146	129	135
Total client net equity increase (US$)[b]	233 600	214 914	283 500
Client net equity increase divided by invested capital	0.6	0.4	0.7
Total MEDA programme cost (US$)	–	33 346	52 500
Client NEI and total MEDA cost (US$)	–	6.4	5.4

Source: MEDA Bolivia annual evaluation, fiscal year 1996
[a]'Client' refers to farm family. Average client net equity increase represents the net margin that the farmer receives from planting one hectare of beans.
[b]The average client net equity increase multiplied by the number of families assisted

ASOMEX and its shareholders

All the investment funds necessary to start ASOMEX were gained through the sale of shares in the company. Approximately US$40 000 in shares were sold, with prices set by law and approved by the shareholders themselves. These shareholders are the key source of external support for ASOMEX, as they provide guidance, planning and management input for the company. In theory, this of course is based not on donor mentality but on the shareholder's self-interest in the profitability of the company. ASOMEX did in fact distribute dividends to its shareholders (in 1995), paying them 50 per cent of the year's profits, and capitalizing the other 50 per cent. Currently, ASOPROF owns 58.09 per cent of the shares in ASOMEX, MEDA 17.45 per cent, and individual shareholders a total of 24.46 per cent.

The ASOMEX board of directors is made up of three shareholder representatives: the MEDA Bolivia director, the ASOPROF director, and the representative of the individual shareholders, who is also the current manager of ASOMEX. Board of directors meetings are supposed to be held at least once every three months but have occurred less frequently. MEDA is committed to improving the coordination and quality of these meetings, which are beginning to occur monthly. Meetings of all shareholders are set to occur once a year.

Generally, the monitoring and planning processes have been weak. ASOMEX management is responsible for providing its board of directors with monthly financial statements and monthly export figures. On many occasions there were no numbers to present, and meetings were not held. Similar evidence of poor monitoring and planning is that the annual shareholders meetings have not been held in several years. ASOMEX has not been providing a regular annual report to shareholders, as it should.

A key weakness in the structure of ASOMEX's ownership has led to these problems. Shareholders with any significant ownership in the company are a small circle of four closely connected institutions and individuals. This situation is clearly not in the best interest of ASOMEX. Having a larger number of independent individual shareholders with a greater share in company ownership could enhance the company's performance.

ASOMEX and its personnel

ASOMEX initially shared a management team with ASOPROF, consisting of director, accountant and secretary. This gave the company the benefit of a team with years of experience working in the bean business. However, the shared staffing arrangement also had its drawbacks, and in retrospect was probably a mistake. ASOMEX was held back from becoming independent, and decisions were made that favoured ASOPROF, sometimes to the detriment of ASOMEX. Staff loyalties naturally lay closer to ASOPROF; finances were blurred, and ASOMEX suffered from poor financial records and accounting.

Finally, in 1997, with encouragement from its board of directors, ASOMEX established an independent management team. The biggest push came from MEDA, with ASOPROF agreeing. ASOMEX acquired its own staff team of three – manager, secretary-accountant and export specialist. In early 1998, after having encountered several staff problems, ASOMEX hired a new team. The manager, who owned close to 10 per cent of the shares in the company, was identified from among the shareholders.

Although it was a good move, transition to independence was difficult. It became clear that ASOMEX had been absorbing some costs that rightfully belonged to ASOPROF. ASOPROF was also collecting all the government export incentive money for exports channelled through ASOMEX. In dealing with this and other issues, ASOPROF exerted a great deal of pressure. This pressure was compounded by the fact that ASOPROF was both the majority shareholder and the largest client. MEDA found itself caught up in trying to maintain good terms with ASOPROF for continued cooperation in common projects and funding sources, while at the same time trying to act in the best interests of its company, ASOMEX.

At present only the manager can qualify for any financial incentive based on performance. The board of directors plans to change the current bonus structure to a percentage of profit. The division of labour in the management team does not make it appropriate to give other employees profit-based incentives.[10] Moreover, it is highly unlikely that anyone in that sector or industry is paid on commission.

At this point, the manager has identified that job satisfaction is a far more effective form of motivating staff. ASOMEX provides its staff with a pleasant work environment, good working conditions, a fair approach towards employees, and the opportunity to learn as part of the work. This is of significant value, given the difficult conditions prevalent in many other workplaces in the area.

ASOMEX and its producer clients

Briefly introduced here are the major ASOMEX clients, their relationship to ASOMEX, and key factors contributing to the success that ASOMEX has had in marketing and exporting. Information on client impact and satisfaction with BDS is detailed in the 'Impact' section in 'Best practices'.

ASOMEX clients are associations of producers. Current clients are:

- *ASOPROF (Asociación Nacional de Productores de Frijol – National Association of Bean Producers),* 1800 members. ASOPROF was started through MEDA's work in introducing edible beans to the lowlands of Bolivia as a winter crop. Its objective is to improve the socio-economic conditions of small-scale peasant producers. All of ASOPROF's product is exported through ASOMEX, and has been since day one that ASOMEX was set up.
- *ASOHABA (Asociación de Productores de Haba – Association of Broad Bean Producers),* 304 members. ASOHABA is a newer association of broad bean producers in the region of Potosí. Its producers live in 19 different highland communities. ASOHABA, which began in 1995 with financial assistance from the European Union, works with MEDA's PRO-COR programme. ASOMEX is confident that ASOHABA has a high-quality product with good export potential despite the management difficulties it has experienced.
- *Fernheim (Paraguayan Mennonite peanut producers),* approximately 5000 farmers. Fernheim has just begun to market through ASOMEX, which is acting as its broker, setting up Fernheim with buyers in the Andean market. With a potential for marketing 500 tonnes of peanuts annually, Fernheim could become a very valuable client for ASOMEX.
- *ASOFAM (Asociación Nacional de Fabricantes Artesanos de Muebles – Association of Artisan Furniture Makers),* 26 highly skilled artisans who construct high-quality, high-end furniture, is a past client. The association is hoping to expand its exports in the near future and is again looking to ASOMEX as one of its main possibilities for a marketing company.

Although no direct transactions have yet occurred, a relationship is developing with another potential client:

- *FEDEAGRO (Federación de Asociaciones Agropecuarias – Federation of Associations of Agricultural Producers),* 732 small-scale farmer members in approximately 15 different communities in the state of Chuquisaca. The farmers produce corn, peanuts, beans and hot peppers, and FEDEAGRO provides technical assistance and a common marketing entity.

Overall, ASOMEX believes that clients should have the following key factors for success:

- ability to produce a high-quality product
- dependability to meet ASOMEX and buyer deadlines
- dependability to meet buyer demand and product specifications
- a strong management system and an efficient production process
- ASOMEX's contribution in bringing producers a fair price for their product.

Although none of ASOMEX's clients has had a perfect record in all of these areas, all are aware of these important factors and are working to integrate them into their organizations.

Best practices

Financial strategy

ASOMEX's structural beginnings were an important element in determining its financial strategy. The services that ASOMEX now provides were initially carried out in a more limited form under MEDA's observation and supervision, within ASOPROF. Thus, before the BDS package was developed to the point of ASOMEX becoming a self-sufficient company, it had the benefit of starting out and developing within an association, aided by grant money from MEDA and other NGOs (Lutheran World Relief and Catholic Relief Services). The feasibility of forming a marketing company to serve ASO-PROF and others had already been shown to be financially viable. Debt incurred in the development and learning stages stayed with ASOPROF, enabling ASOMEX to begin with a clean financial slate.

ASOMEX's entire start-up capital was raised by selling company shares. No grants or donations were incurred to finance it as a separate company. Its six shareholders have forced ASOMEX to be financially accountable and have put it under constant pressure to make a profit; development objectives take second place.

The current financial strategy

ASOMEX's financial strategy comprises a variety of elements, some of which the company has followed since its initiation and others that have been learned along the way. One key element is its 'bare-bones' operation. ASOMEX has minimal operating costs, a staff of three and a shared office.

ASOMEX keeps its services focused. It sets prices to recover 100 per cent of the costs and achieve a profit margin. Financial records show losses for three of the six years for the company; however, this is not related to incorrect price setting. Rather, the losses can be attributed primarily to ASOPROF's low production volume during several poor growing seasons and a number of poor management decisions.

Maintaining its commitment to work with small producers, ASOMEX relies on their associations to minimize costs. The association bears the cost and effort needed to coordinate quality work of the individuals and to gather the finished product. By choosing clients who have developed a good capacity for marketing and exporting, ASOMEX can save itself the costs of trying to work with ill-equipped producers.

ASOMEX presently faces severe financial constraints. It needs to diversify yet needs significant funds to take advantage of new opportunities as an intermediary and export processor, where capital demands are high up front. In ASOPROF's special relationship with ASOMEX, ASOPROF allows ASOMEX to make use of some of its own working capital in carrying out the export processing, resulting in further financial dependence. Also, ASOMEX exports follow ASOPROF's harvests, and it has incurred losses when ASO-PROF did not produce as expected (see Figures 3.1 and 3.2). Its key strategy to avoid seasonal lulls and losses is to pursue a broader product and client base, focusing on agricultural products and adding medium-scale producers.

Analysis of profitability
ASOMEX has demonstrated an ability to recover costs and sustain itself financially in three of its six years of operation. Its effectiveness, however, is difficult to assess. Until 1997, ASOMEX was operated jointly with

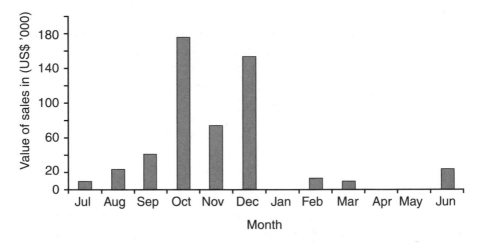

Figure 3.1   *ASOMEX's value of monthly exports, fiscal year 1997/8*

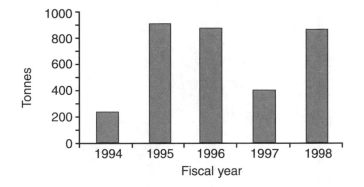

Figure 3.2   *ASOMEX bean exports, fiscal years 1994–98 (volume)*
Source: ASOMEX annual evaluation report 1998

ASOPROF; financial records were poorly kept and somewhat distorted because of an unclear division between the two institutions.

A major factor making the financial records of limited value in providing cost-effectiveness indicators is Bolivia's tax incentive and export bonus structure, which seems to promote some rather unconventional accounting practices. The quantity of export bonus received is determined by the amount of expense incurred in the export. This is an incentive to overstate costs of export and weakens the incentive to minimize costs.

ASOMEX does not record costs and revenues as they pertain to each of the three types of services offered, or the elements within each. It is therefore not possible to discuss the cost effectiveness of each type of service individually. ASOMEX cannot say conclusively which of its services are most profitable, or if some are incurring losses.

Company strengths in achieving cost efficiency lie in 1) a bare-bones operation, 2) the highly focused BDS package, 3) its history of a cost-recovery pricing strategy, 4) carefully chosen producer-association clients, and 5) the company's commitment to devising new strategies to improve itself.

Profits have been unstable, in large part because of the overdependence on ASOPROF as the major client (Figure 3.3). The profit fluctuations of ASOMEX reflect the trends of ASOPROF, as well as some poor interinstitutional accounting and management practices. For example, in 1997 ASOMEX would have shown a profit; however, it was discovered that the company had not recorded a past loan of US$40 000. The entire amount was written down in 1997.

The value of total equity in ASOMEX started out strong with good profits in its first full year of operation, 1994 (Figure 3.4). However, total equity started to erode as the company failed to diversify its base of producer clients, and it experienced losses.

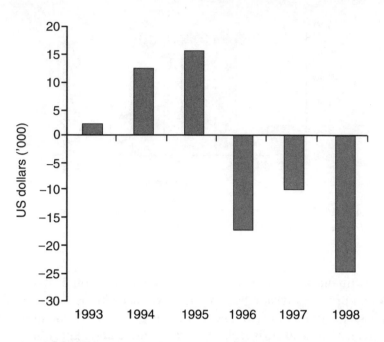

Figure 3.3   *ASOMEX net profit, fiscal years 1993–98. Based on ASOMEX*
Estados Financieros 1993, 1994, 1995, 1996, 1997, 1998

The trend in ASOMEX's debt:equity ratio has been upward (Figure 3.5). This is the result of the combined effect of assuming higher levels of debt, accumulated to provide new operating capital in years of insufficient profit or of losses.

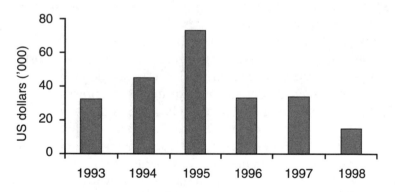

Figure 3.4   *ASOMEX total equity, fiscal years 1993–98. Based on ASOMEX*
Estados Financieros 1993, 1994, 1995, 1996, 1997, 1998

The company's return on equity has not fared well. Figure 3.6 and Table 3.3 show that ASOMEX has not been profitable in three years of negative returns.

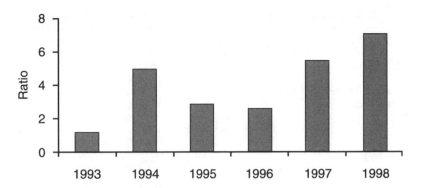

Figure 3.5   *ASOMEX debt:equity ratio, fiscal years 1993–98. Source: ASOMEX Estados Financieros 1993, 1994, 1995, 1996, 1997, 1998*

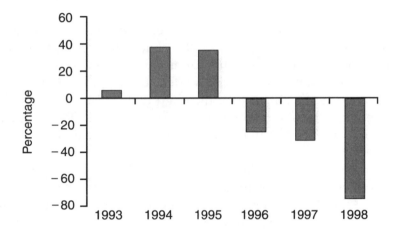

Figure 3.6   *ASOMEX return on equity, fiscal years 1993–98. Based on ASOMEX Estados Financieros 1993, 1994, 1995, 1996, 1997, 1998*

Table 3.3   Financial indicator summary, fiscal years 1993–98

Year	Net profit (US$)	Total equity (US$)	Return on equity (%)	Total liability (US$)	Debt:equity ratio
1993	1901	32 520	6	32 974	1.10
1994	12 306	44 826	38	281 521	4.87
1995	15 582	72 959	35	201 947	2.77
1996	(17 426)	33 033	−24	86 405	2.60
1997	(1899)	34 027	−30	184 777	5.43
1998	(24 693)	15 224	−162	106 804	7.02

ASOMEX has not fared particularly well in meeting its annual targets (Table 3.4). Because 1997 was the first year with a reasonably reliable accounting system and with all financial data available, 1997 is taken as an example.[11]

51

Table 3.4   ASOMEX target performance (all three categories of service are included)

Performance Indicators	FY 1997 target	FY 1997 actual	Percentage of target
Value of sales (US$)	456 000	272 787	59.82
COG sold	366 300	215 000	58.70
Volume of sales (metric tonnes)	3500	392	11.20
Accounts receivables clients	85 000	64 050	75.35
Inventory	12 000	0	0.00
Gross margin	88 700	58 420	65.86
Profit	8300	−19 189	−231.19
Return on equity	0.04	−0.30	−425.00
Active buyers	10	9	90.00
New products	3	0	0.00

As reported in MEDA's annual evaluation report for 1997

ASOMEX faced considerable management challenges during the year (MEDA financial year July 1996–June 1997), and only in the third quarter did MEDA receive financial information from the company. This, coupled with poor climatic conditions that negatively affected bean production, resulted in less than desirable performance for the year (Table 3. 4).

It certainly would not be accurate to say that ASOMEX has operated at an optimum of cost efficiency. In fact, the value of the company has been dropping rather than increasing.

Evidently, a number of factors have contributed to why ASOMEX has not achieved more financial success and better cost effectiveness. All of ASOMEX's major stakeholders now agree that ASOMEX would have run more efficiently if it had had an independent administrative team much earlier in its life. A separate accounting system would have helped the company immensely, and tighter supervision and monitoring of the company's operation and costs would probably have made ASOMEX more efficient, and might have helped to avoid some of its losses.

ASOMEX now has its own accountant, who has greatly improved the quality of the company's financial records. A much better financial monitoring process is now in place, with more accurate, timely accounts. The company continues to search for more producer clients and is exploring avenues through which to secure more working capital. The current management is making considerable effort in many of the problem areas and is confident that change will make ASOMEX profitable once again. Like many young companies, ASOMEX has had its share of financial challenges and is still on a learning curve. Its shareholders are willing to give it more time to climb out of the business-cycle downturn that it has faced recently, and will push the company towards reaching a high level of profitability and cost effectiveness.

ASOMEX outreach

The associations that ASOMEX serves represent many small and medium-sized producers who, in turn, represent entire families that are benefiting from the marketing work of ASOMEX. Table 3.5 estimates the magnitude of ASOMEX's impact, by multiplying the number of producer members (mostly rural men) by a conservative estimate of the size of a Bolivian family.

Table 3.5   ASOMEX clientele

Client association	Years in which association has been a client						Association members (no. households)	Estimated total beneficiaries (no.)
	1993	1994	1995	1996	1997	1998		
ASOPROF	✔	✔	✔	✔	✔	✔	1800	9360
PRISMA		✔	✔	✔			approx. 150	750
ASOFAM				✔	✔		26	130
ASOHABA				✔	✔	✔	304	2128
Fernheim[a]						✔	approx. 5000	–
Totals							2280 (+ 5000)	12 368

[a]Fernheim is not in the target group because it is made up of medium-scale producers and located outside Bolivia, in Paraguay.

ASOMEX's target group is very broad – Bolivian small producers. The company has decided to focus its efforts on agricultural marketing, which reaches the majority of Bolivia's rural population. Table 3.6 gives a general idea of the rural population in areas where ASOMEX is working, and the percentage of the population with which it works.

Table 3.6   Percentage of target group served, by region

State	Province	1992 rural population (no.)	1998 rural population (est. no.)	Target population being served (no.)[a]	Local target group served (approx. %)
Potosí	Linares	52 535	60 150	304 (× 7) – 2128	3.5
Chuquisaca	Hernando Siles	30 125	34 492	582 (× 7.4) = 4307	12.5
Chuquisaca	Luis Calvo	15 199	17 402	61 (× 7.4) = 451	2.6
Santa Cruz	Cordillera	88 628	101 475		
Santa Cruz	Florida	16 955	19 413		
Santa Cruz	Nuflo de Chavez	52 334	59 920	1800 (× 5.2) = 9360	4.8
Santa Cruz	M.M. Caballero	12 853	14 716		

1992 rural population figures, with estimated population figures for 1998.
[a]Target population served is based on the number of client association families in the region, multiplied by the average family size. (Sources of statistics: *PROCOR Diagnósticos Socioeconómicos*, MEDA, FDC and CIDA, 1998; *Estadísticas Socio-Económicas 1996;* Müller y Asociados 1997.)

It is also important to note that the outreach of ASOMEX goes beyond the numbers of association members receiving its marketing services. Often the producer associations will buy the produce of non-member producers to bring their volume up, allowing more people to benefit from the marketing service. Furthermore, when ASOMEX introduces a higher price for the producers' product than other intermediaries normally offer, the effect is an overall increase in the price for producers, thus indirectly benefiting non-member small-scale producers as well.

Demographics and socio-economic condition of clients

ASOMEX has not studied the demographic variables of the population it serves. As a profit-oriented company, it does not track client demographics or socio-economic variables.[12] ASOMEX is certainly generally aware of the conditions of poverty that prevail in the areas in which it works, and this awareness forms much of the motivation for the company's existence.

For this case study, general socio-economic indicators have been gathered for some of the regions in which ASOMEX has active clients. Although the statistics presented are not specifically based on ASOMEX producers, they do help to paint a general picture of the conditions that people in those communities face.[13] The producer associations with which ASOMEX works represent typical small campesino producers in the regions highlighted below. Two communities and a province are presented as samples of socio-economic conditions for each of three ASOMEX client associations (Table 3.7).[14]

Most producers in the rural areas of Santa Cruz where ASOPROF works have more land than farmers elsewhere in the country. Average producers being served in this region have between 20 and 50 hectares per family, although not all of the land may be under cultivation at any one time. This is in contrast to regions such as Chuquisaca, where average land ownership is between 0 and 20 hectares. The members of ASOHABA and FEDEAGRO are more representative of the level of poverty of the average Bolivian rural small-scale producer. ASOFAM, however, although it had humble beginnings, has become very successful and is best classified as urban middle class.

Client impact and benefits

As ASOPROF is the primary client of ASOMEX and is the company's sustenance, the following focuses principally on the impact on ASOPROF farmers.

Economic impact

The trends and data presented here are taken from interviews with ASOPROF member farmers, a study done by CIAT (International Centre for Tropical Agriculture) published in 1999,[15] and ASOPROF statistical reports and files. Seven variables were examined to glean an idea of impact: hectares cultivated, number of farmers cultivating beans, yield, farmer income (looking at price and cost per hectare), education, health and community change.

Measuring ASOMEX impact is a difficult task. Weather patterns play the largest role in affecting crop production and yields. Overall, when taking into

Table 3.7 Socio-economic conditions in communities where ASOMEX producer clients live

	San Julián, Santa Cruz (ASOPROF region)	Puna, Linares, Potosí (ASOHABA region)	Hernando Siles, Chuquisaca (FEDEAGRO region)	National averages[a]
Average family size	5.2	7	7.4	NA
Average annual income (US$)	NA	479	NA	2617 (real GDP per capita)
Infant mortality (no. per 1000 live births who die before age 1)	90	123	89	71
Child malnourishment	NA	60 per cent of children under 5 are malnourished, 38 per cent are chronically malnourished and stunted in growth	NA	11 per cent of children under 5 are malnourished
Life expectancy at birth (years)	NA	54	NA	60.5
Literacy (per cent)	75	50.77	59	83
Education (per cent)	none: 22.5 elementary: 52.1 secondary: 24.3 university: 0.9 technical: 0.2	NA	NA	66 per cent of age 6–23 enrolled in some type of education
Piped water (per cent)	29	NA	NA	63
Average land size (hectares)	20–50	4	NA	NA
Mechanized cultivation	well over 20 per cent	minimal	15 per cent	NA

[a]*Human Development Report 1998,* UNDP, 1998
NA – information not available

consideration the variables of weather, disease, market conditions, bean variety, season, location and inputs, the measurement of impact becomes extremely difficult and potentially impossible.

When asked why they grow beans, the most common response was that there was no other crop to grow in winter and that beans were an excellent option in crop rotation, allowing farmers' yearly earnings to increase significantly.

Overall, the number of hectares cultivated for beans has increased since 1993 (Table 3.8). Some farmers are dedicating more land to beans, others are cultivating more land overall, and more producers are beginning to plant beans as a crop. Mechanization has also played a role; it is on the rise among farmers and, in their opinion, it facilitates an increased amount of bean cultivation.

Table 3.8   Bean production statistics

Year	Quintal price (US$)	Cost per hectare (US$)	Total cultivated (ha)	Producers (no.)	Yield (quintals per ha)	Income est. per ha (US$)	Bean varieties (no.)
1990	16.10	240	1000	700	21.7	110	2
1991	10.50	240	1989	1781	21.7	−13	2
1992	11.40	240	1350	777	22.0	10	3
1993	14.60	240	2600	1550	25.0	124	3
1994	17.10	250	3026	1500	25.0	176	5
1995	13.80	260	3750	1700	24.0	72	6
1996	16.10	270	2745	1600	36.0	311	6
1997	15.20	280	3000	1800	21.0	39	4
1998	17.10	280	3150	1800	15.0	−24	5

This table was compiled from data gathered by field research in January 2000. Sources included interviews with farmers, ASOPROF, ASOMEX and MEDA Bolivia staff, and ASOMEX and ASOPROF records.

The shift to planned production is clear. Farmers are aware of prices and market trends, and ASOPROF works to keep them informed of such. Planned production can be seen as an indirect impact of ASOMEX, because it provides the buyers for Bolivian beans, which in turn gives ASOPROF the ability to offer price contracts and information, and to concentrate its time on technical assistance and credit rather than marketing.

Another indicator of ASOMEX's impact is the number of producers cultivating beans. The number of associations working with ASOPROF, and thus ASOMEX, grew from 16 in 1993 to 21 in 1998.

Overall, it is difficult to measure trends in yield. Among the many factors that affect bean yield are of course weather patterns, disease and the crop-management techniques of individual producers. In addition, the quality of seed is key.

When examining incomes, prices and costs play the primary role (Figure 3.7). Costs for farmers have remained relatively stable over the past six years; prices, on the other hand, have fluctuated. Two important factors are not visible in the figures in Table 3 8. First, the prices are an average, as are yields, and farmers may have had a better harvest and better prices for the crop to which they planted the most hectares – which would give them a better income than shown. Second, beans fill a seasonal gap in the agricultural production calendar, allowing cultivation during winter – commonly a fallow season. The impact of a second crop is not evident in the income figures, which look at income per unit of beans and over a specific time period.

Table 3.8 includes one other indicator of interest – bean varieties – which was not discussed with farmers. This indicator demonstrates an overall upward trend, which is excellent for ASOMEX. The fact that ASOMEX continues to find markets for increased quantities and varieties of beans has a positive local impact.

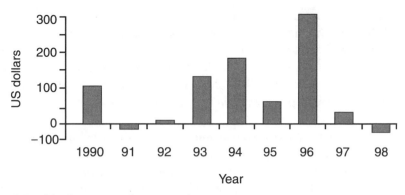

Figure 3.7   *Net income estimate per hectare*

Social impact

Measuring social change is a challenge. ASOMEX does not collect impact data of any type, and ASOPROF does not record social indicators. The analysis here is based solely on anecdotal evidence from interviews and discussions.

It is possible that with the increase in income that farm families have received through selling their beans, they have had the opportunity to increase their education level.[16] A few of those interviewed noted increased opportunity for technical assistance and training courses for themselves, and women mentioned the classes that ASOPROF has been providing. In ASOPROF's opinion, when families have extra income, they will spend it first on their production process (such as buying a tractor) and their second priority is often education. Among those interviewed in the CIAT study, parents had an average of two years of education and children 7.5 years.

Increased consumption of beans is assumed to improve nutrition. To examine the impact of beans on family health it is necessary to look at the adoption of beans into the local diet. All families interviewed had either continued or increased their levels of consumption. Many stated that beans had not been a common part of the diet but that they were slowly becoming accustomed to the food and it was being assimilated. In the study completed by CIAT (interviewing 367 urban housewives and 261 rural housewives), results showed that over 75 per cent of rural families and 84 per cent of the poorest families consumed beans. In the rural sector, beans accounted for 30 per cent of the daily protein requirements. In the urban context, beans have also been adopted, with 50 per cent of families consuming them, fulfilling 17 per cent of their daily protein requirements. This is a positive impact on health for both rural and urban Bolivians, due in part to the work of MEDA, ASOPROF and ASOMEX.

Impact on other clients

The work that ASOMEX carried out with MEDA's PRISMA members in 1994–96 had a positive impact on many of the participants. ASOMEX did not simply act as an intermediary for the PRISMA microentrepreneurs but involved them in the marketing and exporting process, educating them along the way. The producers who were able to export their product felt this was a major achievement, helping to build their confidence as entrepreneurs. Unfortunately the work with PRISMA was not financially sustainable and ended after the pilot project; however, the benefits of improved capacity remained.

ASOFAM, which was formed by some of the most successful furniture producers of the PRISMA programme, worked with ASOMEX in 1996 and 1997 but has not recently done so because members have been content to focus their efforts on local marketing. However, ASOFAM is once again considering the services of an export company.

In its relatively short experience with ASOHABA, ASOMEX has been helpful to the member producers. Before working with ASOMEX, the producers faced selling their crops to intermediaries who often paid poor prices.

It is too early to obtain any impact information on FEDEAGRO, which is currently adopting new crops, including peanuts, chickpeas, and hot chillies, for which ASOMEX is carrying out market research and identification of foreign buyers.

Benefits on a broader scale
ASOMEX has also contributed to the wider society in a number of ways. Already touched upon is the fact that it adds some much-needed competition to the intermediary market. This has had a large-scale impact on the market, bringing prices up among other intermediaries, thus benefiting many more producers active in the same market. The local bean industry benefits by encouraging more efficient practices, and producers benefit from having additional options for selling their product.

Another contribution to the wider society is the foreign exchange earned. Most of the marketing that ASOMEX carries out involves exporting, thus earning important foreign exchange for Bolivia. The value of goods that ASOMEX exports is an indicator of the foreign exchange contribution: in 1994/5, the foreign exchange earned was US$228 000; in 1995/6, US$390 000; and in 1996/7, US$286 494.

ASOMEX has also served as a valuable experience for MEDA and has furthered MEDA's capacity to build sustainable delivery institutions. MEDA has learned much in establishing ASOMEX and is working to improve its services and operation.

Appropriateness of the service
ASOMEX has demonstrated innovation and flexibility in meeting the diverse needs of its clients. ASOPROF needs a reliable export processing service provider at a reasonable price. ASOFAM needs a company that can undertake in-depth market research, identify appropriate foreign buyers and

set up distribution channels. ASOHABA needs an intermediary with fair prices that will handle the entire market research and exportation process. Fernheim needs someone to put it in contact with potential buyers and assist in negotiating with them. In exercising some flexibility in working out an appropriate service for each client association, ASOMEX has been able to maintain a relevant set of interventions for its clients.

Where ASOMEX's service can at times be less appropriate than desired by clients is not in the types of interventions themselves but in how well they have been carried out.[17] One client association has voiced complaints about ASOMEX's export process not always operating smoothly. There have been problems in the timely passage of payment from foreign buyers to the specified bank accounts of the producer association, the slowness significantly inconveniencing all involved. There are also complaints of poor coordination along the product transportation route, causing missed connections and delayed shipments – none of which convey a positive image to the waiting buyer. Some of these problems are due to poor management on ASOMEX's part. More strict and continuous monitoring of the process can reduce the difficulties. Sometimes things are beyond ASOMEX's control, such as flooding causing impassable roads (very common in Bolivia) – and simply the nature of the export business. ASOMEX management is working to eliminate as many of these problems as possible.

Is ASOMEX achieving its maximum development impact? Despite some of its problems, it is providing a much-needed service to an often-overlooked group of people. Small-scale producers certainly have demand for the service; only some can pay for it. There are some complaints from clients, but when asked for an overall impression of how worthwhile it is to work with ASOMEX, these same clients are pleased. Volume must be increased and quality of service improved. The current level of impact is already impressive, having benefited several thousand small-scale producers, and the potential for much larger outreach in the future is high.

Sustainability

Economic sustainability
Despite ASOMEX's less than impressive financial record, the company has been able to survive its first six years of existence, through indirect assistance from MEDA and profit from operations in 1993–95.[18] The board is confident that there is great potential for the company, with these early years serving as years of building the company and learning. They see ASOMEX as being on the brink of a new stage in improved performance. In looking at the possibility for continued sustainability of the young company, what is important is ASOMEX's ability to identify weakness and mistakes of the past and respond effectively to overcome them.

The cost effectiveness section showed the company's economic position to be unstable and, were these trends to continue much into the future, ASOMEX would not be financially sustainable. However, the company clearly recognizes the major reasons for its instability of recent years – the failure to achieve its objective of a broadened producer-client base and the lack of funds to take advantage of new opportunities. The current priority of ASOMEX is to correct these problems. There is no guarantee that diversification will be a winning strategy that will succeed in eliminating instability. However, it appears to be a reasonable and necessary move, and when combined with several other courses of action (improving financial management, obtaining further sources for capital funds) it should improve the company's performance.

The fact that ASOMEX has been highly demand driven contributes to its sustainability. As originally designed by its clients, pursuing strategies of a flexible marketing service tailored to client needs is a valuable factor in sustainability. Also, the demand-driven strategy for identifying new producer clients based on existing buyer demand should prove valuable. Sources of revenue (both producer and buyer clients) are increasing and are expected to continue growing. Table 3.9 shows that new producer clients have been added each year.

Table 3.9 Active clients – product associations and export countries

Year	Active clients (new clients in italics)	Countries exported to (new markets in italics)
1993	ASOPROF	Bolivia
1994	ASOPROF, *PRISMA*	Bolivia, Colombia, Hong Kong, Italy, Japan
1995	ASOPROF, PRISMA	Argentina, Bolivia, *Brazil,* Colombia, Japan, *Spain*
1996	ASOFAM, *ASOHABA,* ASOPROF, PRISMA	Argentina, Brazil, Colombia, Japan
1997	ASOFAM, ASOHABA, ASOPROF	Argentina, Brazil, Colombia, *Italy,* Japan, Spain
1998	ASOHABA, ASOPROF, *FEDEAGRO, FERNHEIM*	Brazil, Colombia, *France,* Japan, *Venezuela*

ASOMEX's clients have demonstrated their willingness to pay by their continued demand for the service. The second column in Table 3.9 shows the continuity in clients. Other small producers and producer organizations would like to have access to a marketing service but cannot afford to pay prices based on cost recovery, or are not export ready. Existing and potential clients say they find ASOMEX prices for its services to be reasonable and slightly better than those of competing companies.

The sustainability of ASOMEX depends on its capacity to maintain a good working relationship with its suppliers, especially ASOPROF. Good relationships with clients involve ASOMEX looking for new buyer markets and new products, and meeting the demands that both its producer and its buyer clients place on it.

Internal operation, and stakeholder communication and commitment
ASOMEX, between its board of directors and its management team, has always intended to develop annual plans, strategize regularly, and constantly innovate to keep services relevant and in demand. However, planning and strategizing are generally not priority areas in the local Bolivian context, making it a struggle for ASOMEX to follow through on its intentions in this area. All of the shareholders are committed to maintaining their shares in the company. Despite having some complaints in its dealing with ASOMEX as a service provider, ASOPROF holds firm to its desire to remain a key shareholder. It has a lot of interest in the company and sees good potential in its future.

Company evolution, shifts and future prospects
ASOMEX has developed, modified and improved its marketing service package over the past few years. Its business development service now offers three variations of marketing services, along with market research and other useful information. The client base is growing, and ASOMEX has begun serving the small producers in several new regions (Table 3.10).

Table 3.10   States where ASOMEX producer clients reside

Year	State (expansion into new regions in italics)
1993	Chuquisaca, Santa Cruz
1994	Chuquisaca, *Cochabamba, Potosí,* Santa Cruz
1995	Chuquisaca, Cochabamba, Potosí, Santa Cruz
1996	Chuquisaca, Cochabamba, Potosí, Santa Cruz
1997	Chuquisaca, Cochabamba, Potosí, Santa Cruz
1998	Chuquisaca, Cochabamba, *Oruro,* Potosí, Santa Cruz and *Paraguay*

Although ASOMEX's client base continues to focus on small producer associations, the company is open to serving the marketing needs of larger producers. The recent development of Fernheim as a producer client represents ASOMEX's move into the arena of medium-scale producers. ASOMEX does not plan to make a major shift to higher-income producers. Ultimately, the commitment to serving small producers is maintained by MEDA's and others' positions on the board, as well as by the fact that ASOMEX's key marketing activity is niche marketing for crops grown primarily by small producers.

In addition to new clients developing on the brokering and export-processing front, ASOMEX sees opportunities to take on further intermediary activities. However, ASOMEX cannot fully take advantage of these opportunities because it lacks working capital. It is looking for an equity investment, a loan or possibly a grant to provide it with the needed capital. MEDA, a possible loan source itself, is also actively searching for funding for ASOMEX. This critical need must be resolved in the near future.

There is consensus among management and shareholders that ASOMEX has good potential to grow as a company and to greatly increase its outreach in the future. ASOMEX sees a number of opportunities to develop new export lines for new products. Stakeholders agree that there is much untapped demand for ASOMEX's services. With the new skilled and independent management team, improved accounting procedures and greater guidance from its board, all stakeholders are expecting successful years for ASOMEX in the near future.

Conclusion

The ASOMEX study has highlighted many elements of programme design and strategy that contribute to success in serving small producers by delivering a business development service. At the same time it is clear that ASOMEX is a far from perfect company. Both ASOMEX's strengths and its weaknesses provide valuable insights and lessons for others attempting to establish self-sustainable programmes that deliver business services with positive development impact. In summary:

ASOMEX strengths

- initial development and learning phases done under parent association, so that when the company started it had already shown potential for financial viability and could start debt free and grant free
- access to NGO expertise in developing sustainable businesses
- NGO role as shareholder to push for development objectives
- shareholder structure to encourage efficiency and profit
- proof demonstrated that a market exists for edible beans, thus creating competition in the industry (more companies serving small producers, including Bolivian Shoji and Bolsemilla)
- major client input in BDS design (created in part by clients)
- pricing structure based on cost recovery
- ability to recognize financially non-viable extensions of service and refusal to offer them
- keeping BDS small and highly focused on profitable elements only
- streamlined operation
- offering arm's-length service from a single location
- good working conditions, facilitating dedicated staff
- sufficient flexibility to meet service needs of different clients
- incorporation of demand-driven business strategies

- work done with producer associations rather than individuals to minimize difficulties and costs of working with individual small producers
- ability to reach large numbers of small producers
- associations' responsibility for needs of the individual small producer
- innovative in responding to new demand opportunities
- positive impact results on producer incomes, level of production, and indirectly on education and health
- ability to fulfil the typically overlooked needs of small producers.

ASOMEX weaknesses

- lack of working capital to take advantage of new business opportunities
- failure to seriously pursue a broadened client base
- overdependence on ASOPROF
- insufficient overseeing by the owner
- lack of well-defined goals and well-developed, feasible plans for achieving them
- failure to take full advantage of economies of scale
- poor accounting procedures in the past
- overly prolonged period of shared administration with ASOPROF
- ongoing weakness in planning implementation processes
- lack of control over accounts receivable
- periods of poor communication between shareholders and management
- practical problems in distribution channels affecting service quality
- lack of capacity to give attention to special needs of disadvantaged groups
- no collection of impact data or impact assessment
- lack of division in recording costs and revenues between the various types of services offered and various elements of each service; relative profitability of various services unknown
- lack of price risk management by both ASOMEX and ASOPROF.

The trade-off between development impact and sustainability

Throughout the case study, issues have arisen that have involved a conflict between achieving maximum development impact and attaining profit. As with any company, the bottom line of sustainability through profit comes first, and development must take second place as a priority. Time and resources are not available in the company setting of ASOMEX to monitor impact, nor to make special effort to serve the most disadvantaged small producers. Even making the suggestion to the ASOMEX manager that it could incorporate attention to special needs (such as gender considerations) met with an indignant response that no profit-oriented company could be reasonably expected to do so. Experience has shown that small producer organizations or small enterprises need to have achieved a certain level of success in their business before they work with ASOMEX. This certainly does not mean that all are well off. Many individuals in the client associations are in fact very poor. But they must be a part of an association that is relatively efficient, stable and well organized, has a high-quality product, has some understanding of market dynamics, and has a profit margin large enough to justify paying for a marketing service.

The trade-off between development impact and financial sustainability does not mean to say that in focusing on cost effectiveness and profit ASOMEX cannot have strong development impact. Through the dedication of its shareholders and managers, ASOMEX has maintained its focus on small producers, despite the more profitable alternative of larger producers. Clearly ASOMEX plays an important development role in serving many small producers with a much-needed marketing service that would otherwise be difficult or even impossible for them to have access to. Thousands of small producers have achieved exportation through ASOMEX, access to better prices for their product, and higher income as a result. This valuable development impact from a self-sustaining BDS delivery company makes ASOMEX a fine model indeed for others to learn from.

Notes

1 'Colonizer farmers' refers to internal migrants from the high Andes. Some of the existing settlements were established by the government and others were spontaneously settled. The 'beans' referred to throughout the case study are dry beans. ASOMEX has worked with a number of bean varieties over the years including negro, mantequilla, haba, rojo tinto and carioca. Most of the exports have been rojo tinto and carioca, whose markets are found principally in Brazil, Colombia and Japan.
2 Although it grew from MEDA's work in the region, ASOPROF is officially completely independent of MEDA and is no longer part of MEDA Bolivia's country programme.
3 See the section entitled 'Marketing and delivering the business development services-package' for further information on ASOMEX's work with PRISMA.
4 See 'The Bolivian bean industry' in the annexe for an overall view of the activity.
5 The struggle between maximizing profit and offering the most producer-friendly prices possible is a debate that has come up in board meetings. The outcome of these discussions has been that ASOMEX needs to keep in mind the satisfaction of clients to maintain them over the longer term. The pricing strategy has an important role to play here, although it is difficult to achieve an optimal balance between company profit and client satisfaction.
6 Supporting data are presented in the 'Impact' section.
7 MEDA's 'Approach to Institutional Development in Microenterprise Finance Programmes: From Project through Programme to Business' (internal publication).
8 Ibid.
9 See the timeline 'MEDA in Bolivia' in the annexe for more detail on MEDA's role.
10 This was the opinion of ASOMEX's general manager, as well as of the MEDA Bolivia country manager at the time ASOMEX was formed.

11 Financial data gathered from MEDA sources do not match data gathered direct from ASOMEX sources because each operates on a different financial year. MEDA's financial year runs from July to June; ASOMEX operates on the calendar year.

12 Socio-economic variables are available in only a limited form through MEDA's impact indicators of ASOPROF. These are presented in Table 3.2 in the 'ASOMEX and MEDA' section.

13 Source of community profile data: *PROCOR Diagnósticos Socioeconómicos*, MEDA, FDC and CIDA, 1998.

14 Community profiles are sketchy because the available data are limited.

15 The CIAT study conducted in 1997/8 was based on detailed interviews with 593 ASOPROF members and family members. Its focus was to measure the impact of beans in Bolivia since MEDA introduced the crop in the mid-1980s.

16 The correlation between increased income levels and increased educational opportunities is not proved in this case. Education levels may have increased over the period for demographic reasons, for general economic reasons unrelated to the initiative, or because of greater government and donor investment in education.

17 Although clients have had some frustrations with ASOMEX, presumably their choice to continue working with it means that it remains the preferred option over export firms focused on big business.

18 See the section 'ASOMEX and MEDA' for a description of the indirect assistance MEDA has offered ASOMEX over its lifetime.

Annexe The Bolivian bean industry

Industry activity and value-added chain

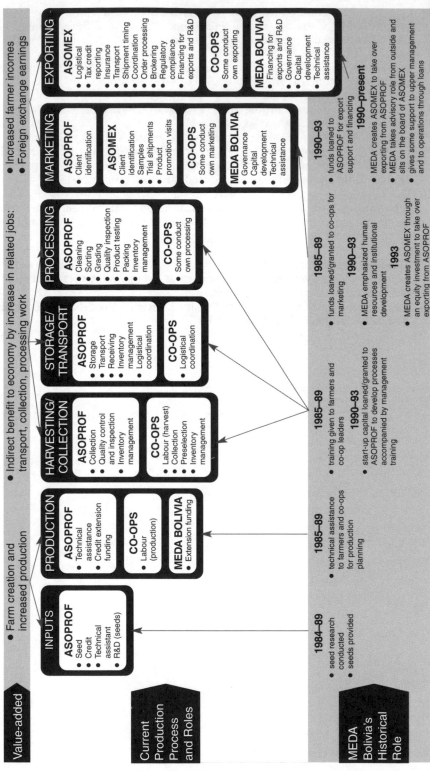

Annexe MEDA in Bolivia

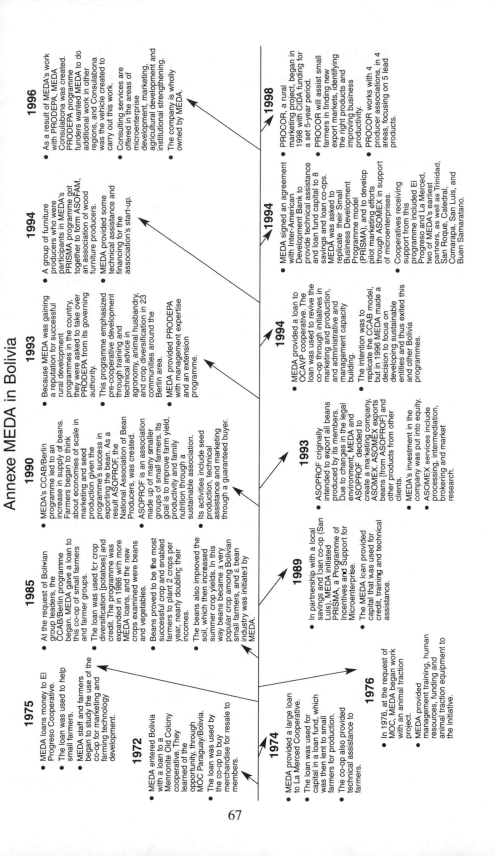

1975

- MEDA loans money to El Progreso Cooperative.
- The loan was used to help small farmers.
- MEDA staff and farmers began to study the use of the co-op for marketing and farming technology development.

1972

- MEDA entered Bolivia with a loan to a Mennonite Old Colony cooperative. They learned of the opportunity, through MOC Paraguay/Bolivia.
- The loan was used by the co-op to buy merchandise for resale to members.

1974

- MEDA provided a large loan to La Merced Cooperative.
- The loan was used for capital in a loan fund, which was then lent to small farmers for production.
- The co-op also provided technical assistance to farmers.

1985

- At the request of Bolivian group leaders, the CCAB/Berlin programme began. MEDA gave a loan to this co-op of small farmers and farmer groups.
- The loan was used for crop diversification [potatoes] and credit. The programme was expanded in 1986 with more MEDA loans, and the new crops examined were beans and vegetables.
- Beans proved to be the most successful crop and enabled farmers to plant 2 crops per year, nearly doubling their incomes.
- The beans also improved the soil, which then increased summer crop yields. In this way beans became a very popular crop among Bolivian small farmers, and a bean industry was initiated by MEDA.

1989

- In partnership with a local savings and loan co-op (San Luis), MEDA initiated PRISMA, a Programme of Incentives and Support for Microenterprise.
- The MEDA loan provided capital that was used for credit, training and technical assistance.

1990

- MEDA's CCAB/Berlin programme led to an increase in supply of beans. Farmers began to think about economies of scale in marketing and seed production given the programme's success in exporting the bean. As a result ASOPROF, the National Association of Bean Producers, was created.
- ASOPROF is an association made up of many smaller groups of small farmers. Its goal is to improve farm yield, productivity and family nutrition through a sustainable association.
- Its activities include seed production, technical assistance and marketing through a guaranteed buyer.

1993

- ASOPROF originally intended to export all beans produced by its members. Due to changes in the legal environment, MEDA and ASOPROF decided to create a marketing company, ASOMEX. ASOMEX exports beans [from ASOPROF] and other products from other clients.
- MEDA's investment in the company was put into equity.
- ASOMEX services include processing, intermediation, brokering and market research.

1993

- Because MEDA was gaining a reputation for successful rural development programmes in the country, they were asked to take over PRODEPA from its governing authority.
- This programme emphasized pre-cooperative development through training and technical advice in agronomy, animal husbandry, and crop diversification in 23 communities around the Berlin area.
- MEDA provided PRODEPA with management expertise and an extension programme.

1994

- MEDA provided a loan to OCAVP cooperative. The loan was used to revive the co-op through initiatives in marketing and production, and administrative and management capacity building.
- The intention was to replicate the CCAB model, but in 1996 MEDA made a decision to focus on developing sustainable entities and thus exited this and other Bolivia programmes.

1994

- A group of furniture producers who were participants in MEDA's PRISMA programme got together to form ASOFAM, an association of wood furniture producers.
- MEDA provided some technical assistance and financing for the association's start-up.

1994

- MEDA signed an agreement with Inter-American Development Bank to provide technical assistance and loan fund capital to 8 savings and loan co-ops. MEDA was asked to replicate their Small Business Development Programme model (PRISMA), and to develop pilot marketing efforts through ASOMEX in support of microenterprises.
- Cooperatives receiving support from this programme included El Progreso and La Merced, two of MEDA's earliest partners, as well as Trinidad, San Roque, Caledral, Comarapa, San Luis, and Buen Samaratano.

1996

- As a result of MEDA's work with PRODEPA, MEDA Consulabona was created. PRODEPA programme funders wanted MEDA to do additional work in other regions, and Consulabona was the vehicle created to carry out this work.
- Consulting services are offered in the areas of microenterprise development, marketing, agricultural development and institutional strengthening.
- The company is wholly owned by MEDA.

1998

- PROCOR, a rural marketing project, began in 1998 with CIDA funding for a set 5-year period.
- PROCOR will assist small farmers in finding new export markets, identifying the right products and improving business productivity.
- PROCOR works with 4 producer associations, in 4 areas, focusing on 5 lead products.

1976

- In 1976, at the request of MOC, MEDA began work with an animal traction project.
- MEDA provided management training, human resources, funding and animal traction equipment to the initiative.

4 Increasing the volume and value of smallholder coffee in El Salvador

LISA STOSCH and ERIC L. HYMAN[1]

Introduction

THIS CASE STUDY analyses a business development services project that assisted small-scale coffee producers and processors in El Salvador. NGOs played a facilitative role by assisting cooperatives that provided members with services. For sustainability, the cooperatives recovered costs through profit margins on processing and marketing and interest spreads on loans. Key lessons learned include the importance of a subsector approach for building capacity, the need to plan for external risks, appropriate roles of service providers and facilitators, value of indirect cost recovery, validity of subsidies in postwar reconstruction, advantages of centralized credit administration, profitability of some improved environmental practices, and how expansion and replication increased cost effectiveness and impact.

The project was designed and implemented by EnterpriseWorks Worldwide and its local affiliate, Servicios Empresariales de Mesoamérica (SEM).[2] Coffee is the leading export of El Salvador. The country had 9600 coffee farms in 1998, earning approximately US$1500 each.[3] About 90 per cent of the coffee farms were less than 14 hectares (CSC 2000). In the 1998/9 season, small-scale producers grew 15 per cent of the country's total coffee production.[4]

The project focused on small-scale coffee producers because of the large potential to improve their productivity, product quality, income and employment. The subsector was still recovering from 12 years of civil war in El Salvador (1979 to 1990) and extensive government control over coffee prices and sales during the 1980s. The project also had environmental objectives: 1) promoting shade-grown varieties of coffee for biodiversity and income diversification from the tree crops; 2) integrated pest management; and 3) treatment and safe disposal of other processing wastes, which are a major pollutant in El Salvador (Mencía 1995; Arturo 2000).

Most coffee produced in El Salvador consists of *arabica* varieties, which grow well in shade and at high elevations. Arabica is used in gourmet coffee and can be sold at a premium price if the quality is good. It is also mixed with lower-quality *robusta* varieties in mainstream coffee. However, only about 1 per cent of Salvadorean coffee was sold to high-value gourmet or organic markets.

Unprocessed ripe coffee fruits are called coffee cherries because of their red colour. The coffee processing stages are parchment coffee, green coffee and roasted coffee (whole beans or ground).[5] Most of the coffee produced in

El Salvador was exported as green coffee, but some low-quality, ground roasted coffee was produced for the domestic market.

The domestic market price of coffee in El Salvador varied with the processing, with the largest mark-ups occurring after the coffee was exported. The wholesale price of ground roasted coffee in industrialized countries was usually 63 per cent above the green coffee price in El Salvador. Here are the prices per kilogram of intermediate coffee products in 1998/9:

Unprocessed coffee cherries (domestic market – buyers further
process the cherries into parchment or green coffee and export it) US$1.34
Parchment coffee (domestic market – buyers further process the
the parchment into green coffee and export it)   US$1.85
Green coffee (export market)   US$2.22
Ground roasted coffee in El Salvador (domestic market – low
quality and small quantities)   US$4.54

Coffee processing is one of the most polluting industries in El Salvador. Many small processing facilities dumped untreated waste on land or in water. Coffee processing wastes exerted a high oxygen demand.[6] More than 90 per cent of the country's rivers were already contaminated (Kovaleski 1999). In 1998, the government required all industrial processors to prepare and implement plans for reducing pollution.

The project was designed by the Inter-American Development Bank (IDB) with extensive input from EnterpriseWorks Worldwide. In January 1995, IDB provided a grant for a three-year project (later extended to four and a half years) to SEM and UCAFES (a second-tier cooperative or association of cooperatives representing both large- and small-scale coffee farmers). IDB awarded a technical assistance contract to EnterpriseWorks Worldwide.

The purpose of the project was to assist seven existing, first-tier cooperatives that process and/or market coffee from 850 small-scale farmers. The original seven cooperatives were Berlín, Cuscatlán, Grano de Oro, Jucuapenses, La Esperanza, Nonualcos and La Unión. However, La Esperanza was dropped in 1995 because of its financial and managerial problems. A new cooperative, La Palma, established with European Union funding in 1996, was later added to the project.[7] Also during the project period, Grano de Oro folded and Siglo XXI was established as its smaller successor.

EnterpriseWorks began the project with a subsector study that identified the main constraints for small-scale coffee farmers in El Salvador:

● limited access to annual working capital credit and longer-term fixed capital credit for expansion or renewal of plantings

- insufficient extension services
- dearth of well-functioning, local processing facilities for small-scale producers
- lack of timely market information (Amorín et al. 1995).

Before this project, four of the cooperatives sold unprocessed coffee cherries, two sold parchment coffee to large companies that processed it into green coffee for export, and one sold ground roasted coffee on the domestic market. None produced significant quantities of export-quality green coffee. La Unión and Nonualcos previously produced parchment coffee and both needed improved plant facilities. La Unión's wet-processing facility was bombed during the civil war and was not functioning efficiently. Nonualcos needed upgraded processing equipment to improve efficiency and address environmental concerns.

Project description

Table 4.1 lists the services the project has provided and the number of cooperatives receiving them. Table 4.2 lists the project funders and their financial contributions, and Table 4.3 the partner organizations implementing the project and their contributions. Figure 4.1 shows the relationships among funders and partners, and the timeline in Figure 4.2 gives an overall history of the project.

Business development services and credit provided

The business development services that the project provided helped the cooperatives to improve their technical and management skills, build and upgrade processing equipment, and gain access to new markets. They enabled the cooperatives to increase member income by selling processed parchment coffee instead of unprocessed coffee cherries to the large processing and export companies. Member farmers also benefited from centrally provided credit and training and extension services, and bulk purchases of farm supplies through the cooperatives.

Technical assistance for coffee farmers

The project completed an on-farm diagnostic analysis for each member who received a loan. This included soil analysis, examination of pest and disease problems and harvesting practices, and recommendations for organic and chemical fertilizer and integrated pest management techniques.

Since 1991, Salvadorean coffee farmers have paid for agricultural extension services from PROCAFE indirectly through a levy on coffee exports.

Table 4.1   Business development services and credit provided by the project

Type of service and recipients	Specific services	Number of cooperatives
Technical assistance for coffee farmers	• Prepared assessments and soil analyses to determine specific needs of participating farmers	6
	• Provided customized extension services to help coffee farmers in harvesting, pruning, pests and diseases, and fertilizer use	7
	• Promoted use of by-product pulp from processing as organic fertilizer	4
	• Supplied parasitic wasps to reduce pesticide use	7
	• Conducted 1377 field visits and training events	6
Credit for coffee farmers	• Offered farmers one-year loans for working capital	6
	• Offered farmers long-term loans for rehabilitation of unproductive coffee stands or expansion	6
Capital investment and technology transfer for cooperatives	• Improved wet-processing plant facilities	2
	• Built new wet-processing plants	2
	• Provided new or improved facilities to process small quantities of parchment coffee into green coffee for the domestic market	5
	• Established new facilities for final processing of green coffee and prepared operating manuals on processing	4
	• Upgraded a final processing facility	1
	• Built biological control laboratories for production of parasitic wasps to control coffee borers	3
Institutional capacity development for cooperatives	• Provided new computers, customized software, and training for accounting and loan administration	6
	• Remodelled offices, agro input sales areas, and training areas	6
Marketing assistance for the cooperatives	• Advised cooperatives on marketing parchment coffee to export companies	7
	• Provided advice to cooperatives on marketing ground roasted coffee on the domestic market	7
	• Linked the cooperatives to UCAFES through fax machines for rapid communication of marketing information	7
	• Established a coffee marketing committee and encouraged collaborative marketing by the cooperatives	7
	• Distributed materials on marketing and price information	7
	• Produced a marketing video	7

Source: G. Amaya and J. Gemeil personal communication 2000

The project funding gave members of six cooperatives access to more extension services than other farmers. Project funding enabled each cooperative to hire an agronomist to provide these services. PROCAFE trained the agronomists and the project provided each cooperative with a motorcycle for the agronomist.

Table 4.2　El Salvador project funders (March 1994 to December 1998)

Name	Type of organization	Funding (US$)
Inter-American Development Bank	multilateral development bank	1 326 154
European Union	multilateral government donor	200 000
EnterpriseWorks Worldwide	non-governmental organization	91 069
Rotary clubs: of Stowe, Vermont, and San Salvador	community service organization	8000
Total		1 625 223

Source: SEM 1999

Table 4.3　Counterpart funding for the El Salvador project (US dollars)

Name	Type of organization	Counterpart funding
SEM	non-governmental organization	in-kind contribution
Berlín, Cuscatlán, Jucuapenses, La Palma, La Unión, Nonualcos, Grano de Oro	cooperatives	88 600
COMERCAFE	private marketing company established by EnterpriseWorks Worldwide	in-kind contribution
Consejo Salvadoreño de Café (CSC)[a]	government and industry council that analyses and recommends policies, distributes market information and inspects quality of coffee exports	in-kind contribution
Muyshond-Avila and Industrias Columbus	private processing and exporting companies	in-kind contribution
UCAFES	second-tier cooperative (Union of Cooperatives)	15 000
PROCAFE[b]	privatized agricultural extension services	35 322
Total		138 922

Source: SEM 1999
[a]CSC was funded by a US$0.0007 levy per kilogram exported.
[b]PROCAFE was funded by a government levy of US$0.02 per kilogram of coffee exported.

The agronomists advised farmers on coffee seedling propagation, pruning, crop diversification and shade tree planting. Before the project, many small farmers were frustrated because they could not afford to follow through on many of PROCAFE's recommendations. Project credit has enabled farmers to adopt many of these recommendations. The agronomists also served as credit promoters, identifying and assessing potential loan clients and helping farmers with loan procedures. PROCAFE provided assistance from more experienced specialists as needed through a collaboration agreement with EnterpriseWorks Worldwide and SEM. After the project ended, three of the

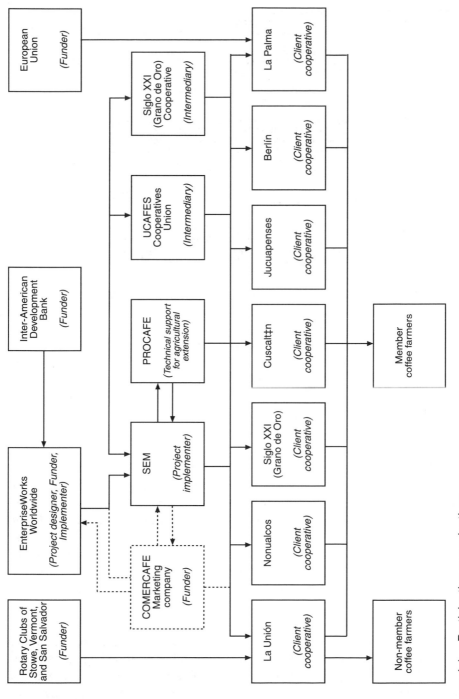

Figure 4.1   Participating organizations

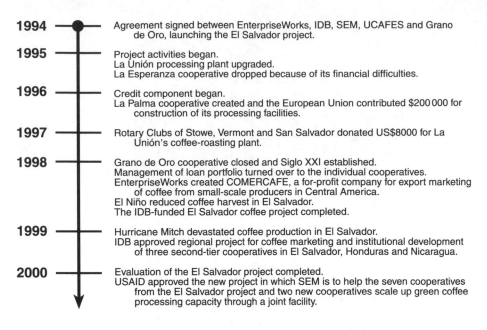

1994	Agreement signed between EnterpriseWorks, IDB, SEM, UCAFES and Grano de Oro, launching the El Salvador project.
1995	Project activities began. La Unión processing plant upgraded. La Esperanza cooperative dropped because of its financial difficulties.
1996	Credit component began. La Palma cooperative created and the European Union contributed $200 000 for construction of its processing facilities.
1997	Rotary Clubs of Stowe, Vermont and San Salvador donated US$8000 for La Unión's coffee-roasting plant.
1998	Grano de Oro cooperative closed and Siglo XXI established. Management of loan portfolio turned over to the individual cooperatives. EnterpriseWorks created COMERCAFE, a for-profit company for export marketing of coffee from small-scale producers in Central America. El Niño reduced coffee harvest in El Salvador. The IDB-funded El Salvador coffee project completed.
1999	Hurricane Mitch devastated coffee production in El Salvador. IDB approved regional project for coffee marketing and institutional development of three second-tier cooperatives in El Salvador, Honduras and Nicaragua.
2000	Evaluation of the El Salvador project completed. USAID approved the new project in which SEM is to help the seven cooperatives from the El Salvador project and two new cooperatives scale up green coffee processing capacity through a joint facility.

Figure 4.2   *Timeline of activities and events in the project's history*

cooperatives retained a full-time agronomist, covering the cost from their own resources. The other three cooperatives went back to relying on more limited extension assistance from PROCAFE for their members.

Coffee bushes begin producing at around 3 years of age, reach peak production after four to five years and remain productive until they are about 30 years old. The project improved coffee production by helping farmers to plant more bushes and improve harvesting practice. Member farmers planted 56 additional hectares of shade-grown coffee during the project, a 2.5 per cent increase. La Unión and Grano de Oro both had nurseries for coffee seedlings. PROCAFE provided them with certified seeds and the nurseries grew the seedlings for six months before sale. Farmers also replaced some old, unproductive stands. The project promoted retaining or planting fruit trees to provide shade for coffee plants and diversify farmer income. For maximum quality, farmers were instructed to harvest only fully ripe coffee cherries, which required several pickings through the stand.

The coffee borer, a serious pest that can destroy a coffee crop, can be controlled with pesticides or parasitic wasps. PROCAFE installed biocontrol laboratories at Cuscatlán, Grano de Oro and La Unión to propagate parasitic wasps. Parasitic wasps enabled participating farmers to reduce the use of toxic pesticides by 25 per cent. The most widely used pesticide for the coffee borer was endosulfan, which can be fatal to people.[8]

Credit for farmers

The project included a revolving fund to provide coffee farmers with working capital loans (one year) and fixed capital loans (up to five years) to rehabilitate existing stands and plant new ones. The loans were expected to benefit at least 500 farm households in six of the cooperatives.[9] For fixed capital loans, borrowers had to provide land, other collateral or a guarantee from a co-signatory. The first loans were made in 1996 and UCAFES, the union of coffee cooperatives, disbursed the loans and collected repayments with technical assistance from SEM (Royo Llop 1997).

From 1996 to 1998, the project made 325 working capital loans amounting to US$231 000 and 133 fixed capital loans for more than US$272 000. At the end of 1998, UCAFES had received full repayment on the loans due through that date (SEM 1999).

At the end of 1998, UCAFES turned the credit portfolio, collateral and guarantees over to the six cooperatives, as planned. At that time, the total cash value of the loan fund was close to US$568 000. Borrowers had to make subsequent loan payments to their cooperative, which was required to use the money for additional working capital loans. Before the loan funds were transferred, each cooperative had to do the following:

- demonstrate the solvency of the existing loans
- establish written policies and rules for handling delinquent loans
- reach an agreement with its general assembly on how the credit fund would be managed
- open a bank account exclusively for the loan fund
- obtain the credit committee's approval on new loans
- require borrowers who received new loans to pledge their coffee production as collateral.

SEM trained the six cooperatives in loan administration. Each cooperative signed a contract accepting responsibility and agreeing to specified loan terms (duration, disbursements, interest rate, repayment schedule, and penalties for delinquent borrowers). The cooperatives paid the administrative and legal costs of decentralizing the loan funds. On new loans, they were expected to charge borrowers an interest rate 2 to 3 per cent higher than their cost of funds. The average interest rate was 24 to 26 per cent, well above the inflation rate and the rates charged by most NGOs in the country.[10] The cash transferred to the cooperatives was 132 per cent of the nominal value of the original loan fund. After adjusting for inflation, the real value of the amount transferred was US$524 998, still 122 per cent of the original fund. In addition, accounts receivable from loan repayments not yet due exceeded US$318 000.

Unfortunately, the loan performance deteriorated after responsibility was decentralized to the first-tier cooperatives. By the end of 1999, the delinquency rate for members of five of the six cooperatives ranged from 9 to 26 per cent and averaged 15 per cent. Loan performance was worse for the sixth, Grano de Oro, which was unable to collect 70 per cent of its members' fixed capital loans. External factors were very unfavourable in 1998 and 1999, but the cooperatives' inexperience in credit management also played a role. The world market price for coffee fell sharply in 1998 and Hurricane Mitch devastated El Salvador's coffee production in the 1998/9 season. The poor loan performance of Grano de Oro was a major factor in the cooperative's closure and subsequent restructuring as a smaller cooperative, Siglo XXI.

Credit administration is a common problem for first-tier (primary) cooperatives because of the high administrative costs and the inherent conflicts of interest between cooperative management and cooperative members.

Several other options might have been preferable for the post-project loan fund.

- Creating one new entity staffed with experienced credit administrators to manage the loan funds on behalf of all the cooperatives.
- Transferring the loan funds to each cooperative provisionally for one year. Once a cooperative demonstrated a good track record, the permanent transfer would take place. This might have resulted in some cooperatives gaining loan management responsibility while others would not (Gálvez 2000).
- Transferring the loan funds as planned, but with the project's credit committee providing continuing training and follow-up.
- Hiring a consultant to assist the cooperatives through the transition and help them to develop a strategy for restructuring problem loans.
- Turning over responsibility for the loan funds to an existing microcredit institution.

Capital investment and technology transfer for cooperatives

As a result of the project, three cooperatives (La Palma, Grano de Oro and Cuscatlán) began selling parchment coffee for the first time, and two others that had already been producing parchment coffee (Nonualcos and La Unión) were able to increase their production and efficiency. Project assistance enabled five cooperatives (all except La Palma and Grano de Oro) to begin selling ground roasted coffee on the domestic market.

The upgraded wet-processing facilities at La Unión and Nonualcos included investments in coffee-receiving areas, depulpers, water pumps, spinners, fermentation tanks, washing tanks, predrying patios and mechanical dryers that increased gains in efficiency. Fewer coffee cherries were needed to produce the same amount of parchment coffee. Before the project, the cooperatives used 6.96 kg of cherries to make 1 kg of parchment coffee. The amount of cherries needed was reduced by 10 per cent through more efficient equipment and better-trained workers. Also in 1995, La Unión lost 5180 kg of potentially saleable coffee in its waste pulp. The project addressed this problem by installing a trap to recover this coffee before the pulp entered the storage tank. New equipment and improved quality control at La Unión and Nonualcos also reduced the rate of damaged coffee from 15 per cent to 5 per cent. The introduction of helicoidal conveyors, paddles, and gravity flow for coffee transport and efficient washing and pulping reduced water consumption by two-thirds.

The project enabled Grano de Oro to build one of the region's most modern and environmentally sound small-scale wet-processing plants. This plant had the capacity to produce nearly 227 300 kg of parchment coffee per year (in green coffee equivalent). To conserve diesel – a costly and dirty fuel – the project supported construction of a 112.5-kilowatt substation for the plant. Grano de Oro also received funding to build an irrigation system for watering 25 000 coffee seedlings. The cost of upgrading the La Unión and Nonualcos plants and building the Grano de Oro plant was approximately US$101 000. The total processing capacity of these three plants increased 139 per cent (SEM 1999).

In 1996, a wet-processing plant was constructed for La Palma. This cooperative now produced gourmet coffee and mainstream coffee. La Palma then paid another processor to transform its parchment coffee into green coffee. In its first year of production, La Palma sold gourmet-quality green coffee to a foreign buyer at US$0.87/kg above the typical price for 'strictly high-grown' coffee. As a result, La Palma was able to pay its members a premium price for their coffee cherries, and this reportedly caused other coffee buyers in the area to pay higher prices as well.

The project installed low-cost, wastewater treatment facilities for the four cooperatives with wet-processing plants. The wastewater was channelled into a lagoon and treated with lime to reduce its acidity. Over 24 hours, sediment settled to the bottom and fine solids rose to the top. Then the sediment was removed and added to the pulp removed earlier in the wet process. The resulting pulp mixture was used as an organic fertilizer for coffee since it contained nitrogen, phosphorus and potassium, but it could not completely replace chemical fertilizer. The four cooperatives stored the pulp and gave it away to their members. The marginal cost of pulp production was mainly the labour required to store it and clean the storage facilities once a year, only US$0.01/kg in 1998/9.

After the pulp was removed, the wastewater flowed through a series of pits where it was oxygenated and gradually evaporated or percolated through the soil. Organic matter remaining in the pit was removed at the end of the processing season. The total cost of pollution control, including labour and chemicals, averaged US$0.14/kg of parchment coffee (Mencía 1995). More sophisticated biological treatment methods that relied on micro-organisms to dissect coffee processing waste were used in Costa Rica, but they were too expensive for small processors in El Salvador.

Before the project, only Nonualcos had a dry-processing facility that could produce significant quantities of green coffee and it needed an equipment upgrade to meet export quality standards. Nonualcos also needed final processing equipment to produce small amounts of ground roasted coffee for the domestic market. The project provided Berlín, Cuscatlán, Jucuapenses and La Unión with equipment for dry processing, roasting and grinding. La Palma and Grano de Oro did not receive processing equipment because La Palma sells its parchment coffee to exporters and Grano de Oro was undergoing restructuring.

One of the most important issues the project had to address was quality control. Common quality control problems before the project included the following:

- *Storage before processing and during sun drying.* When coffee cherries were stored or dried on the ground rather than on a cement patio, dirt and debris were introduced. The coffee could also pick up undesirable odours and flavours from the soil.
- *Overfermentation.* The wet process had to be carefully controlled to avoid overfermentation since parchment coffee continues to ferment in storage. Maintaining proper storage conditions and limiting storage time were critical.
- *Failure to do sun drying.* Coffee would not mature properly if sun drying were skipped before second-stage drying.
- *Moisture content too high or low.* The optimal moisture content of parchment coffee after the second stage of drying is 11 to 12 per cent and it was often too high or too low.
- *Fuel vapours from the dryer.* Fuel vapours from a mechanized dryer, if not properly vented, can spoil the taste of coffee.
- *Packaging for storage and transport.* When parchment or green coffee is transported in a container that holds or previously held other products, it can pick up undesirable odours and flavours if it is not properly packaged.

Capacity building for cooperatives

Before the project, some of the cooperatives did not conduct annual audits and had poor internal controls and financial systems. The project required each cooperative to contract with an external auditor and undergo annual audits. The project provided business management advice and training for the cooperatives. All seven cooperatives received a computer; fax machine; and customized software for accounting and loan administration and a database on member production.

Before the project, six of the cooperatives sold unprocessed coffee cherries to intermediaries at a relatively low price. The intermediaries accumulated sufficient coffee cherries to sell to large companies for processing into green coffee and export. Lack of market information hindered the cooperatives' ability to get good prices. The project increased the bargaining power of the cooperatives with green coffee processors and exporters by creating a marketing committee to negotiate prices and terms of sale for parchment coffee. It also saw the potential for new products in the country, such as frozen coffee drinks and coffee-flavoured foods and beverages.

La Unión was the first of the cooperatives to sell its own brand of ground roasted coffee on the domestic market. It explored new retail outlets at the country's main airport, supermarkets, restaurants and food stands.

Coffee produced with environmentally sound practices could bring a better price in niche markets. ECO-OK was an environmental certification programme operated by a Salvadorean NGO (SalvaNatura) with an international NGO (Rainforest Alliance), the Network of Agricultural Conservationists and PROCAFE. It was funded by the Global Environment Facility.[11] SalvaNatura charged a sliding fee based on farm size for doing initial assessments of farms. In 1999, it sold ECO-OK coffee at a premium of US$0.22 per kilogram.

Each farmer in the SalvaNatura programme received a socio-environmental management plan that he had to follow to qualify for the ECO-OK seal. SalvaNatura also certified coffee-processing plants, charging cooperatives an annual fee for use of the ECO-OK stamp on product packaging. La Unión paid the inspection fees for having all member farms certified by ECO-OK. Many La Unión members are in areas important for biodiversity, such as the Apaneca-Ilamatepec corridor and the Central American biological corridor. Berlín also started the ECO-OK process.

Outreach and impact

The number and type of producer participants who received at least US$20 in additional income as a result of the project includes owners and workers of the farms belonging to the cooperatives, workers at the processing plants, and non-member farmers who sold coffee cherries (Table 4.4). Non-members received immediate payments based on the value of their unprocessed coffee cherries, while cooperative members received an additional 10 per cent for their coffee after it was processed and marketed.

Another goal of the project was to strengthen the cooperatives by expanding the membership. The number of member farms increased by 246 per cent in 1996/7 but fell by 37 per cent in 1997/8 and by an additional 29 per cent in 1998/9. The large increase in membership was mainly from the addition of the

Table 4.4   Producer participants

Producer participants	1995/6	1996/7	1997/8	1998/9
Member farms	<u>463</u>	<u>1604</u>	<u>1010</u>	<u>714</u>
Male owners[a]	366	1267	798	564
Female owners	97	337	212	150
Male workers[b]	401	1388	874	618
Female workers	62	216	136	96
Non-member farms[c]	<u>0</u>	<u>0</u>	<u>58</u>	<u>50</u>
Male owners	0	0	46	40
Female owners	0	0	12	10
Male workers	0	0	35	30
Female workers	0	0	23	20
Processing plant workers	<u>69</u>	<u>42</u>	<u>40</u>	<u>40</u>
Male	69	42	40	40
Female	0	0	0	0
Total producer participants	532	1646	1108	804

[a]Based on loan records, 21 per cent of member farm owners were women and 79 per cent were men.
[b]Assumes that each farm has one owner and one worker earning US$20 or more in incremental income per
  year. On average, women provide 34 per cent of the total labour time in coffee production.
[c]Includes only non-members selling coffee to La Unión; estimate based on purchases from non-member farms
  divided by an average of 727.3 kg per non-member farm.

new La Palma cooperative. The subsequent declines were due to the restructuring of Grano de Oro and severe weather problems.

The workers included seasonal and part-time workers and paid labourers as well as unpaid family members. Labour accounted for 65 per cent of the costs of small-scale coffee farming. The total labour required to produce 100 kg of green coffee was 2.4 person-days, including harvesting and post-harvest labour.[12] More efficient technology resulted in a loss of 27 jobs at Nonualcos, but since that processing plant was unprofitable it might otherwise have had to close.

Production and sales

As with any agricultural commodity, coffee revenues varied from year to year due to factors beyond a project's control. Figure 4.3 gives a picture of the fluctuations in coffee production in El Salvador over a long term, from 1978/9 to 1998/9. Unfavourable weather (El Niño in 1996/7, La Niña in 1997/8, and Hurricane Mitch in 1998/9) had a major effect on Salvadorean production. Compared with 1996/7, the national coffee harvest fell by 16 per cent in 1997/8 and by 28 per cent in 1998/9. In 1998, the world market price of coffee fell by 22 per cent from the previous year due to excess inventories in the consuming countries and bountiful harvests in the largest producing countries. The combined effect made 1998/9 a difficult year for both producers and cooperatives.

Table 4.5 shows the quantities of coffee sold by the seven cooperatives and their gross revenues from the 1995/6 production year through 1999/2000. It shows how project assistance enabled the cooperatives to move along the

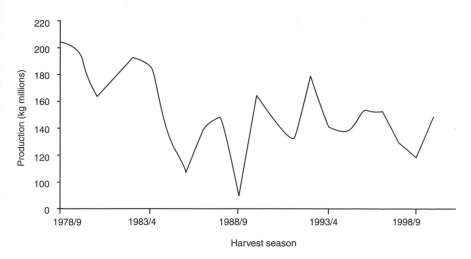

Figure 4.3   *Coffee production in El Salvador, 1978/9–1998/9*

value chain, selling fewer coffee cherries and more parchment coffee and ground roasted coffee. In 1996/7, Cuscatlán gained access to the Nonualcos processing facilities for parchment coffee production. During its first year (1998/9), Siglo XXI sold only unprocessed coffee cherries; it began producing parchment coffee in 1999/2000. Five cooperatives sold some parchment coffee in 1999/2000.

Table 4.5   Production and gross revenues for the seven cooperatives

	1995/6	1996/7	1997/8	1998/9	1999/2000
Production (kg)					
Unprocessed cherry coffee	710 663	315 764	335 435	291 422	369 217
Parchment coffee	306 259	762 297	565 520	614 013	741 929
Roasted coffee	0	0	909	6838	9910
Gross revenues (US dollars)					
Unprocessed cherry coffee	1 336 046	682 366	711 123	390 506	ND
Parchment coffee	584 955	1 715 169	1 419 455	1 135 924	ND
Roasted coffee	0	0	4569	31 043	ND
Total gross revenues	1 921 001	2 397 535	2 135 147	1 525 573	ND

Source: EnterpriseWorks Worldwide's annual Impact Tracking System
ND – no data

Table 4.6 lists the estimated incremental gross revenue that the project brought in for the cooperatives. The income gain is calculated by multiplying the average incremental production over the baseline by the average price of each product in each year. Because of the annual variations in coffee harvests and prices, the baseline production was the average of the two years before the project's investments in establishing or upgrading processing plants – 1994/5

81

Table 4.6 Incremental gross producer income gains from coffee sales by the seven cooperatives, 1996/7 to 1998/9 (US dollars)

Stage of processing	1996/7	1997/8	1998/9	Cumulative
Unprocessed cherry coffee	(348 822)	(342 204)	(230 555)	(921 581)
Parchment coffee	748 893	341 521	341 431	1 431 845
Roasted coffee	0	4569	31 043	35 612
Total income gains	400 071	3886	141 919	545 876

Source: EnterpriseWorks Worldwide's annual Impact Tracking System
Incremental production over the baseline (average for 1994/5 and 1995/6) multiplied by the average price of each product in each year

and 1995/6 for Cuscatlán, La Unión, Nonualcos and Grano de Oro, and 1996/7 and 1997/8 for Berlín and Jucuapenses. Since La Palma did not exist before the project, all of its production was counted as project impact.

Since investments in the processing plants were not completed until 1996/7 and farmers did not receive project loans until 1996, the first year of incremental income was 1996/7. Producer earnings were high that year but dropped in 1997/8 before rebounding somewhat in 1998/9. Some cooperatives earned additional income by selling agro-inputs and coffee seedlings to members, but this income was not counted in Table 4.6 because the revenue the cooperatives earned balanced out the cost to the member farmers.

Producer cost savings

Table 4.7 lists the cost savings to the producers due to the project. Farmers saved money through integrated pest management, reduced water use and partial substitution of coffee processing pulp for chemical fertilizer. Most of the pulp was given free to cooperative members, but they were responsible for transporting it – usually at the same time they bought supplies from the cooperatives or delivered their coffee cherries. Farmers also saved money by buying supplies at lower prices through the cooperatives, but this was not counted because of lack of information.

The processing plants saved labour through use of new equipment. Several cooperatives saved money through more efficient water use. Helicoidal conveyors, paddles and gravity flow eliminated using water to transport coffee through the plant. The average water saving was 9.16 litres per kilogram of coffee cherries.

Total monetary benefits

Table 4.8 lists the total monetary benefits from the project – the sum of the producer cost savings and producer income gains. Benefits first accrued in 1995/6, increased 151 per cent in 1996/97, fell 58 per cent in 1997/8 and rebounded 49 per cent in 1998/9. Further economic benefits are expected for the years to come.

Table 4.7 Producer cost savings for the farmers and cooperatives, 1995/6 to 1998/9 (US dollars)

Item	1995/6	1996/7	1997/8	1998/9	Cumulative
Farmers					
Reduced pesticide use	1398	1407	1416	1425	5646
Reduced chemical fertilizer use	266 783	268 442	270 101	271 760	1 077 086
Subtotal for farmers	268 181	269 849	271 517	273 185	1 082 732
Cooperatives					
Labour saved in processing	1800	7247	7320	6131	22 498
Reduced water consumption in processing	2539	6319	4696	5147	18 701
Subtotal for cooperatives	4339	13 566	12 016	11 278	41 199
Total	272 520	283 415	283 533	284 463	1 123 931

Source: EnterpriseWorks Worldwide's annual Impact Tracking System

Table 4.8 Total monetary benefit, 1995/6 to 1998/9 (US dollars)

	1995/6	1996/7	1997/8	1998/9	Cumulative
Total monetary benefits	272 520.00	683 486.00	286 418.00	426 381.00	1 668 805.00
Benefits per participant	273.89	210.30	131.63	271.93	–

Source: EnterpriseWorks Worldwide's annual Impact Tracking System

Recognition of project achievements

The achievements of the El Salvador project have been recognized in several ways:

- In 1998, PROCAFE recognized a member of Nonualcos as 'Small-Scale Coffee Farmer of the Year' for achieving a high yield.
- In 1998, IDB cited the El Salvador project as one of its four most successful small projects in Latin America and the Caribbean.
- La Unión received an honourable mention for its conservation practices from the Salvadorean Executive Secretariat of the Environment.

Parallel, expansion and replication activities

The El Salvador project did not have the resources to work with all the country's coffee producers. Opportunities existed to expand, which would benefit more cooperatives and farmers within and outside of the country. During and after the initial project, EnterpriseWorks Worldwide and SEM began other activities in the region: establishment of a for-profit export marketing company; a regional project for green coffee marketing in El Salvador, Honduras and Nicaragua; construction of a joint green coffee processing facility for nine cooperatives in El Salvador; and replication projects in Guatemala and Haiti.

Regional coffee marketing company

In the last year of the El Salvador project, EnterpriseWorks Worldwide established a for-profit coffee export marketing company to benefit smallholder farmers throughout Central America and Mexico. EnterpriseWorks provided the capital to start the company, Comercializadora Regional de Café (COMERCAFE). The company began operations on a pilot scale in 1998. Based in El Salvador, its first director was an expatriate businessman with extensive contacts in the coffee industry. Although he left in 1999, his work resulted in commitments for coffee purchases through 2002. The second director was a Salvadorean national.

COMERCAFE served as a broker for green coffee exports, linking local producers with international buyers. It had a cupping facility to test the quality of coffee and helped the parties to negotiate, prepared the necessary paperwork for export, and arranged shipping. COMERCAFE did not sell coffee produced by the cooperatives participating in the original El Salvador project because none produced significant quantities of export-quality green coffee. It provided the seven cooperatives with a marketing manual and other market information.

The EnterpriseWorks Worldwide regional coffee project

Before the end of the El Salvador project, EnterpriseWorks Worldwide began planning a regional project for export marketing high-quality, green coffee from second-tier cooperatives in several Central American countries (Amaya and Gemeil 1997). The IDB multilateral investment fund supported this subsequent regional project covering El Salvador, Honduras and Nicaragua (IDB 1998; 1999). The US$2.3 million initiative (US$1.6 million from IDB and US$0.7 million in local counterpart contributions) focused on export marketing of organic and gourmet coffees in the USA and Europe. This project extends from May 1999 to April 2002.

The regional project is strengthening one second-tier cooperative in each of the three countries. The three are the Union of Cooperatives of Agrarian Reform Producers, Processors and Exporters (UCRAPROBEX) in El Salvador, the Coffee Cooperatives Center of Honduras (CCCH) and the Promoter of Cooperative Development of Nicaragua (PRODECOOP). The regional project also provides technical assistance for coffee processing, emphasizing quality and environmentally sound technology.

The EnterpriseWorks Worldwide and USAID project in El Salvador

EnterpriseWorks Worldwide submitted a proposal to the US Agency for International Development (USAID) El Salvador mission for a follow-on project to establish a joint facility for processing green coffee that would serve nine cooperatives (Amaya and Gemeil 2000). USAID gave EnterpriseWorks Worldwide a grant of US$400 000 for the project in 2000. This project is assisting the seven cooperatives from the first IDB-funded El Salvador project and two others – San Pedro Puxtla in Ahuachapán and Perquín in Morazán. The nine cooperatives joined forces in a new second-tier cooperative, Central de Cooperativas de Caficultores de El Salvador (CEN-CAFES). This second-tier cooperative serves only small farmer cooperatives. UCAFES served a mix of large and small coffee farmers, which created some internal conflicts. The project extends from July 2000 to July 2002.

The nine cooperatives will bring their parchment coffee to a single dry-processing facility operated by CENCAFES. The two cooperatives not in the earlier project will receive additional technical assistance and wet-processing equipment for parchment coffee production. The nine cooperatives will jointly market their coffee. A specialized microfinance provider, Ayuda-ACCION, will administer loans for farmers belonging to these cooperatives.

The Guatemala project

A small project in Guatemala followed the model of the El Salvador project. This US$96 384 project was implemented with US$75 000 from the Starbucks Coffee Company plus counterpart funding. This replication project assisted two small cooperatives in the Jalapa area of Guatemala – Las Flores and Los Corteces. The cooperatives are members of the Association of Small-Scale Coffee Producers of Guatemala (ASPECAGUA). The National Coffee Association of Guatemala (ANACAFE) and EnterpriseWorks worked together to design and build two new, small facilities for parchment coffee production.

These facilities adopted the technologies employed in the El Salvador project for water conservation, water pollution control, and by-product pulp recovery. Construction was completed at the end of 1997. Both facilities were able to overcome initial quality control problems and Starbucks purchased their entire output from the 1998/9 and 1999/2000 seasons.

The two processing plants have increased the incomes of 213 smallholder coffee farmers. The cooperatives were repaying the construction costs through loans at an interest rate of 21 per cent per annum. The repayments were made into a revolving loan fund managed by ASPECAGUA that will be used to help cooperatives in the association build processing plants (Gemeil 2000; Stosch 2000).

The Haiti Bleu project

With USAID funding, EnterpriseWorks Worldwide collaborated with the South-East Consortium for International Development (SECID) and the

Fédération des Associations Caféières Natives (FACN) on a coffee subsector study in north and south-east Haiti in 1999. In 2000, as part of a US$704 700 project, SECID awarded EnterpriseWorks Worldwide a contract to train FACN to apply the study's recommendations for improving the quality of the crop and the grading, storage, dry and wet processing, and export marketing of Haitian Bleu coffee.

Project strategy and sustainability

The El Salvador project combined business development services with credit for smallholder farmers and capital investment grants for cooperatives. EnterpriseWorks Worldwide was primarily a business service facilitator.[13] It designed the project, raised funding and provided technical and managerial assistance to its local affiliate, SEM. In turn, SEM served as a service facilitator providing primary cooperatives with technological and managerial assistance. All of the cooperatives offered farmers extension services, recouping costs indirectly through a margin on processing and marketing of coffee and membership fees averaging US$11 to US$23 per year. Some cooperatives made a profit by selling agro-inputs to members.

During the project, SEM provided credit. Afterwards, the loan fund was transferred to the first-tier cooperatives. At the time of the transfer, no loan defaults had occurred and the value of the loan fund had grown. However, after the first-tier cooperatives assumed management of the loan funds, the delinquency rate increased substantially owing to a severe hurricane, a sharp decline in the world market price for coffee and the cooperatives' inexperience in loan administration.

The project used a subsector approach to identify and overcome problems affecting small-scale coffee production, processing and marketing. SEM was able to operate with a small staff because, rather than providing services to farmers direct, it coordinated the services and collaborated with other donor agencies, non-governmental organizations, the private sector, government agencies and cooperatives.

The project developed relationships among the cooperatives for economies of scale in processing, efficient provision of technical and managerial assistance, sharing of market information and collaborative marketing to increase their bargaining power. Since three of the cooperatives were too small for commercially viable wet processing, the project brokered processing agreements between them and larger cooperatives.

The processing agreement between the small Cuscatlán cooperative and the larger Nonualcos cooperative was mutually beneficial. Nonualcos charged a fee of US$0.18/kg of parchment coffee to process Cuscatlán's coffee cherries. Cuscatlán sold most of the parchment coffee to a dry processor and exporter, retaining a small portion for final processing for the domestic market. Cuscatlán was able to add value to members' coffee without high capital or operating costs. Nonualcos benefited from the extra income from better use of its processing plant.

Unfortunately, another collaboration proved unsuccessful. Two small, isolated cooperatives, Berlín and Jucuapenses, contracted with La Esperanza for processing services. La Esperanza ran into financial problems early in the project and creditors seized its assets, including the coffee that the two cooperatives had delivered. SEM's attempts to recover the value of the seized coffee were unsuccessful, but it did help the two cooperatives renegotiate their bank loans to avoid bankruptcy.

SEM removed La Esperanza from all further project activities and recovered a project motorcycle and computer. However, Berlín and Jucuapenses were no longer interested in collaborating with other cooperatives. Instead, they paid private companies to process their coffee cherries. Problems like the one with La Esperanza could have been avoided by insisting that the larger cooperative post a financial guarantee for the coffee delivered for service processing.

Sustainability of SEM

In November 1996, ATI/El Salvador was transformed from a branch office of an international NGO into the Salvadorean NGO, SEM, enabling it to receive funding direct from donors. EnterpriseWorks Worldwide covered SEM's expenditures that were not funded by other donors, including the costs during the interim between the two IDB grants. EnterpriseWorks Worldwide's financial support to SEM amounted to US$43187 in 1997, US$39329 in 1998, US$60093 in 1999 and US$23400 in 2000. SEM also managed a revolving loan fund for coffee cooperatives, using funds contributed by COMERCAFE. SEM will keep the interest earned on these loans to cover general office costs and retain the principal repayments in its loan fund.

As NGOs facilitating business development services, rather than private companies delivering those services, EnterpriseWorks Worldwide and SEM will continue to need donor funding to assist additional coffee cooperatives in El Salvador and other countries. COMERCAFE, the for-profit marketing company, is also expected to generate some operating revenue for the NGO activities.

Sustainability of the cooperatives

All of the cooperatives had serious financial problems before the project started, and some were facing bankruptcy, partly because of the 12-year civil war that had devastated public infrastructure, disrupted agriculture, industry and domestic consumption, and damaged some of the cooperatives' processing plants. The project's approach to ensuring sustainability of the first-tier cooperative was primarily to improve its revenue from processing and marketing, membership fees and interest on loan funds that it managed.

The cooperatives and their members received subsidized technical and marketing assistance. The cooperatives received grants for fixed capital investments to upgrade or build new processing facilities (ranging from US$46 700 to US$161 300). The cooperatives were expected to repay the fixed capital investments with interest into revolving funds for future loans to member farmers. After the project ended, three cooperatives used their own funds to retain the project agronomists. Members of the other three cooperatives returned to relying on PROCAFE for extension services.

Grano de Oro had serious debt problems before the project started, and its financial position subsequently deteriorated further because of managerial problems and the insolvency of many of its member farmers. The high default rate in fixed capital loans to its members increased its financial problems and created internal conflicts. In 1998, these problems made it necessary to close Grano de Oro. A new, smaller cooperative, Siglo XXI, was created to replace it, but only financially solvent members of Grano de Oro were allowed to join. SEM was represented on the board of this new cooperative and intended for it to become a model in systems, controls and management. SEM took over responsibility for the loan fund that had been transferred to Grano de Oro and later turned over the capital from this fund to UCAFES to compensate for Grano de Oro's outstanding debts.

Sustainability of the marketing company

In its first year of operation, COMERCAFE's total costs were close to US$123 000. In its second year, costs fell to around US$65 500, largely because the new director received a lower salary and commission than his predecessor. COMERCAFE sold US$5.5 million of coffee in its first year, earning over US$53 000 in gross revenue. In 1999, its gross revenue was nearly US$57 000 and it provided market-brokering services for 22 cooperatives in El Salvador that produced export-quality green coffee.

EnterpriseWorks Worldwide and SEM used some of COMERCAFE's net revenue to fund development in El Salvador and Bolivia. The eventual ownership of the marketing company has not been decided. One proposal is to sell or give shares in COMERCAFE to the second-tier cooperatives in the regional project. Profits earned before the transfer would be donated to SEM's revolving loan fund. An alternative is for SEM to retain ownership of COMERCAFE and use some of its revenue to support its not-for-profit activities.

Lessons learned and conclusions

Some important lessons can be learned from the initial project in El Salvador. EnterpriseWorks Worldwide began the project design with a subsector study with substantial input by the stakeholders. A whole-subsector approach can have large economic benefits, but it often takes considerable time and effort.

After project funding was secured, EnterpriseWorks Worldwide and SEM conducted a detailed assessment of needs for each cooperative. The assessments found that establishing a new wet-processing plant would not be viable for the smallest cooperatives. Farmers who received project loans also benefited from individual site assessments.

Like other crops, coffee is subject to risks such as weather, pests, diseases and changing world market price. Severe weather adversely affected the impact of the project. The collapse of the International Coffee Organization's quota and price mechanism in 1989 reduced world market prices. While the project plan and needs assessment discussed risks, the project did not include interventions that could have mitigated risks, such as establishing a reserve fund for each cooperative, trying to obtain crop insurance from private companies or government, or hedging by arranging advance sales at an agreed price.

Although coffee farmers were not generally the poorest of the poor in El Salvador, most smallholder coffee farmers lived below the poverty line. The project targeted clients with the potential to substantially increase their productivity, product quality, income and employment.

EnterpriseWorks Worldwide and SEM facilitated technical and managerial assistance to first-tier cooperatives that provided business development services to their members. This allowed the local NGO to keep its staff size small. This was possible because coffee farmers had already been organized into cooperatives (organizing new cooperatives is costly). Partnerships with other organizations built on the comparative advantage of each partner.

It is often more efficient and effective for one organization to provide a whole package of services to rural enterprises rather than relying on a separate provider for each service. Collaborations between small cooperatives and large ones can be cost effective and sustainable but can run into problems if any of them are having financial difficulties. Written contracts with financial safeguards can be developed to protect all parties. Having a first-tier cooperative represented on the project's advisory committee can help to ensure that the interests of the other client cooperatives are considered, but it can also result in conflicts of interest. Relying on second-tier cooperatives may be preferable because it would keep beneficiary interests separate from intermediary functions.

Integrated business service delivery by one provider can allow indirect cost-recovery mechanisms that are efficient and sustainable. Charging separate fees for each service often elicits more resistance from low-income producers and is less efficient because of higher administrative costs.

Six cooperatives that the project assisted were in a precarious financial position when the project was designed and might have faced bankruptcy in the absence of the assistance. Because of the special circumstances of reconstructing a war-torn economy and the weak state of the subsector, IDB provided its support as non-reimbursable grants through an NGO, rather than loans to the government. In effect, the capital investments for the processing facilities were also grants, although the cooperatives were supposed to pay the amounts back to a revolving loan fund for farmers. The subsequent regional project that IDB funded was also a grant, but it did not subsidize processing investments, just technical assistance.

The Committee of Donor Agencies for Small Enterprise Development has raised questions about donor subsidies for business development programmes because of concerns about economic efficiency, sustainability, scale of outreach and possible displacement of private sector services. However, reconstructing an economy after war or a natural disaster is a legitimate use of donor subsidies that should not be considered in the same category as subsidizing business development services under more routine circumstances.

Business development services and credit are complementary. Many farmers would have been unable to take full advantage of extension services and improved inputs without credit. Low-income farmers need long-term financing for large fixed-capital investments, but loans with a long repayment period can cause problems for credit providers.

Small processing facilities can sometimes be upgraded and can be better for the environment, affordable and even profitable. Adopting better technology can generate by-products for sale, or reduce production costs through more efficient use of resources. Some international consumers are willing to pay a premium price for a product with less negative environmental impact or a positive impact on resource conservation or biodiversity. Although these niche markets are small, they are growing rapidly.

By collaborating with the privatized agricultural extension agency funded by an export levy, the project avoided duplicating services and kept costs lower. Three of the cooperatives continued to provide the more intensive extension services for their members after the project ended. The rest received regular services from the privatized agency.

The project initially administered the loan fund with input from an advisory committee. Loan loss rates were low during SEM's administration. At the end of the project, responsibility was transferred to the first-tier cooperatives and default rates went up. Unusually bad weather and a large drop in the world market price of coffee played a major role in the increased default rates. However, SEM also thought that the cooperatives were not ready to take on loan management. Credit administration was often problematic for first-tier cooperatives because the interests of management at times conflicted with those of the voting members.

It might have been more efficient and sustainable to provide credit through a specialized microfinance provider, although the external risk factors would still have posed a problem. A larger and more diversified credit portfolio that included loans for other agricultural crops as well as non-agricultural purposes might have faced less risk.

While cost recovery from services is important, NGOs that facilitate or provide business services for low-income microentrepreneurs and farmers will continue to need funding from donors or private contributors to reach more people in the future. It is much more difficult to recover costs for facilitating business services than for providing them. SEM earned some income by contracting out its professional services in other countries.

A for-profit marketing company may have greater incentives and skills to operate efficiently than an NGO marketing unit. It is also more likely to be sustainable and taken seriously by private buyers. In an era of declining donor funding, NGOs may increase their sustainability through entrepreneurial funding, such as operation or sale of a for-profit company. However, the start-up costs and time required to achieve profitability in a business venture should not be underestimated and capital of the private company should not be siphoned off to fund the NGO. An expatriate businessperson with substantial marketing contacts was essential in COMERCAFE's start-up phase. Responsibility was successfully transferred to a host country national director at substantially lower cost.

Expanding to other countries in the region can increase the efficiency and effectiveness of export marketing. Replicating pilot activities in new locations and expanding into other activities in the subsector can expand outreach and scale up benefits. Although they involve more risk than the well-proven interventions, research, development and pilot activities are important functions not filled by most NGOs or government agencies.

Worldwide, much work needs to be done to put the principles behind the report of the 1992 United Nations Conference on Environment and Development (Agenda 21) into practice. Since then, globalization of the world economy has increased and developing countries have sought greater integration into international trade. Some of the opposition to globalization has centred around concerns about the effects on low-income, small-scale producers and the local and global environments.

This study shows a case in which increasing exports from a developing country can raise the incomes of small-scale producers without negative environmental impacts. To achieve these objectives, however, it was necessary to increase the value added locally through further processing and boost the competitiveness of small-scale production and processing by transferring appropriate technologies and making training and technical assistance, credit, business management assistance, and marketing services available. NGOs can help to bridge these gaps.

The case study also has some important implications for the donor guidelines for business development services for small enterprises. To the extent that private markets for BDS exist, building their capacity can be an efficient and effective way to foster economic development. However, developing the market for BDS should be viewed as a means to an end, rather than an ultimate goal.

Special challenges are involved in reaching rural microenterprises and the agricultural sector compared to urban small enterprises, which are more likely to be served by private sector BDS providers.

A systems approach with multiple, coordinated interventions and a greater NGO or public role in service provision may be needed to develop a whole subsector of rural production. Some of these services may be short term, but others may require a longer, continuing role.

Increasing cost recovery in NGO programmes through direct fees for services or indirect mechanisms is one element of sustainability. Another approach may be for NGOs to spin off commercial ventures that provide business services. The NGO can eventually either exit entirely or use some of the profits generated to cover its own operating costs.

BDS and credit are complementary, but it may be best for BDS facilitators or providers to link up with a specialized microfinance institution that has greater expertise in loan administration, the volume of loans needed to achieve economies of scale, and a more diversified loan portfolio.

Notes

1 The authors would like to acknowledge the assistance of Víctor Mencía (SEM) and the staff of SEM. Helpful comments were received from Gilberto Amaya (EnterpriseWorks Worldwide), Pam Fehr (MEDA), José Gemeil (EnterpriseWorks Worldwide), Sunita Kapila (IDRC), Steve Londner (TechnoServe) and Don Mead (Michigan State University).
EnterpriseWorks Worldwide received core funding from the US Agency for International Development through Cooperative Agreement DHR 5455–00–9082–00–PCE/A/00/96/90021/00.
2 EnterpriseWorks Worldwide was formerly known as Appropriate Technology International (ATI) and SEM as ATI/El Salvador.
3 All monetary values are in US dollars using an exchange rate of 8.75 colones per dollar. The exchange rate was stable between 1994 and 2000.
4 Since the coffee-processing season is November to February, a production year spans part of two calendar years.
5 The first stage (wet processing) involves depulping, washing, drying and fermenting the cherries, and results in parchment coffee. The second stage (dry processing) includes cleaning, dehusking and sifting of parchment coffee to produce green coffee, named for the greenish cast of the beans. The third stage (final processing) involves roasting and, in some cases, grinding and is generally done in industrialized countries.
6 The 547 000 tonnes of coffee processed in Central America in 1998 resulted in discharges of 1.1 million tonnes of pulp that polluted 110 000 cubic metres of water

per day over six months. These discharges were equivalent to the sewage produced by a city of 4 million people (Rice and Ward 1996).

7　Subsequent references to seven cooperatives include La Palma.

8　Small-scale coffee farmers in Latin America generally did not use the recommended protective masks, clothing and boots when applying pesticides. In 1993 and 1994, more than 200 human poisonings in Colombia, four fatal, were attributed to this pesticide (Rice and Ward 1996).

9　La Palma was not included in the credit component.

10　The inflation rate averaged 5.5 per cent per year from 1994 to 1999.

11　The Global Environment Facility is implemented by the United Nations Development Programme, the United Nations Environmental Programme and the World Bank.

12　One worker can harvest a 48-kg bag of coffee cherries in a day.

13　Tanburn et al. (2001) contains complete definitions of business development service terms.

References

Amaya, G. and J. Gemeil (1997) 'Regional program for small-scale coffee producers', EnterpriseWorks Worldwide, Washington, DC.

Amaya, G. and J. Gemeil (2000) 'Proposal to USAID for development of small-scale coffee farmers of El Salvador', EnterpriseWorks Worldwide, Washington, DC.

Amorín, C., J. Chavarría and V. Mencía (1995) 'Análisis del subsector del café de El Salvador', EnterpriseWorks Worldwide, Washington, DC.

Arturo, R.A. (2000) 'Contaminación del agua en El Salvador', United Nations Office for Project Services, El Salvador.

[CSC] Consejo Salvadoreño de Café (2000) 'El cultivo del café en El Salvador', Consejo Salvadoreño de Café, El Salvador.

Gálvez, G.C. (2000) 'Evaluación ex-post-programa IDB-UCAFES-Grano de Oro', Sistemas Empresariales de Mesoamérica, San Salvador.

Gemeil, J. (1998) 'Proyecto para la fabricación e instalación de tres tostaduras de café', Inter-American Development Bank, Washington, DC.

Gemeil, J. (1999) 'Non-reimbursable technical cooperation funding, regional initiative for the integration of small-scale coffee cooperatives in processing and marketing', Inter-American Development Bank, Washington, DC.

Gemeil, J. (2000) 'Starbucks project report', EnterpriseWorks Worldwide, Washington, DC.

Kovaleski, S. (1999) 'Salvador's river of poison', *Washington Post* 18 March, p. A15.

Mencía, V. (1995) 'El tratamiento de las aguas provenientes del beneficiado de café', Sistemas Empresariales de Mesoamérica, San Salvador.

PROCAFE (1998) *Boletín Estadístico de la Caficultura Salvadoreña*, Fundación Salvadoreña para Investigaciones del Café, San Salvador.

Rice, R. and J. Ward (1996) *Coffee, Conservation, and Commerce in the Western Hemisphere*, Smithsonian Migratory Bird Center and Natural Resources Defense Council, Washington, DC.

Royo Llop, N. (1997) 'Evaluation of the credit program and institutional strengthening of UCAFES and Grano de Oro', Sistemas Empresariales de Mesoamérica, San Salvador.

[SEM] Sistemas Empresariales (1999) 'Informe final de ejecución de programas', Sistemas Empresariales de Mesoamérica, San Salvador.

Stosch, L. (2000) 'Coffee and tree crops product and commodity report', EnterpriseWorks Worldwide, Washington, DC.

Tanburn, J., G. Trah and K. Hallberg (2001) *Business Development Services for Small Enterprises: Guidelines for Donor Intervention*, Committee of Donor Agencies for Small Enterprise Development, Washington, DC.

5 Empowering Ghana's cereal producers in the marketplace

JONATHAN DAWSON

The context

The problem

Small-scale farmers make up 60 per cent of Ghana's farming population and contribute nearly half of the country's GDP. Yet they have little economic clout and remain classic 'price-takers', generally isolated from market information and profitable market opportunities. According to a 1995 World Bank report, the two most vulnerable occupational groups in the country are food- and export-crop farmers, of whom 39 and 37 per cent respectively had annual incomes below the poverty line.[1]

An important reason that the smallholders lack clout is that traditionally they have been limited to being primary producers only. Without access to storage and processing facilities, smallholders had little choice but to sell their crops to traders, who then sold to large commercial firms that dominate high-value processing and marketing. Moreover, the cash requirements of most smallholders generally force them to sell their produce at harvest time when prices are lowest. Later, many must buy back these same basic foodstuffs from the traders, paying significantly more than they originally received. Consequently, poor households are often unable to purchase enough to meet their basic needs, and many end up hungry and malnourished.

The low prices that farmers receive for their produce also restrict the financial and human resources they are prepared to invest in farming. This is because many farmers cannot afford adequate agricultural inputs for their needs, and where they expect to receive only low prices for their crops, they are unwilling to expend their limited resources on harvesting and post-harvest activities. As a result, post-harvest losses in Ghana are heavy, with grain loss running as high as 30 per cent.

Farmers could increase their power in the marketplace by establishing groups and cooperatives. Thus they could pool their resources, gain access to bank credit, acquire production and processing equipment, purchase inputs in bulk, and get higher prices for their produce through collective processing and marketing. However, since the liquidation of the Alliance of Ghana Co-operatives in 1957 and the transfer of its assets of over £4.5 million (much of which was made up of members' savings) to a highly politicized rival body, farmers have been understandably suspicious of formal cooperatives. Currently, the cooperative movement in the country is weak, with relatively few groups active.

TechnoServe

Established in 1968, TechnoServe promotes the creation and strengthening of rural, agriculture-based enterprises by

- providing direct technical and managerial assistance to existing enterprises
- promoting and assisting the establishment of individual or cooperative enterprises
- promoting links between client enterprises and large-scale commercial marketing companies
- strengthening the capacity of local enterprise-support institutions
- providing financial intermediation to improve the access of client enterprises to credit.

TechnoServe has an enterprise-development methodology for all its activities worldwide, based on subsector analysis, the delivery of integrated technical assistance and financial intermediation to client enterprises, and replication of successful models of assistance. In a recent change of strategy, and in addition to its traditional focus on group enterprises, TechnoServe has started supporting individually owned enterprises that deliver services to the rural poor. It is expected that the general capacity-building activities for groups, which have been central to TechnoServe's approach, will be phased out over a number of years through a process in which TechnoServe's roles will be transferred to other support organizations in the country.

Established in 1971, the Ghana programme is TechnoServe's oldest programme worldwide. It operates an annual budget of US$2 million and has almost 100 staff, including two expatriates and a local team with specialities in agronomy, engineering, marketing, finance, accounting, sociology and management information systems. Funding sources include the United States Agency for International Development (USAID), the government of Ghana, numerous private foundations, churches, and members of the communities in which TechnoServe works.

For much of its history, TechnoServe-Ghana has implemented programmes covering many activities, including charcoal making, sugarcane syrup production, vegetable production, pottery making and rabbit rearing. In recent years it has focused on a few subsectors to achieve greater impact. Core activities at present are

- non-traditional export crop development
- cereal crop storage and marketing
- palm oil production and marketing.

TechnoServe-Ghana operates in 210 rural communities throughout the country, directly assisting 76147 clients and direct beneficiaries and an estimated 318437 indirect beneficiaries, half of whom are women.

Business development services that the project provides

TechnoServe-Ghana's cereal crop storage and marketing programme – here-after called 'the project' – has evolved in response to changing conditions and lessons learned (see section 'Support to farmer groups'). The project intro-duced inventory credit to Ghana, and since 1989 has focused on helping to provide this financial service. Inventory credit uses stored produce as collat-eral for commercial loans. The project acts as an intermediary between the groups it supports and financial institutions. The groups receive a loan equal to 75 per cent of the harvest-time price of the produce stored in group-man-aged warehouses. This loan is distributed pro rata among members according to the amount of grain they store. Group members can either redeem their crop as food in the period before the next harvest or sell it at the higher, lean-season price. The financial institution is repaid (capital and interest) after the stored produce is sold or redeemed. The remaining income is distributed pro rata among members after a fee is deducted for crop treatment and storage.[2]

The success of the credit scheme depends on other services that the proj-ect provides. Capacity building is necessary to enable farmers' groups to develop a constitution, elect officials, conduct regular meetings, keep records, manage loans and undertake other activities. The project has also helped to improve crop treatment and storage techniques, thus reducing post-harvest losses and permitting farmers to hold their crops until market prices rise. Previously farmers stored crops in their own houses, and infestation and spoilage were common.

The project helps farmers to develop links with large-scale, formal-sector buyers of their produce to maximize income from their crops. It is also sup-porting a new umbrella organization of its client groups, the Farmers' Service Multipurpose Co-operative Union (FASCU), to strengthen their capacity for autonomous development.

One effect of inventory credit has been to increase the volume of grain stored after harvest. The increased volume available, however, reduces the value of grain in the lean season. Realizing that this would be the case, the project seeks other value-adding activities for its cereal crop-producing farmer groups. These activities include mechanically drying grains, introduc-ing new maize varieties and grading maize for niche marketing.

This case study focuses on project activities in the subsector from the time when the inventory credit model was introduced in 1989. It has been pre-pared by analysing project documents, interviewing project staff and visiting project sites in November 1999.

Rates of exchange

Sharp devaluation of the Ghanaian cedi (GHC) in recent years and the asso-ciated price inflation make comparisons over time using this currency misleading (Table 5.1). Therefore, most values are given in US dollars. Although using the dollar somewhat distorts the picture on the ground, since smallholder farmers do not immediately or fully see their incomes adjusted by the new rates, the distortion is usually not great.

Table 5.1   Value of the Ghanaian cedi against the US dollar and cedi inflation rate, 1992–99

Year	Cedis to US$1 (no.)	Inflation rate (%)
1992/3	500	10
1993/4	800	25
1994/5	1100	25
1995/6	1500	60
1996/7	2000	47
1997/8	2250	27
1998/9	3150	18

Cereal crop storage and marketing project: a description

Brief history of the project

Early TechnoServe support in the mid- to late 1980s was through participation in a programme with other agencies to disseminate 'green revolution' technologies in an attempt to replicate Asia's success in increasing agricultural production. Those technologies were immediately popular and farmers doubled or tripled their yields. However, marketing proved a problem, and the principal effect of the bumper crops, particularly maize and sorghum, was to depress local prices and reduce farmer incomes. Consequently, credit repayment was poor, and TechnoServe staff were compelled to assume debt collecting and advisory responsibilities.

In response, TechnoServe discontinued facilitating access to production credit and focused instead on helping farmers to obtain loans to store and market their grain to earn greater profits and improve their food security. This new model – inventory credit on stored produce – has remained the core element of TechnoServe's support to cereal producers to the present.

TechnoServe's new support model was launched on a pilot basis between 1989 and 1992, working with groups in the Central, Volta and Eastern Regions. Initially commercial banks were unwilling to provide credit for the scheme without a full loan guarantee, having incurred losses in several previous credit programmes for smallholder farmers. The Dutch Ecumenical Development Cooperative Service provided the necessary guarantee facility and the Agricultural Development Bank of Ghana (ADB) provided loans for the project.

The economic impact of the pilot project was limited, although it had some achievements. TechnoServe's private sector approach of promoting commercial bank loans and market rates for inputs was not readily accepted. This was because maize was a primary food crop for farmers in the target areas, and getting them to adopt a commercial attitude towards its production and marketing was difficult. Furthermore, many communities in these areas had benefited from a history of relief programmes providing heavily subsidized credit, agricultural inputs and food supplements.

The desire to work with more commercially oriented farmers and to expand its services to other areas led the project to begin operations in 1992/3 in the Brong-Ahafo Region, where the highly productive 'maize triangle' is located. The scheme immediately had greater impact there on participating farmers' incomes and on the number of participating farmers and farmer groups.[3]

TechnoServe began operations in the Upper West Region in 1991 in a World Bank-funded initiative implemented jointly with the Department of Cooperatives. The aim of this project was to train farmer groups to take over and manage the assets of the state-owned Farmers' Service Company (FASCOM). Inventory credit was part of the assistance package and was used to fund the storage of maize, sorghum, groundnut and rice.[4]

To diversify its sources of finance for the initiative, the project obtained funds from the Ghana Ecumenical Church Loan Fund on more favourable terms than those provided by ADB. Seeing the success of the model, together with its consistent realization of 100 per cent repayment rates, ADB dropped its loan guarantee requirement and in 1995 recommended funding the project-supported groups.

A number of factors have combined to stimulate the significant increase in the volume of stored cereal crops (and the resulting fall in profitability of inventory credit) from the mid-1990s:

- the introduction by ADB in 1997/8 of an inventory credit scheme for traders to buy maize stocks in bulk
- the import of maize (a particularly serious problem during the 1998/9 season), which had a distorting effect on the market
- the generally good harvests of the past two growing seasons[5]
- the significant growth in the geographical spread of the project and the number of participating farmers and farmer groups. This was facilitated in part by the pilot project of a World Bank-funded initiative, the Village Infrastructure Project (VIP), implemented by a number of support agencies, including TechnoServe. Under this pilot, new financial resources were mobilized, four rural banks introduced inventory credit into their portfolio, and the number of participating groups experienced rapid growth
- the launching of another inventory credit programme by the Adventist Development and Relief Agency in the maize triangle in 1997. This programme now covers 75 farmer groups

- widespread adoption of the crop treatment and storage techniques introduced by the project in collaboration with the Ministry of Food and
  Agriculture (MoFA) by non-participating farmers. These farmers use these
  techniques without taking inventory credit.

The combination of these factors, together with the bumper harvests in
1997/8 and 1998/9, meant that over those two years inventory credit delivered
meagre returns and ADB was left with large deposits of grain that it could
not sell.

Those years may have marked the beginning of the end of the viability of
inventory – or they may have been just a blip in the long-term trend.
However, the project managers always recognized that the scheme's profitability was of limited duration, and consequently they worked to identify
other potential value-adding activities for their client farmers (see
'Promotion of other value-adding activities for small-scale cereal crop
producers').

Support to farmer groups

Establishing and strengthening farmer groups has been central to
TechnoServe's traditional approach in developing successful rural enterprises
(although a new orientation in global policy will phase out general capacity
building for farmer groups and emphasize support for group and individual
enterprises). The process of mobilizing and strengthening groups varies little
among the various TechnoServe-supported activities.[6]

Many of the groups working with TechnoServe were in existence before
the project came to Ghana, although they were generally less active. To qualify for TechnoServe support, a group must

- have a formal constitution and democratically elected leaders and hold
  regular meetings
- be recognized by financial institutions and have operated a bank account
  for at least six months
- be willing to invest equity capital in group enterprises
- be willing to sign a formal management assistance agreement with
  TechnoServe and pay a fee for TechnoServe services
- have a savings scheme for its members to ensure they continue to store
  their crops without the need for credit when profit margins from inventory
  credit fall.

TechnoServe's business advisers (BAs) – mostly university-level extension
staff – are responsible for supporting the groups. A team of BAs based at each
TechnoServe zonal office has a range of skills including community

animation, sociology, agronomy, engineering and accounting. On average, each BA supports ten groups.

Experience has demonstrated that internal group cohesion, transparency and trust among members are central to the success of group economic activities. Over the past decade, TechnoServe has devoted progressively greater efforts to engendering these attributes among its client groups. Its support has shifted from being purely technical to a more balanced approach, reflecting the importance of effective community mobilization and organization. It has also placed greater emphasis on training women, who typically have less access to formal training than their male counterparts. Each group maintains its books and accounts using a system developed by TechnoServe. The BAs train and supervise the farmers in all aspects of accounting and record keeping. The accounting system has been simplified over time, both to increase the ability of group members to maintain and use their records to inform business decisions and to reduce the time the BAs spend on training and technical assistance.

The project also provides several project-specific services.

- It supplies critical market information on prices, including information on import shipments or other potentially market-distorting events. This helps the groups decide when to sell their stored grain.
- It trains the groups in tracking local market trends themselves.
- It works with the groups to establish and strengthen umbrella organizations that will be able to take over the functions currently performed by the project. One such body, FASCU, has been established in the Brong-Ahafo Region. Opportunities are being explored in the north for forming a company – with farmers and TechnoServe sharing the equity investment – to take over crop marketing.

TechnoServe's support of FASCU has been through advising it on developing a constitution and working methods and by funding a visit of two members of the FASCU executive to a similar but more established organization in Nigeria. The project is conscious of the need to allow FASCU to develop in an organic manner and at a pace that is comfortable for its members. Consequently, TechnoServe has not developed a blueprint for it.

Farmer groups pay fees for TechnoServe's assistance. This is to recover costs for TechnoServe and to imbed a commercial attitude among the farmers. In 1998/9 this fee was GHC 250 (US$0.08) per bag stored.

Improved treatment and storage

Smallholders were largely unfamiliar with effective storage techniques for cereal crops before the project started. Typically, part of the crop was stored at home after harvest for consumption, but it could not be held long without suffering from post-harvest losses, which were generally high, reaching 30 per cent in some cases.

The project worked with experts from the Post-Harvest Management Division of MoFA to develop improved treatment and storage techniques for the groups. The techniques developed involved drying the crops either on patios (concrete strips constructed for the purpose) or in cribs resting on pal-lets to allow ventilation. The patios were new to Ghana, but the cribs had been used previously. The project has significantly increased crib use and also promoted an improved, rodent-free model.

Drying time depends on the crop: rice and groundnut take about three weeks, and maize up to two months. The crops are then shelled or husked, cleaned of all foreign matter and taken to the group warehouse where they are checked for moisture content, insect infestation, mould and broken ker-nels. This is done by a group member trained by the project in quality control. A MoFA-trained group member then sprays with insecticide the grain that meets quality standards. Farmers are now largely able to obtain chemicals and spray their crops without any help from the project.

In most cases, group members provide storage facilities – either rooms in their houses or other buildings. Occasionally premises are hired for this.

Building materials for 40 storage warehouses were provided as a grant under the VIP pilot phase, and participating communities built these voluntarily. In the 1998/9 season, 33 more warehouses were built using funds from TechnoServe's Development Assistance Project and materials and labour from participating communities.

Three hermetically sealed grain-storage cocoons from the USA were introduced under the VIP pilot phase. These structures control insects by preventing outside entrance of oxygen. Studies are under way to determine their economic feasibility for crop storage.

Intermediation between groups and financial institutions

The project acts as an intermediary between client groups and financial institutions, without which the inventory credit scheme would not be possible.

- First, before the harvest, the BAs find out how much grain the groups intend to store and how much credit they will need. The project uses these projections to negotiate commercial facilities with the lenders.
- Second, the BAs inspect the crops as they are deposited at the storage facilities to verify that both quantity and quality agree with the inventory declaration.
- Third, the project monitors group records and activities to ensure that loan repayments are made to the bank before the group members are paid for their crops, thereby ensuring that the loans are repaid on schedule.

Several participating financial institutions, particularly rural banks and the NGO Sinapi Aba Trust, which has been lending to groups in the north since 1997/8, have extension staff who participate in the monitoring activities. In fact the project has trained staff of a number of financial institutions in these skills. However, these extension staff are too few and do not have the necessary logistical support to cater for the entire project coverage. Without the intermediation role of the project there is no doubt that the participating financial institutions would suspend inventory credit for smallholders.

The project provides these services without charge. An attempt to charge the institutions a fee was dropped when ADB indicated that it would increase the interest charged to producer groups by 2 per cent to cover this. The project considers that the interest rate charged to farmers is already high, and increasing it would not be justifiable.

Marketing support

The project links its client groups with large-scale grain buyers to develop reliable markets, reduce transport and other transaction costs, and obtain higher prices. Deals have been successfully brokered by the project with two such buyers. In 1998/9, a single buyer bought all the maize in the maize triangle sold by the groups. Other marketing avenues are being explored. Members of the FASCU executive also are increasingly participating in meetings between the project and potential clients.

Promotion of other value-adding activities for small-scale cereal crop producers

It has always been clear that the profitability of the inventory scheme would decline over time as the volume of grain stored at harvest time grew. Consequently, an important element of the project's long-term strategy has been to identify and develop other value-adding activities in the subsector. TechnoServe is currently exploring several such activities. The economic viability of mechanical maize drying is being studied. Newly harvested maize takes around two months to dry with sun drying, and a certain level of spoilage and breaking of kernels is inevitable. Maize dried with mechanical dryers is of higher quality and reaches the market at a time of relative scarcity – and thus earns a high premium. If mechanical maize drying is deemed viable, individual farmers will be invited to develop business plans, and the project will help them to get credit and identify suitable technology.

The project is also helping cereal farmers to exploit high-value niches for food and drink products. A multinational corporation with a production plant in Ghana is working with farmers to identify the potential of specific varieties of maize for commercial beer brewing, poultry feed and children's food. The project is also investigating the possibility of the farmer groups themselves grading their grain. This would give them access to higher-value markets for top-quality crops.

Project management

At the apex of TechnoServe's structure is the head office in the United States, which comprises regional offices for Africa and Latin America; the marketing, finance, human resources and administration departments; and the office of the president. TechnoServe maintains an extensive field presence for project implementation through ten country offices or affiliates in Africa, Asia, Latin America and Poland. TechnoServe-Ghana has a head office in Accra; zonal offices in Kumasi, Techiman and Tamale; and subzonal offices in Wa and Bolgatanga (reporting to the Tamale zonal office) and Cape Coast (reporting to the Kumasi zonal office). The head office comprises the finance, research and development, and Microenterprise Development Assistance Service (MIDAS) departments.

TechnoServe plays a leading role in identifying and developing potentially profitable economic activities. Since poor farmers themselves do not generally have access to the information or resources necessary to identify and test market opportunities, TechnoServe sets itself the task of doing this for them. Although client farmers and the BAs inevitably feed into this process, it is the research and development and the MIDAS departments that lead it. This appears inevitable in view of the role that TechnoServe seeks to perform: professional researchers have much better access than farmers or project field staff to information on macroeconomic trends, potential market niches and appropriate technology. They are also better placed for the financial analysis required to gauge the profitability of potential activities.[7]

Both the research and development and the MIDAS departments are well equipped for the role of identifying and developing new business ideas. Their staff includes economists, agriculturists, technologists and a healthy mix of those with private sector and NGO experience. They also have funds to hire specialist consultancy advice where necessary.

Once new business concepts have been introduced there is a notable level of participation in their implementation and development by both client farmers and TechnoServe staff at zonal and subzonal levels. The BAs and the farmer groups, for example, played an important role in developing FASCU. Village-level meetings recognized the need for the umbrella organization to increase the number of groups the project reaches. Responsibility for all operational matters (holding elections, arranging meetings, developing agendas, establishing fees, deciding on policy, and so on) was left entirely to the client groups.

At zonal and subzonal levels, monthly strategy meetings are held involving all TechnoServe staff where ideas for new activities or for innovations in existing ones are discussed. Those agreed upon are included as proposals in the monthly reports made to head office. These reports also include impact-monitoring data on a wide range of performance indicators collected by the BAs. TechnoServe-Ghana issues progress reports on all its activities every six months.

Periodic cost-effectiveness analysis may be carried out at key moments in the life of a project to appraise project strategy and achievements. This operation employs a standard methodology worldwide for evaluating all TechnoServe activities.

Project performance

For the most part, the data used here are derived from project records of actual costs and benefits. Reference is also made to a cost-effectiveness analysis of the inventory credit programme that TechnoServe recently completed. This has projected expected costs and benefits to the year 2011 to arrive at a cost-effectiveness ratio.

Impact

In describing the project's impact, data will be disaggregated between two distinct zones: the north and the south. Disaggregated data are available since 1992/3 for the south but only for 1997/8 and 1998/9 for the north.

In the north there is only one growing season, production levels of crops stored (maize, cowpea, rice, groundnut, millet and sorghum) are relatively low, and project impact is primarily in terms of improved food security; up to 60 per cent of cereal stored under the project is redeemed. Any stored crops that are sold are managed individually, as most farmers redeem some of their crop to sell in local markets to handle their periodic needs for cash.

There are two growing seasons in the south (major and minor), maize is the only grain stored, yields are relatively high, and the larger portion of stored produce is sold. Generally the groups handle the selling, and where possible they sell in bulk.

Participating groups and farmers

Figures 5.1 and 5.2 show the growth in participation since the project was launched in the maize triangle in 1992/3. Participation fell after 1993/4, after more than doubling in the south between 1992/3 and 1993/4. The fall in participation was caused by bad weather in several years in the mid-1990s that produced low yields and consequently higher harvest-time prices: farmers had little surplus crop to sell and little incentive to hold it in view of the relatively high price offered at harvest time.

Favourable weather and large harvests contributed to the sharp increase in project coverage from 1997/8. However, the primary factor was the large increase in the size of TechnoServe's programme: staff numbers grew from 43

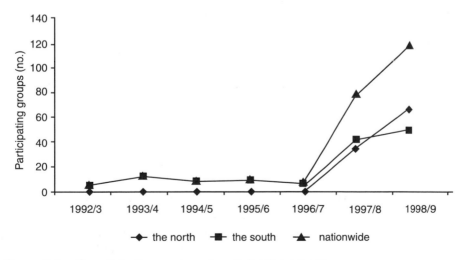

Figure 5.1   *Growth in the number of participating groups*

105

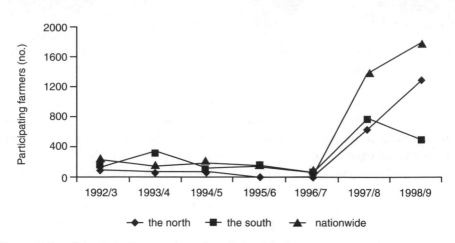

Figure 5.2   *Growth in the number of participating farmers*

in 1996 to 71 in 1997, 85 in 1998 and 97 in 1999, and the project spread to areas serviced by its newly opened offices in Bolgatanga, Cape Coast and Kumasi.

The fall in participation in the south in 1998/9 was due to several factors that led to a flooding of the market and reduction in profit margins from inventory credit: the expanded availability of inventory credit to traders from banks; maize imports; good harvests; extension of the project's reach; and adoption of project techniques by non-participating farmers. The effect of these factors was stronger in the south, where the commercial grain market is more developed. The extremely high interest rates – currently running at 43 per cent relative to an inflation rate of 18 per cent – also discourage participation in the inventory credit scheme.[8]

The number of women participants has grown with the project, reaching 50 per cent in 1997/8 (57 per cent from the north, 44 per cent from the south) before dropping to 41 per cent in 1998/9 (43 per cent north, 35 per cent south). The main reason that women were not recorded as participants in the early years of the project is that men controlled household resources and therefore grain stored was registered under their names. Women have become more active in the groups and correspondingly more likely to store crops under their own name as the project has gone on.

Credit mobilized

Trends in the volume of credit to farmers mirror the patterns of growth of the project (Table 5.2). Following strong growth in credit volumes between 1992 and 1994, poor harvests in two of the succeeding three years substantially reduced credit demand. This changed from 1997/8 with the increase in size and geographical coverage of the project. The relative rise in the amount of credit taken in 1995/6 and 1996/7 compared with 1994/5 can be explained by the groups' participation in VIP.

Table 5.2 Total inventory credit mobilized (US$)

Area	1992/3	1993/4	1994/5	1995/6	1996/7	1997/8	1998/9
North	–	–	–	–	–	33 140	54 889
South	21 120	45 000	7042	22 050	18 482	83 727	62 742
Nationwide	21 120	45 000	7042	22 050	18 482	116 867	117 631

However, the average amount of credit that farmers take is falling (Table 5.3). This is due to the increased size of the project in the north, where farmers typically use less than half the amount of credit, compared with those in the south, and to a reduction in the use of credit in the south because of the falling profit margins.

Table 5.3 Average inventory credit per farmer (US$)

Area	1992/3	1993/4	1994/5	1995/6	1996/7	1997/8	1998/9
North	–	–	–	–	–	51.40	42.0
South	148.7	142.4	56.8	153.0	355.4	108.0	124.2
Nationwide	148.7	142.4	56.8	153.0	355.4	82.0	65.0

Loan repayment rates on inventory credit have generally been steady at 100 per cent. The only exception are several groups in the Techiman area that have outstanding interest payments from the 1997/8 season. This has only recently come to light and is being dealt with.

Crops stored

Production levels in the north are relatively low (Table 5.4). Despite the fact that the north had more than twice as many participating farmers in 1998/9, northern farmers stored only 60 per cent more crop than their southern counterparts.

Farmers in the north, unlike those in the south, store a number of crops other than maize (Table 5.5).

All the crops stored in the north are produced by participating farmers, all of whom take inventory credit. In the south, however, stored grain falls under three categories:

- maize produced and stored by participating farmers for which inventory credit is taken
- maize produced and stored by participating farmers but for which no credit is taken. This is called 'simple storage', and a fee is charged only for treatment and storage
- maize purchased by groups from non-participating farmers to meet the credit allocated by the financial institution. This is called 'buy–sell'. In some cases, groups deliberately overestimate their storage needs to generate

Table 5.4   Total volume of crops stored (tonnes)

Area	1992/3	1993/4	1994/5	1995/6	1996/7	1997/8	1998/9
North	–	–	–	–	–	447	692
South	281	941	260	443	200	1055	1160
Nationwide	281	941	260	443	200	1502	1852

Table 5.5   Crops stored in the north (tonnes)

Crop	1997/8	1998/9
Maize	362.43	291.38
Groundnut	43.3	334.4
Rice	24.8	50.9
Cowpea	13.63	10.46
Millet	2.4	3.44
Sorghum	0.44	1.42
Total	447	692

extra income from the buy–sell operations or to compensate for unexpectedly low demand for storage by members.

Between 1992 and 1994, all farmers in the south took inventory credit for all their stored produce. Simple storage was introduced in 1994/5 but has never accounted for more than 6 per cent of the total maize stored.

Buy–sell operations accounted for 11 per cent of the total maize stored in 1992/3, 10 per cent in 1993/4 and 19 per cent in 1994/5. However, it dropped sharply after that, reaching zero in 1998/9. This is probably because of the falling profits from inventory credit.

Sharp differences exist between the north and the south in how farmers use stored grain (Tables 5.6, 5.7). A significant proportion of maize in the north is redeemed mainly for household consumption, although some is sold to meet cash requirements. In the south all stored maize is sold cooperatively, except in exceptional circumstances.

The majority of farmers in the north redeem some of their grain (65 per cent in 1997/8 and 78 per cent in 1998/9), but relatively few farmers in the south do so. A small but growing proportion of farmers in the south store their grain in the group warehouse and benefit from cooperative marketing without taking inventory credit. With credit being so expensive, this is a more profitable course for those who can afford to store without taking loans.

If, as appears likely, the margins from inventory credit continue to fall, the number of farmers involved in simple storage in the south is certain to grow. The project has reduced the loan available to farmers from 75 per cent of the total value of stored grain to 60 per cent, to be lowered further afterwards. Client farmers in the south appear to be in broad agreement with the

Table 5.6   Crops sold or redeemed (percentage)

Area	1992/3	1993/4	1994/5	1995/6	1996/7	1997/8	1998/9
North	–	–	–	–	–	61.4	42.6
South	100.0	93.7	84.2	93.7	100.0	100.0	100.0

Table 5.7   Farmers redeeming or simply storing inventoried crops

	1992/3	1993/4	1994/5	1995/6	1996/7	1997/8	1998/9
North							
Total participants	–	–	–	–	–	645	1305
ICP* redeemers	–	–	–	–	–	420	1020
Simple storers	–	–	–	–	–	0	0
South							
Total participants	143	316	124	144	52	775	505
ICP redeemers	0	45	33	21	1	0	0
Simple storers	0	0	20	15	7	20	33

*ICP – Inventory Credit Programme

proposal and are keen to reduce their dependence on credit. Their group savings schemes will help to reduce their dependence on the banks. Cuts in credit levels will be considerably more difficult to achieve in the north.

Benefits

Calculating the benefits of the project is a highly complex process involving many variables, such as various prices for different crops; differential benefits of selling and redemption, buy–sell and simple storage; income to groups and individual farmers; timing of selling; and prevailing market prices. A summary of the total project benefits is presented here rather than a step-by-step account of how the benefits have been calculated (Table 5.8, Figure 5.3.)[9]

Table 5.8   Financial benefits per 135-kg bag of maize from inventory credit sales, redemption and simple storage (US$)

	1992/3	1993/4	1994/5	1995/6	1996/7	1997/8	1998/9
North							
IC* sales	–	–	–	–	–	12.99	1.21
IC redemption	–	–	–	–	–	10.74	0.42
Simple storage	–	–	–	–	–	25.86	14.71
South							
IC sales	11.84	5.89	17.52	3.72	16.30	0.61	8.08
IC redemption	0.80	(0.17)	10.82	1.56	8.75	0.09	3.71
Simple storage	25.68	15.19	24.06	13.12	33.40	14.91	17.61

The 'maxi bag' traditionally used in Ghana weighs 135 kg.
*IC = inventory credit

Simple storage is the most profitable option, yielding in most cases more than double the returns of inventory credit. Similarly, holding produce to sell when prices peak can bring significantly higher returns than the savings generated by redemption.

The year-on-year percentage differential between harvest and selling prices was as follows:

1992/3	74.0
1993/4	78.5
1994/5	269.5
1996/7	120.0
1997/8	41.5
1998/9	81.0

Trends in prices and benefits are subject to a number of variables, the most important of which are the size of the harvest, the scale of inventory credit allocations nationwide, and market-distorting maize imports. The relative effect of these factors on prices and benefits, however, has not been determined and no simple, linear pattern is evident in the data available (Table 5.7, Figure 5.3). Recently, though, the trend in harvest and selling prices and incremental benefits from inventory credit has been downward. But the times might have been exceptional and prices might rise again.

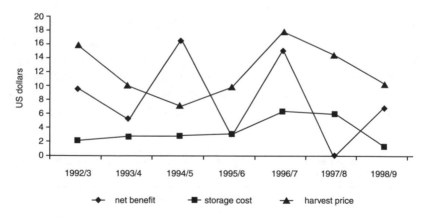

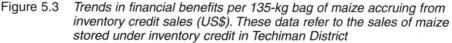

Figure 5.3   *Trends in financial benefits per 135-kg bag of maize accruing from inventory credit sales (US$). These data refer to the sales of maize stored under inventory credit in Techiman District*

It seems more likely that the key variable in the fall in prices and benefits is the widespread adoption of inventory credit by larger economic entities. The introduction of ADB's scheme for traders in the 1997/8 growing season coincided with the beginning of the fall in returns. And it is likely that traders will continue to buy large volumes of grain using inventory credit.

There is no discernible narrowing of the differential between harvest and selling prices. The more significant trend appears to be a progressive erosion of both. It may be that the market for grains is now saturated and that prices will not generally rise again except in years of poor weather when harvests are relatively low. It should be noted in this context that the recovery in profitability during 1998/9 was due to a sharp fall in storage cost, not to an increase in the differential between harvest and sale prices. This followed the building of 33 warehouses during the 1998/9 season. With these warehouses, storage costs will remain low, increasing the margins for farmers.

The project had an important impact on the incomes (or, in the case of households redeeming crops, reduced outgoings) of participating farmers (Table 5.9). Between 1992/3 and 1996/7, average household incomes for farmers in the south rose by 10 to 29 per cent from inventory credit selling and 12.5 to 27 per cent for simple storage. The margins were higher for simple storage, but the volumes were lower. The benefits from redemption were modest.

Table 5.9   Average annual financial benefit per participating farmer from inventory credit sales, redemption and simple storage (US$)

	1992/3	1993/4	1994/5	1995/6	1996/7	1997/8	1998/9
North							
IC* sales	–	–	–	–	–	13.00	1.21
Increment as % of family income	–	–	–	–	–	10.56	0.32
Redemption	–	–	–	–	–	10.74	0.42
Increment as % of family income	–	–	–	–	–	2.25	0.08
Simple storage	–	–	–	–	–	0.00	0.00
Increment as % of family income	–	–	–	–	–	0.00	0.00
South							
IC sales	145.70	111.83	182.38	75.94	429.05	6.42	129.79
Increment as % of family income	15.00	15.00	27.00	10.00	29.00	0.50	9.00
Redemption	–	(1.58)	66.89	15.92	26.24	–	–
Increment as % of family income	–	(0.21)	10.00	2.00	2.00	–	–
Simple storage	–	–	182.88	159.19	248.09	184.39	266.87
Increment as % of family income	–	–	27.00	20.00	17.00	12.50	18.00

*IC – inventory credit

It is too early to draw conclusions for the north that can be generalized since data are available for only the last two growing seasons. Nonetheless, the 10.5 per cent increase in the average household income of participants in 1997/8 must be counted as a remarkable achievement.

Four additional benefits from the project, but for which data are not available, are worthy of mention. First, the inventory credit model introduced by the project has been adopted on a much larger scale and extended to other food and cash crops. While it is true that this may have contributed to undermining the benefits accruing to the participants in the TechnoServe project, its long-term impact on the wider Ghanaian economy is likely to be favourable.

Second, a higher proportion of the food grains produced in the north now remains in the region after harvest. Traditionally, traders bought most of the grain harvested in the north, transported it south for storage, and later sold it in the north during the lean season. Poor households, as a consequence, had to pay an extra premium to cover transport costs. By improving the capacity of farmers to store their grains, the project has helped to enhance food security in the region.

Third, as a result of the treatment and storage techniques introduced by the project, post-harvest losses have fallen sharply to no more than 3 per cent of the crop.

Fourth, there is no doubt that participating farmers have become more businesslike in their farming activities as a result of the training the BAs provided. There is evidence that awareness about trends in the costs of inputs and market prices has increased and that this knowledge is being used in choosing what crops to grow.

Cost effectiveness

As indicated above, TechnoServe estimates the net benefits accruing to participating farmers, year by year, as well as annual estimates of project costs.

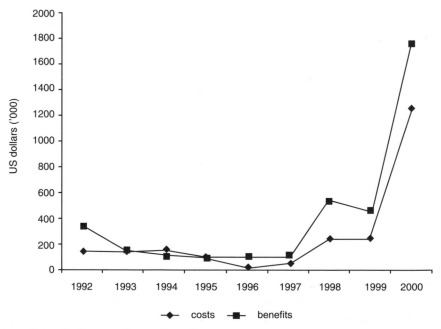

Figure 5.4   *Project costs and benefits*

112

According to their calculations, the total project costs between 1992 and 1999 (US$1 754 708) exceeded benefits (US$1 238 445) by a factor of 1.41:1. Moreover, the margin between the two has grown over time (Figure 5.4). This is because the profitability of inventory credit is declining, and most of the recent growth in the project has been in the north, where the surpluses have been relatively small.

A recent analysis by TechnoServe expected the project to prove cost effective. Projecting project costs and benefits until the year 2011, it arrived at a cumulative ratio of quantifiable benefits to costs of 1.01:1.[10]

However, this finding is based on several assumptions. First, the benefits are projected to remain strong until the year 2011, the final year of their period of analysis. Although some reduction in benefits is built into the projection, this appears to significantly understate the likely decline, especially given the sharp drop in profitability of inventory credit over the past two years.

Second, the analysis assumes that no new expenses will be incurred by the project after 2001, as project functions are expected by then to have been transferred to umbrella organizations such as FASCU. Although Techno-Serve recognizes that this is not attainable within the time frame envisaged, it has not included any costs for continuing activities in the calculations.

Finally, the analysis does not include data for 1989–92, when the model was being tried out, when the project's impact was considered to be low and consequently when costs would have exceeded benefits. This was considered a pilot phase or an action–research period and is thus not included in the final calculation.

Despite these limitations, the quantifiable financial returns of inventory credit to direct project participants are not expected to match project costs until about 2010. A case may be made that the gap between costs and benefits is covered by other benefits that the project has not been able to track – such as widespread adoption of improved treatment and storage by smallholders not directly working with the project and replication of the inventory credit model. The limited resources available for assessing impact, together with problems of attribution, make it impossible to verify this hypothesis.

Sustainability

Any discussion of sustainability must begin with the question, sustainability of what? Support to cereal crop producers has taken several forms. Constraints in grain marketing led the project to move from promoting increased production to facilitating inventory credit for storage and marketing. Now, as the returns from inventory credit begin to fall, the project is exploring opportunities for value-adding processing and marketing activities. However, it is likely to be difficult to deliver sustainable benefits along these lines to smallholder maize farmers, because maize processing and marketing are highly commercialized, with many large processors and traders against whom smallholders will have to compete.

The barriers to entry into inventory credit are not high enough to restrain competition. Traders benefit from inventory credit from banks, and in the maize triangle farmers with no direct contact with the project have adopted the new treatment and storage techniques without taking credit. Widespread imitation of any innovation that the project introduces in the maize subsector is inevitable. The weak market position of smallholders relative to large-scale farmers, processors and traders means that it will be difficult for the project to identify activities for its clients whose benefits will not be usurped by other, more powerful market players.

So, while the project may take credit for introducing inventory credit as an important financial product in Ghana, it appears likely that in the maize sector the principal recipients of such credit are likely to be large-scale operators. Nonetheless, even under such a scenario, smallholders may benefit in the longer term from reduced differentials between harvest and lean-season prices – a core aim of the project.

Benefits may well continue to accrue sustainably to small farmers in two important areas. First, farmers in the north growing crops other than maize are unlikely to face high levels of competition from large operators. Here, smallholders may continue to capture the principal benefits. Second, many farmer groups have adopted the facilities and techniques for simple storage of crops. This is likely to continue to be a widespread, long-term, sustainable feature of smallholder activity – at least in the south of the country.

Another question relating to sustainability concerns the future role of FASCU and similar organizations that might take over the responsibilities of the project. At present it is unlikely that FASCU or any other body will be able to assume any significant role in the near future. In the first place, FASCU is the only umbrella organization that has yet been established, and discussions on establishing others are still at an early stage. Second, FASCU itself has no secretariat, premises, vehicles, equipment, salaried staff or large flow of income. The capacity-building requirements for this organization to take over the functions of a well-funded international NGO are enormous and long term in nature.

TechnoServe's effort to transfer its group capacity-building activities to indigenous agencies has not succeeded. Attempts to encourage other agencies to play a more active role have been unsuccessful because these activities are difficult and expensive to conduct and few organizations in the country have the resources to undertake them.

In view of the uncertain future of inventory credit, the role of these organizations is not clear. Financial intermediation, which is essential for inventory credit, is beyond their capacity, as they would not have the expertise, logistical support or staff numbers this task requires. However, it is possible to envisage a scenario in which the role of financial intermediation would diminish in significance. The project is currently exploring new economic activities for its clients and, in line with TechnoServe's new global policy, will increasingly seek to promote individually owned enterprises.

If farmers move rapidly to simple storage, with project interventions increasingly directed towards the support of individually owned enterprises, the range of services to be transferred to other actors will be greatly reduced. FASCU and other organizations could then limit their role to storing and marketing crops. These activities appear more amenable to management by farmers' organizations: they can be centrally planned without huge expense; they do not require resource-intensive outreach work with groups; and they have the potential to be commercially viable, covering all administrative costs and generating a profit. This appears feasible in the south. However, in the north, where dependence on inventory credit and logistical problems associated with crop marketing (smaller and more dispersed stored crops) are greater, returns are lower and the institutional framework is generally weaker. In short, if inventory credit remains popular in the north, a realistic strategy for its long-term sustainability when the project closes will need to be developed.

Lessons learned

Inventory credit is a potentially important tool for supporting smallholders . . . Inventory credit has proved of great value to participating farmers, whose annual household incomes increased by as much as 29 per cent in the south and 10.5 per cent in the north. Food security has also improved significantly in the north. Moreover, the benefits have spread beyond the direct participants, since many farmers without formal contact with the project have adopted the new treatment and storage techniques.

. . . but its direct benefits may be short term in nature. With the replication of the inventory credit model by other agencies, price differentials have come down and the direct benefits to project participants appear to have been relatively short term. Do the last two years represent a blip or are returns from inventory credit, in fact, already fading? The bigger lesson is that where the model is adopted by financial institutions lending to large-scale operators, the volume of grain stored will increase sharply and the differential between harvest and lean-season prices will drop.

Effective democratic structures in the village are valuable in empowering rural producers socially and economically . . . The project has had a marked impact on the capacity of its client groups. Groups with accountable leadership and transparency of operations developed autonomous, self-help activities such as group farms and buying of expensive equipment like corn

115

mills and power tillers. Farmers, both as groups and in the context of FASCU, are exploring the potential for cooperatively purchasing inputs and crop marketing in bulk.

Farmers are apparently using the skills in record-keeping and analysis of costs that they acquired from the project in deciding how to allocate their resources. Signs are appearing of a growing understanding of trends in the relative profitability of various crops, and agricultural activities are changing accordingly.

. . . but the venture can be long term and expensive. Developing such village structures takes time and resources. Groups working for less than seven years with TechnoServe did not feel confident enough to operate independently. This was not primarily because they feared that group dynamics would disintegrate without the supervision of an external referee (although, in some cases this might be the case), but rather that without TechnoServe support they would not be able to identify new economic activities and evaluate their likely profitability.

The extension services that the BAs provide to strengthen the capacity of the client groups have used up most of the project's funds. TechnoServe is increasingly aware that the high cost of these services makes cost effectiveness difficult to achieve. This realization has been an important consideration in the organization's decision to phase out general group-strengthening activities and to focus more on providing support to group and individually owned enterprises.

The operation of an inventory credit scheme for smallholders using commercial banks appears to be dependent on the ongoing presence of an intermediary support agency . . . There is no doubt that without the services that the project and financial institutions currently provide, the inventory credit scheme would collapse. The organizational and support needs of smallholders are considerable, and even the most efficient and committed of lenders have neither the resources nor the logistical support to provide the services that the project currently supplies.

. . . but responsibility for some of the elements of the support programme may be transferable to local organizations. Early efforts by the project to transfer service provision to local NGOs were unsuccessful, as these institutions had neither the commitment nor the resources required to take over the responsibilities. A new exit strategy has been developed, based on building the capacity of FASCU and perhaps farmers' marketing companies for service delivery. It seems unlikely that such organizations could ever be expected to take over the role of financial intermediation. This requires technical skills and logistical facilities that only international NGOs have. However, with appropriate support, farmers' umbrella organizations could take over such functions as crop storage and marketing operations.

TechnoServe's long-term strategy of identifying agencies to which it could transfer its group mobilization and strengthening services appears extremely ambitious. This is difficult and expensive work and, as the project is already established, finding local organizations willing and able to take over these roles without international funding will not be easy.

Intermediary organizations have a key role in identifying viable economic opportunities for smallholders ... One of the defining features of poverty in the developing world is isolation from profitable economic opportunities and from information about such opportunities. The twin processes of economic liberalization and globalization are opening up many opportunities (as well as problems) for small producers. A wide range of domestic and international market niches has been created that, with appropriate assistance, small producers have proved able to occupy. In such circumstances, intermediary organizations can play a vital role in linking their clients with new markets and building their capacity to compete successfully in them.

... but they must do so in a businesslike manner. A huge responsibility rests on the intermediary organizations in encouraging their clients to move into new market opportunities. If they miscalculate the prospective benefits of activities they promote, or overlook some threat to their profitability, the losses their clients sustain can be substantial. This is particularly true with organizations like TechnoServe that require clients to make a significant investment in the enterprises they support. The strong private sector background of TechnoServe staff is an advantage in this respect.

Intermediaries need to be able to recognize the limits of their market promotion role. That is, their forte lies in identifying and exploring the profitability of market opportunities, building the capacity of their clients to exploit the opportunities, and linking them with private sector partners (input providers, marketing companies and so on). It does *not* extend to playing an active market role. Indeed, evidence from the project shows that even capacity building for small producers is often provided by the larger companies that they supply – known as 'buyer-mentoring'. This is an idea that the project will be exploring along with new, high-value market niches for its cereal crop producers.

The small-producer support agency must continually innovate. Small-producer markets are rarely static. An innovation – a new technology, a new product, or a new model of assistance – is introduced into the market and soon after, where the barriers to entry are low, imitation and market saturation follow. In such circumstances the role of the support agency is to watch the horizon continually, identifying innovations that clients can adopt and that have the potential to promote their competitive advantage.

A commercial orientation on the part of the service provider can be of great value to its client producers. An important factor in the success of

TechnoServe support to rural enterprises is its commercial approach. Enterprises – individuals or groups – are required to have a bank account, sign a management agreement with TechnoServe, pay fees for services, and invest equity capital in the enterprise. This created problems in the organization's early years in Ghana, where the predominant development ethic was one of subsidy and grant. However, the tide has turned TechnoServe's way, and its businesslike approach has contributed to the high level of ownership among its clients of their group activities.

Support for privately owned enterprises is a legitimate way of addressing rural poverty . . . In a recent shift in its global policy, TechnoServe now supports individually owned as well as group enterprises and is set to phase out general capacity building for its client groups. Two factors inspired this change. First, it is often considerably cheaper and simpler – or more cost effective – to launch and support a private enterprise than a group one. Second, for certain types of activity, it may well be more efficient. For maize-drying businesses, which the project is considering to establish, for example, there are grounds to believe that individual entrepreneurs provide higher-quality services than group-managed enterprises.

. . . but it can entail a trade-off in focusing on poverty and empowering communities. TechnoServe's current strategy to achieve greater cost effectiveness entails trade-offs at two levels. First, the move away from general group mobilization and strengthening will mean that the impact of its interventions in community empowerment will inevitably decline. The activities that the BAs undertake to teach the groups to organize themselves, keep records, and analyse their costs and income, may have been expensive and not cost effective. But they helped to build a foundation for solid community empowerment. Although continuing support to group enterprises will provide an ongoing vehicle for skills transfer, the empowerment dividend associated with general capacity building of groups is bound to be affected.

Second, it is likely that in some parts of the country no economic opportunities will be identified that will merit TechnoServe intervention on the grounds of cost effectiveness alone. These will generally be the poorest and most isolated areas that already lack development services of all kinds. The point here is not to question the reasoning behind TechnoServe's pursuit of greater cost effectiveness; it is rather to recognize that such a shift does involve trade-offs. There are certain deprived areas where the market is most unlikely to be an effective mechanism for delivering services to the poor.

Flexible funding allows projects to explore different strategies and approaches. A lesson from the project concerns the value of flexible funding. TechoServe-Ghana has two main sources of funding: the Title II programme provides 70 per cent, under which TechnoServe imports wheat and uses the proceeds from its sale to fund development activities, and 25 per cent comes from the

USAID office in Ghana under the Trade Investment Reform Programme. TechnoServe enjoys a high degree of flexibility in allocating these funds. This flexibility has permitted it to explore various models of enterprise support and to investigate the profitability of a range of potential economic activities.

Challenges for the future

The project faces three important challenges as it seeks to build on its success:

Identifying new, value-adding activities for farmer groups. The first challenge is to find new value-adding activities for cereal crop farmers as the profitability of inventory credit declines. This is likely to be particularly difficult for maize (the most important crop among participating farmers), as this is a crop in which many large-scale operators are already engaged. Finding niches in which innovations introduced for the benefit of small producers will not be replicated and ultimately usurped by these large operators will not be easy.

Transferring project responsibilities to local organizations. Transferring project functions and capacities to local, private organizations is a laudable goal – particularly when the organizations are representative bodies created by the project's client groups. However, this will not be achieved easily, quickly or cheaply. As noted above, the gap between the current form of FASCU and its envisioned role is vast. Other regions of the country do not have such an organization. With appropriate support, these organizations could gradually increase their capacity to manage the storage and marketing operations. However, this needs to go slowly, at a pace that is comfortable for the new bodies – and certainly with a longer timeframe than provided for in the cost-effectiveness analysis.

Transferring the financial intermediation role to local organizations will be difficult. Previous attempts at this have failed because of a lack of commitment and resources. Perhaps a significant fall in inventory credit demand will remove this problem. However, if inventory credit is to remain an important part of the project, careful thought needs to be given to cost-effective approaches to financial intermediation. Finding solutions will not be easy.

Retaining the poverty focus. The challenge facing the project (and indeed TechnoServe as a whole) as it moves away from its traditional focus on group enterprises is to retain its strong focus on alleviating poverty. It is undeniable that in some circumstances the market can deliver services to the poor. However, in others it cannot. In particular, in some geographical areas cost-effective promotion of new economic activities will probably not be possible.

The challenge for the project in choosing economic activities to promote and individual entrepreneurs to support is to minimize the trade-offs necessary to empower communities, and focus on alleviating poverty.

Notes

1 *Ghana Poverty: Past, Present and Future,* World Bank, Washington, June 1995.
2 An in-depth analysis of the scheme can be found in 'Financing rural growth: rural inventory credit in Ghana', TechnoServe Findings Paper, Norwalk, 1999.
3 Although one of the districts of what is known as the maize triangle falls outside of Brong-Ahafo, in Ashanti Region, all project activities in the maize triangle are undertaken by the Techiman zonal office, located in Brong-Ahafo.
4 Sorghum was dropped from this scheme after it was realized that its price differential between the harvest and the lean seasons was not sufficient to make inventory credit a profitable activity.
5 The ADB scheme is being used for the storage and marketing of maize, fish and coffee and is soon to be extended for use with cocoa. The government of Ghana allocated GHC 40 billion (US$12.8 million) for inventory credit schemes in its 1999 budget. Although this funding has not yet materialized, there is little doubt that inventory credit allocations in the country are set to grow further.
6 In most cases, groups become involved in only one of the activities that TechnoServe promotes – non-traditional export crop development, cereal crop storage and marketing, or palm oil production and marketing – although a small number are engaged in more than one.
7 Both the research and development department and the MIDAS department investigate new, potentially viable rural economic activities. Until recently, MIDAS was concerned only with activities in the field of non-traditional crop exports, but it has now broadened its brief.
8 The falling benefits from inventory credit are illustrated in Figure 5.3.
9 Details of these calculations are available from TechnoServe.
10 In the method TechnoServe uses to calculate cost effectiveness, benefits from the project (actual measured benefits) are subtracted from benefits that would have accrued without the project (based on a calculation of the levels of output, income, employment and so on that would have been likely had there been no project) to arrive at the net benefit that is used in calculating the cost-effectiveness ratio. This ratio is naturally much less favourable than would be achieved by simply subtracting total costs from total benefits.

6 Linking small ornamental fish producers in Sri Lanka to the global market

SANDRA O. YU

Sarvodaya Shramadana Sanamaya

AN ORNAMENTAL FISH FARMING project is being promoted through the economic arm of the Lanka Jathika Sarvodaya Shramadana Sanamaya (LJSSS) as one among several ways of improving the economic lot of the rural poor in Sri Lanka. LJSSS started as the Sarvodaya Shramadana Movement, a people's movement, in 1958, and by an Act of Parliament was incorporated as LJSSS in 1972. LJSSS aspires to strengthen people in spiritual, moral, cultural, political, social, economic and technological spheres through an organization that encompasses people and communities, from the village to national levels. Its basic grassroots unit is the Sarvodaya Shramadana Society.

The economic programmes of LJSSS are handled by the Sarvodaya Economic Enterprise Development Services (SEEDS). SEEDS began its operation as a separate division of LJSSS in 1986 and it now reaches 18 of Sri Lanka's 25 districts, or approximately 300 000 people. LJSSS itself covers all of the 25 districts, or around 500 000 people. It is the hope of SEEDS that the Sarvodaya Shramadana Societies will become self-governing villages, capable of serving their community's economic and social needs. Through these organized societies, a social infrastructure was laid through which SEEDS provides business development services (BDS) to a large population at low cost. It is hoped that the united societies will constitute an economic and political force that can influence sectoral and national economic policies.

This case study of the SEEDS ornamental fish-growing project examines the impact, outreach, cost effectiveness, overall effectiveness and sustainability of the project. It pinpoints lessons and makes observations that can add to current thinking about business development services in general.

Enterprise promotion

SEEDS started its work by offering only microfinance (savings and credit) and training in entrepreneurship. Seeing the need for advisory services to help borrowers, it expanded its services in 1990 to include business development, business information and extension services. Accordingly, SEEDS established three main divisions, each of which handles specific but complementary services. Village banking services are handled by the Rural Enterprises Programme (REP), while training in entrepreneurship and management is carried out by the Management Training Institute (MTI). Extension and business services are under the Rural Enterprise Development Services (REDS).

Realizing that the main rural livelihood of its members – rice production – does not produce an adequate income for rural households, REDS seeks out new and non-traditional business opportunities for rural communities. As part of its business support service, REDS provides business opportunity identification, marketing support, feasibility studies, business plan preparation, and training in technical skills.

In line with this, REDS promotes a number of economic activities, one of which is ornamental fish farming. It has also actively promoted garment, dairy, cashew, betel, tea cultivation and pineapple-growing businesses, supporting them through a full range of assistance. REDS calls these 'major sectors'. They were selected for their market potential, availability of raw materials and land, and potential outreach. For the major sectors, SEEDS aimed at establishing at least 250 new enterprises each year. 'Minor sectors' were also promoted, although on a lesser scale. Ornamental fish farming belonged to this latter category. Others were ornamental plants, cut flowers and retail shops. Priority sectors vary year by year, depending on market conditions, perceived potential and entry of new sectors.

Ornamental fish growing: the development phase

The ornamental fish farming project was conceived in 1995 after REDS staff members attended a conference where this idea was presented as a promising business opportunity. REDS examined its potential and took the following steps during the development stage of the project.

Market assessment

The marketing aspect of the project was handled by the agricultural coordinator, with the assistance of the extension officer of Colombo District. Both spent two weeks collecting technical and market information on ornamental fish farming, including export and local markets, prices, breeds, technology, feeds and disease management. The findings of the study were favourable (see Box 6.1), and they were presented in a report drafted with the assistance of a college student (REDS 1995).

Community needs assessment

To assess community capability, extension and field officers consulted communities informally about their interest in farming ornamental fish as a backyard industry. The findings were favourable.

Box 6.1 The ornamental fish industry in Sri Lanka

Exports of aquarium fish by Sri Lanka have been increasing substantially over the past ten years. The value of ornamental fish exports increased from LKR 30 million[1] in 1981 to LKR 370 million by 1997. This growth has been mainly because existing importing markets have expanded and Sri Lankan exporters have acquired access to new markets. According to the 1999 FAO News Highlights, the export value of ornamental fish and vertebrates worldwide was over US$200 million in 1996. The same report indicated that international trade of aquatic organisms for ornamental purposes increases at an annual rate of 14 per cent. Sri Lanka's share in the world trade, at over 1 per cent, is projected to increase to 10 per cent in the medium term. The largest supplier of freshwater ornamental fish is Singapore, which accounted for 33 per cent of global imports in 1986. Singapore has 130 exporters of ornamental fish compared with Sri Lanka's 14, of which only around five or six export in any significant quantities. The major buyers of ornamental fish are France, Germany, Japan, the Netherlands and the USA.

Thus far, local Sri Lankan production has not been able to fill the volume requirements of export markets. Among the biggest fish export companies are Lumbini Aquarium, O.C. Tropical Fish Aquarium and Lanka Aquarium. Recently a large fish export company, Joan Kees, set up shop in Sri Lanka, and this has given worldwide prominence to the local industry.

Around 75 per cent of ornamental fish exported from Sri Lanka are marine varieties. In recent years, however, Western countries have been putting restrictions on the importation of fish caught from the ocean. This has led the Sri Lankan government to promote freshwater ornamental fish production in the country. Sri Lanka is endowed with favourable climatic conditions that make it suitable for rearing and breeding freshwater fish.

Among the problems of the local industry are inadequate stocks of freshwater aquarium fish, lack of communication between small-scale breeders and established exporters, lack of research and development in freshwater aquarium fish breeding, lack of government support to the industry, and lack of adequate facilities for packaging and air transport.

Sources: REDS 1995, Weerakoon 1998

Development of organizational capability

Given the positive results of the study, REDS officials and staff set about organizing the project and recruiting participants.

Orientation of REDS

REDS sought the assistance of a specialist from the Dehiwala Zoo to train its staff and potential project participants in raising ornamental fish. A two-day training session was held in Godigamuwa, Maharagama, with 12 participants from REDS and Sarvodaya. The participants were taught about fish varieties, constructing cement tanks, feeding systems, breeding systems, pest and disease management, and marketing.

Intensive training for REDS officials

REDS officials sought more thorough and intensive training in ornamental fish growing. They contacted the National Aquarium Research Agency (NARA), which offered longer training programmes on ornamental fish farming. The agricultural coordinator, the district extension officer and another REDS official attended this programme, which was held over six days on three consecutive weekends.

Having acquired solid technical knowledge about ornamental fish farming and an initial network of technical agencies, exporters and academic institutions, REDS proceeded to develop a programme for ornamental fish farming. The following steps were taken.

- It prepared a plan for supporting project participants, consisting of finance, training (both technical and management), and extension services using the resource complement within SEEDS.
- It began contacting prospective buyers and exporters who could work with Sarvodaya members through purchase agreements or outgrowing (described below under 'Market identification').
- It set about publicizing and promoting the project among Sarvodaya members.

Recruitment and training of project participants

Information was spread throughout Sarvodaya's existing organization, which encompassed some 10000 village societies, 25 district offices and several national offices and networks. While REDS also produced flyers to aid the dissemination of information, the main channel for communication was the constant interaction between the national and district offices, the Sarvodaya societies and the members.

Through these channels, REDS announced that it would hold a one-day training programme on ornamental fish farming in the district offices. Hundreds of Sarvodaya members responded and, as a result, REDS conducted one-day training programmes for 345 people, in batches, in nine districts. Although it was hoped that the project would mainly benefit women and youth, the training was open to all interested members. (It was noted that non-traditional products using new technology, such as ornamental fish farming, had greater appeal and success among younger people.) People from NARA, the Fisheries Ministry, AgEnt (a USAID-funded agency) and universities, as well as commercial buyers and exporters taught participants about fish varieties, constructing ponds and tanks, feeding systems, disease management and marketing.

Although 345 people participated in the training sessions, only 115 embarked on the project. Both Sarvodaya members and REDS officers gave several possible reasons for the low turnout of project participants. Some members thought that those located far from the district offices and major markets realized it would be difficult to transport fingerlings and grown fish to and from their homes. Others were discouraged by the difficulty of finding markets. There were also those who found it difficult to handle the technical details. Some understandably found one day of training not enough to provide them with the knowledge and confidence they needed to begin the project. A few seemed to be interested only in putting up an aquarium in their homes.

Project feasibility for individual participants

When 115 participants stated their interest in starting an ornamental fish business, the district extension officers helped each one to assess the feasibility of implementing the project at the participant's location. The extension officers looked at the skills of the participants, their previous business experience, the land on which ponds would be constructed, water quality, available transport and infrastructure facilities. The district extension officers prepared feasibility reports for each of the participants. The participants prepared project proposals, usually to apply for a loan.

Production process and support

Support was given in market identification, financing, technical and management training, and advisory services.

Market identification

Project participants generally had two types of buyers: exporters and local dealers. For exporters, project participants operated through an outgrowing arrangement. Outgrowing is a common arrangement in the ornamental fish industry. As exporters expand their volume, they need larger tracts of land to hold more ponds. With land prices rising in Colombo and nearby areas, the best method for expansion is to contract out the job of growing and breeding fish. Exporters provided participants with the fingerlings to be grown over 45 to 60 days. After the fish were grown, they were sold back to the exporters.

The main varieties of fish produced by the project participants were as follows:

| Mainly for export | Mainly for the domestic market |
| *(45-day growing period)* | *(60-day growing period)* |

Barb (*Barbus* or *Puntius*)	Angel (*Holocantus* and *Pomocantus*)
Guppy (*Poecilia reticulata*)	Carp (*Cyprinus carpio)*
Molly (*Mollienisia*)	Goldfish (*Carrassius auratus*)
Platy (*Xiphophorus maculatus*)	
Siamese fighter (*Betta splendens)*	
Swordtail (*Xiphophorus helleri*)	

Exporters supplied fingerlings under varied terms. Some required that the project participant or outgrower purchase the fingerlings outright. In this case, when the fish were harvested the project participants were free to sell them to whomever they wished. Other exporters, such as Lanka Agua, did not require outright purchase but rather asked for a bond in the form of a bank cheque equivalent to the cost of the fingerlings. Lanka Agua then held this cheque until the fish were harvested and sold back to it. Another, Shoal Aquarium, did not require either outright payment or bond but simply deducted the cost of the fingerlings from its payment to the outgrower upon harvest. The owner of Shoal Aquarium relied entirely on the pressure and influence of Sarvodaya on the project participants to return the grown fish to him and not to sell them to other buyers. Normally the survival rate of fish was 70 to 90 per cent. Figure 6.1 illustrates the outgrowing relationship between outgrower and exporter.

Local dealers paid outgrowers one-and-a-half to two times more than did exporters. However, outgrowers still preferred selling to exporters since they

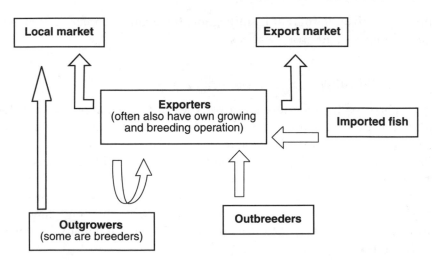

Figure 6.1   *Basic outgrowing arrangement between Sarvodaya project participant-outgrower and exporters*

would buy larger quantities of fish. Some outgrowers sold to both local deal-ers and exporters to maintain their sales volume. They sold a bigger portion of their fish to exporters during the peak export season (early September to mid-April), and to local dealers during the lean export season (mid-April to August). Those who did not have links to local dealers simply experienced a drop in income during the lean season.

REDS played an important role in identifying exporters and local buyers. If problems arose, the REDS district extension officers also provided liaison and arbitrated between parties when necessary. One exporter agreed that his company's relationship with SEEDS could become a commercial one, since SEEDS ensured the reliability of the outgrowers and, through the extension officers, maintained communication between the exporter and the outgrow-ers. He found it more efficient to deal with extension officers, who made enquiries on behalf of the outgrowers, rather than having to deal separately with each outgrower.

Financing

To start fish farming, a person had to construct fish ponds. Two types of ponds were built: mud ponds and cement tanks. Fish varieties such as angelfish, carp and goldfish were raised in mud ponds. Fish raised in cement tanks were found to acclimatize to aquariums more easily, especially when sent to the importing countries. Therefore, those for export – guppies, swordtails, mollies and platys – were raised in cement tanks.

Mud ponds were usually 1000 square feet and could contain as many as 1500 to 2000 fish. The cost of constructing a mud pond 1000 square feet in size would range from LKR 10 000 to LKR 15 000,[1] depending on the materials used for netting. Cement ponds, on the other hand, usually were 100 square feet and could hold around 1000 fish. The cost of constructing a 100-square-foot cement pond ranged from LKR 10 000 to LKR 18 000 depending on whether the walls were made of cement layers with soil filling, which were cheaper, or were entirely of concrete. Cost could be halved if the participants used their own labour in constructing the ponds. An all-concrete pond could last ten years, while one made of cement slabs with soil filling would last five or six years.

Apart from the investment in the ponds, other expenses involved in grow-ing ornamental fish, with sample costs for one cycle, are detailed in Table 6.1.

At the start of the project, the outgrower needed to lay out capital to cover the construction of ponds or tanks and, if payment was immediately required by the supplier, to buy fingerlings. Subsequently, the operation could be financed out of earnings. Further financial needs arose out of the desire for expansion – to construct more ponds or to buy other equipment such as water pumps or oxygen tanks.

Table 6.1 Typical expenses incurred in growing ornamental fish

Cement tank fish per 1000 fingerlings	Mud pond fish per 2000 fingerlings
Fingerlings: LKR 2500	Fingerlings: LKR 4000
Fish food: LKR 350–500 (fish food is often prepared at home upon the instruction of the exporter, NARA or REDS)	Fish food: LKR 400–800 (feeds are cheaper in mud ponds as organic foods are bred in such ponds or are found in surroundings)
Medicine: LKR 100 (necessary only on rare occasions when fish contract some disease)	Medicine: LKR 100 (necessary only on rare occasions when fish contract some disease)
Transportation: LKR 500–600 (purchase of fingerlings, showing fish samples for harvesting, and delivery of grown fish)	Transportation: LKR 500–600 (purchase of fingerlings, showing fish samples for harvesting, and delivery of grown fish)

To support the costs of starting the project, SEEDS provided loans to project participants ranging from LKR 7500 to LKR 25 000. Loans were often used to finance pond construction and purchase fingerlings. These loans matured in two years and carried an interest rate of 24 per cent per annum. The maturity period was appropriate for the project since the greater part of the expenditure consisted of capital investments whose payback period was not immediate. A borrower who established a good record and wanted to expand could take out bigger loans. One participant recently borrowed LKR 50 000.

Technical inputs

Follow-up technical training was found to be important for the businesses, especially since trainees had only the initial one day of training. It was found, for instance, that after the initial training, some participants still did not know how to construct ponds properly or feed the fish adequately. Others sought advice on more specialized topics, such as breeding. These follow-up training sessions lasted one or two days. They were usually held two or three times a year per district. Examples of topics covered were breeding, fish identification, sexing (determining whether a fish was male or female), how to deal with diseases, feeding, marketing and selling.

'Fish clinics' were to form part of the technical support provided to outgrowers. The clinic was set up as a one-day consultation between experts and producers. Experts were invited to a place where they could talk individually with outgrowers with queries. Each expert occupied a booth and the producers consulted the expert who could best help them. So far, the only fish clinic held was in February 1998. Ten experts came from the University of Peradeniya, NARA, AgEnt, the Ministry of Fisheries and export companies. The main areas covered were fish breeding and embryology, ecosystems and environmental conditions, water quality and water management, nutrition and feeding, diseases and prevention, and marketing trends. The turnout exceeded REDS expectations as 133 people registered, over double the 60 that were expected.

REDS further provided information on ornamental fish technology through a SEEDS magazine and through various handouts distributed during training seminars. Participants noted that the only resource materials in the local language on ornamental fish farming that they could use for reference were those that REDS provided. For their regular operation, project participants relied mainly on exporters for technical help.

Extension services

Extension services were provided by the district extension officers, who visited project participants regularly and attended to problems as they emerged. The extension officers were instrumental in maintaining good relations between producers and buyers and in inspiring feelings of confidence among participants.

Sarvodaya members found that having intermediaries such as REDS was important in organizing participants for joint tasks and for consulting exporters. Many Sarvodaya project participants lived far from each other. Therefore, exporters were not willing to collect fish from them, since each might have produced only a small quantity. In contrast, some non-Sarvodaya outgrowers, for instance those by the Mahaweli River System, lived close to one another and, because of their large collective volume, exporters easily organized transport of fingerlings and collection of grown fish. For instance, it took only two days for Lanka Agua to collect grown fish from 57 outgrowers in Mahaweli River System B or from 52 outgrowers in Kothmale. Furthermore, other outgrowers had telephones and could consult the exporters by phone. Sarvodaya members did not have such advantages and therefore frequently needed the help of the extension officers to organize joint transport or to communicate with the exporters.

District extension officers visited project participants once a month, or more frequently during start-up and when problems arose. They checked on the development of projects. They were sometimes overwhelmed by the scope of their work, which included as many as 4000 Sarvodaya members in each district undertaking different REDS-promoted projects. These officers expressed their need for greater technical and managerial skills and knowledge.

Management

Managerial and entrepreneurial training was provided in a more limited manner. Management training was provided utilizing the GTZ-developed training programme Competency-based Economies through Formation of

Entrepreneurs (CEFE) and was implemented by the Management Training Institute. The course was held over a period of 14 days with a one-week break during which participants began to apply their learning back home and gathered information for drawing up their business plans.

Assessment of the project

This project is assessed on its

- impact on the project participants
- outreach
- cost effectiveness
- client perception of the effectiveness of the services received
- potential for sustainability.

SEEDS for the most part has not kept data on the above. Except for findings such as new enterprises created, cost effectiveness per beneficiary or enterprise reached and sample profitability achieved, the accomplishment reports of SEEDS summarized inputs provided rather than output realized. One of the problems cited was the difficulty in reaching its members. Also, SEEDS hesitated to use its limited financial resources for external assessment studies. Recently REDS devised a self-administered survey tool to keep track of people's economic activities, but as it contains only the respondent's name, address and enterprise type, it thus serves as no more than a registry.

Because of this inadequacy of data, a survey was conducted among 30 project participants to find out how they had fared on the above five criteria. The reported findings are deemed indicative only, inasmuch as the sample size is small (26) relative to the population (115). Moreover, the survey was carried out in only four of the eight districts and hence does not represent a balanced picture of conditions in all districts. However, 90 per cent of all project participants are located in these four districts.

Project participants were almost evenly split between men (54 per cent) and women (46 per cent). The highest formal education of any participant was secondary school, and 40 per cent had attended only primary school. Before participants joined the ornamental fish project, their main source of income had been wage employment, which provided an average income of LKR 5598. A few of the respondents had joined at the project's inception in 1994, but most (65 per cent) had been with the project for only two years.

Impact

SEEDS considered ornamental fish farming as one of the more successful enterprises of those they were promoting. In their quarterly reports, SEEDS

130

Table 6.2   Average profitability of various SEEDS-sponsored activities, 1998

	1 Jan–31 Mar	1 Apr–30 Jun	1 Jul–30 Sep	1 Oct–31 Dec
Cut-flower marketing	2440	3130	3093	3010
Ornamental fish farming	8000	7967	7666	8250
Glassware selling	11 920	16 900	16 150	18 220
Compost marketing	–	–	–	12 750

Source: SEEDS quarterly reports

made sample comparisons of average profitability realized by participants in the various districts; Table 6.2 is an example.

In assessing impact, the task of estimating returns to the participants is complicated by the wide variation in the participants' cost and input patterns and by their use of different marketing and pricing strategies. The data used here were derived from the survey and sample computations made by the beneficiaries and the exporters.

On income

Ornamental fish farming has a seasonal market, characterized by approximately seven months of peak and five months of lean export sales. Sales dropped 60 to 70 per cent during the lean season. Thus annual instead of monthly data are used to assess income improvement.

The annualized profit calculation below presents two sample projects. The first had two 100-square-foot cement tanks of guppies, a common start-up scale farmed by outgrowers. The second, operated by one of the interviewed participants, had a 1500-square-foot mud pond containing 5000 platys.

In the first example, the farmer realized from a small scale of two cement tanks a net monthly income of LKR 3950, or LKR 3025 after the cost of capital was deducted. Except for a few fish farmers who had a good mix of local and export buyers and thus could still enjoy good sales during lean export periods, most experienced a 60 to 70 per cent drop in sales during slow months. Assuming a 60 per cent drop in sales, net monthly income during the lean season in Example 6.1 would drop to LKR 2370 or LKR 1445 net of capital cost. Assuming seven months of peak sales and five months of low sales, annual net earnings amounted to LKR 11 415. In Example 6.2, the annual net earnings amounted to LKR 23 670.

Based on the survey, the 20 (of 26) respondents who reported their incomes revealed an average annual income of LKR 27 509 from ornamental fish farming. Two respondents performed exceptionally well – more than LKR 100 000. The rest earned LKR 30 000 or less. The average annual income, excluding the two exceptional performers, was LKR 17 427. Project participants reported that their incomes increased after they joined the ornamental fish project. The pre-project average monthly income was LKR 5598. Average monthly income after joining the project rose to LKR 8300, a

> **Example 6.1   Two 100-square-foot cement tanks (2000 fingerling guppies)**
>
> | | | |
> |---|---:|---:|
> | Sales per cycle (2000 × 80 per cent yield) × LKR 6.50 | | LKR 10 400 |
> | Operating costs | | |
> | Fingerlings | LKR 5000 | |
> | Fish food (average of LKR 0.350 and LKR 0.500 for two tanks) | 850 | |
> | Medicine (average of LKR 0.0 and LKR 0.100 for two tanks) | 100 | |
> | Transportation* | 500 | |
> | Total operating costs | | LKR 6450 |
> | Contribution margin per cycle | | LKR 3950 |
> | Number of cycles per annum | | |
> | Peak export months (7 months/45 days) = 4.7 | | |
> | Lean export months (5 months/45 day × 30%) = 1.0 | | |
> | Total cycles per year = 5.7 | | |
> | Total contribution margin (5.7 × LKR 3950) | | LKR 22 515 |
> | Financing (Capital cost for two 100-square-foot cement tanks, LKR 15 000) | | |
> | Principal payments per year (2-year financing) | LKR 7500 | |
> | Interest at 24 per cent per year | LKR 3600 | |
> | Annual capital costs | | LKR 11 100 |
> | Cashflow surplus | | LKR 11 415 |
>
> *Transportation costs are estimated at LKR 500, but for those with a large har-vested crop of, say, at least 4000 fish, the exporters are willing to collect the fish. Some growers alternatively try to reduce this cost by sharing transport costs with other growers.

50 per cent increase (or 13 per cent real increase after netting out inflation rate).[2]

A summary of the averaged income data is as follows:

Monthly income *before* ornamental fish farming (OF) project	LKR 5598
Monthly income *during* OF project, including other income	8300
Annual income from OF project	27 509
Annual income from OF, without two exceptional performers	17 427
Total value of business investments in OF project	33 130
Total value of new household investments as a result of OF project	19 807

132

Example 6.2   One 1500-square-foot mud pond (5000 fingerling platys)

Sales per cycle (5000 × 76 per cent yield)* × LKR 3.50		LKR 13 300
Operating costs†		
Fingerlings	LKR 5000	
Fish food	2000	
Medicine	100	
Transportation	100	
Total operating costs		LKR 7200
Contribution margin per cycle		LKR 6100
Number of cycles per annum		
Peak export months (7 months/45 days) = 4.7		
Lean export months		
(5 months/45 day × 30 per cent) = 1.0		
Total cycles per year = 5.7		
Total contribution margin (5.7 × LKR 6100)		LKR 34 770
Financing		
(Capital cost for 1500-square-foot mud pond, LKR 15 000)		
Principal payments per year		
(2-year financing)	LKR 7500	
Interest at 24 per cent per year	LKR 3600	
Annual capital costs		LKR 11 100
Cashflow surplus		LKR 23 670

*In general, the survival rate of fish in mud ponds is lower because conditions are less controlled.
†Some of the operating costs are lower on a per unit basis than in the first case. Fish food is cheaper in mud ponds than in cement tanks because the natural environment provides a variety of organic feeds. Transportation cost is also lower because the exporter, given the large volume, collects the harvested fish. Transportation costs here involved collecting fingerlings and sending fish samples to the exporter to verify if they can be harvested.

On productive investments

Those interviewed invested from LKR 10 000 to LKR 500 000 in their ornamental fish operations. Most had at least two or three ponds or tanks. The more successful ones had as many as 15 tanks plus a few smaller ones for breeding. All started out with one or two ponds and gradually increased the number. The average investment made in the ornamental fish project was LKR 33 130.

On household investments

A primary aim of such a project was to improve the living conditions of the participating household. An indication of improvement would be the amount of household investments made out of the project's earnings. Based on the survey, half of the respondents reported an increase in household investments as a result of income earned from the ornamental fish project. The average household investments made by those who reported them was LKR 19 807. It was not clear whether those who did not respond did not make such investments or found the question difficult to answer. Reported incomes and investments were rough approximations since the participants simply made mental notes of their expenses and earnings and rarely kept written records.

On jobs created

Ornamental fish farming is not a labour-intensive activity, since only about three to four hours a day are needed to tend the ponds. One project participant who had 12 ponds hired only one worker throughout a year. Another, with 15 growing tanks and 12 breeding tanks, hired only one or two workers and only during peak season. The survey corroborated this finding, as 80 per cent did not hire full-time workers. If they hired at all, they would do so only during peak season or part-time (56 per cent of respondents).

Outreach

Notwithstanding the favourable increase in participant income, the reach of the project was limited. Since the start of the project in 1995, there has not been a substantial increase in the number of project participants. Only 40 participants have joined the programme, with most of them coming from Colombo District.

Because the ornamental fish project serves mainly the export market, the distance to exporters, who are mostly located in urban centres, is an important consideration. The project could be useful mainly to people who were not too far from the urban centres, particularly those in urban and semi-urban areas. It was not surprising that the new additions to the project came almost entirely from Colombo District.

Though the land requirements of the project would have been ideal for Sarvodaya's rural target groups, this also meant that project participants lived relatively far from one another. The distance between participants in some districts averaged five to seven kilometres, and this prevented participants from cooperating to reduce their costs and increase their profit. As a result, those who were successful were the ones who had the drive to expand their operation and thus achieve economies of scale on their own. Those who wished to pursue ornamental fish farming as subsistence farmers, with three tanks producing fewer than 4000 fish, had to shoulder transportation costs on their own, which could be quite substantial per batch of fish.

Cost effectiveness

The cost of implementing the project is summarized in Table 6.3. The costs are categorized as follows:

- Development costs associated with preparing the project. These included market assessment, network organization and development.
- Maintenance costs incurred in running the programme. These included the salaries of those directly involved and a share of the organization over-head.
- Other direct expenses incurred in activities such as training and clinics on raising fish.

Table 6.3 Summary of project costs and cost assessments

	Cost (LKR)	Beneficiaries (no.)	Cost per person benefiting (LKR)	Fees collected (LKR)	Cost recovery rate (%)
Developmental cost	20 625	115	179	0	0
Market assessment and networking	2160	115	19	0	0
Training, including preparatory work					
Training, 12 participants	13 980	12	1165	0	–
Training, 345 participants reached[a]	139 775	345	405	16 388	12
Users of the training	–	115	1215[b]	–	–
Fish clinic, 133 participants	21 272	133	160	7012	33
Preparation of individual feasibility studies	13 496	115	117	0	0
Total	211 308	115	1837	23 400	11
Monthly maintenance cost	29 049	115	253	0	0

Source of raw data: SEEDS quarterly report and interview with Mr V.N. Jayasinghe, Senior Development Manager.
[a]345 participated in the training, 115 actually used the training to start a business.
[b]LKR 405 for each of the 345 training participants, LKR 1215 if the training cost is calculated per person for only those who started businesses.

Some of the data, such as development costs, and the cost of training that took place in 1995, were mere approximations. The absence of such data (some of which were located in the district offices where the training activities took place) made the task of making accurate calculations quite daunting.

The costs of implementing the project were low. Development costs were estimated at LKR 198 per participant, preparing individual feasibility studies for each participant cost LKR 117, and monthly maintenance added up to only LKR 253 per person. A fish clinic cost only about LKR 160 per

135

participant. Training costs were a bit higher, computed at LKR 405 per trainee, but because turnout for the training course was low, the actual cost per user was even higher – LKR 1215 (see Table 6.3).

Costs for this project were low because it mainly linked project participants to the market and to the technology (the exporters). REDS was a third party that provided supplementary support and troubleshooting to ensure the proper functioning of these links.

The cost of implementing the project, compared with the effect on the participants, was generally positive. The cost of developing the programme, including the initial training cost of LKR 1837 per participant, averaged over one year (which is a shorter time than the actual usability of the learned material), was LKR 153 per participant per month. The monthly maintenance cost of SEEDS per project participant was LKR 253. Added together, the monthly per participant implementation cost was LKR 406. Annually, this amounted to LKR 4872. Comparing this with the annual income of LKR 27509 averaged from 26 respondents, the benefit/cost ratio was 5.6:1 (LKR 27509/LKR 4872).

Despite the improved participant income from the project and the relatively low cost of the project per participant, SEEDS did not try to recover costs through fees. It had achieved a recovery rate of only 11 per cent for the development expenses, including training, and zero per cent for the monthly overhead. Some of the REDS costs could have been recovered from exporters as service fees, if its services had been valued. One of the interviewed exporters was willing to treat its relationship with REDS as a commercial one and pay for the services received through the extension officers. Other exporters were not so willing.

Effectiveness of services

Information on the effectiveness of the services that SEEDS provided was gleaned mainly through participants' satisfaction. As stressed, SEEDS provided integrated support services, including marketing assistance, technical training, financial support, advisory services and management training. Most participants received all these services except management training, which only a few undertook.

The respondents were asked to rank the services they received from SEEDS according to importance on a scale of one to five – five being the most appreciated. It was found that the most important service was financial support (3.76), followed by technical training (3.38), marketing (3.0), and advisory services (2.4). This reflected the critical role of financial help in starting the participants off in the ornamental fish project. Financial support was highly valued as it enabled participants to construct tanks they would not have been able to afford on their own. Other outgrowers had to approach banks to take out a loan, sometimes with the help of the exporter, who had to vouch for the expected revenues from the project.

Technical training was particularly valued. The technical training programme conducted by REDS motivated trainees to set up an ornamental fish farming project or to venture into related activities such as breeding. Still, buyers and exporters provided much of the day-to-day technical input. Some of those interviewed also commented that SEEDS should provide more technical help than the initial one-day training. They recommended a three- or four-day training programme or the one-day programme with regular follow-up sessions in quick succession.

Although REDS had linked most of the project participants to their buyers, participants still gave a low rating to marketing help, and 39 per cent said they had marketing problems.

In terms of satisfaction with specific assistance received, training ranked the highest (3.27) on a scale of one to four, with four being the highest, followed by advisory services (2.95), marketing (2.50), and finance (2.38). Overall satisfaction on the project was high (3.0) with 42 per cent saying they were 'very satisfied' and 38 per cent 'satisfied'.

Interestingly, respondents cited SEEDS as the main source of future financing, the private sector as the main source of markets, and government as the main source of technical training only. The two high performers cited the private sector as their only source for future assistance. This could mean that the assistance SEEDS provided was less adequate for the more complex needs of growing businesses.

Sustainability

The project achieved some measure of sustainability in that it linked project participants with the exporters or buyers who provided technology and a regular market. This was apparent in the low cost of the project to REDS, as it played mainly a third-party role, helping to maintain good relationships and providing supplementary training and technical information.

The sustainability of running the project would be ensured if costs could be recovered. Given the relatively low cost of the project and the high benefit to the participants, this objective seems to be feasible. Since REDS extension services helped exporters to deal effectively and efficiently with outgrowers, it could well be paid by these suppliers for its services. As earlier pointed out, one exporter was willing to pay for such intermediation services.

REDS, however, may need to improve its services to both outgrowers and suppliers. It is aware that it needs to scale up its competency now that many of the microenterprises it has helped are growing into larger concerns and are facing more complex issues than REDS can presently handle. REDS will need to increase its competency if it wishes to be effective with both new clients and those expanding their businesses. This realization has been echoed by some of the district extension officers, who cited the need for greater knowledge about practical management and further technology training.[3]

The sustainability of the industry is another matter, however. The government has given minimal support to this industry; research and development have not been given serious attention. There is, for instance, inadequate research in developing new and better genetic pools of ornamental fish. As a result, it is feared that too much inbreeding has been taking place among freshwater fish in Sri Lanka, especially among guppies, which constitute 60 per cent of Sri Lanka's freshwater ornamental fish exports. Still, because the business has been profitable, people have continued with unguided breeding and growing of fish. Fear has also been expressed that water quality is deteriorating in Sri Lanka because of agrochemical pollutants. This may have caused the recent outbreak of guppy disease.

Prospects for the growth of the industry have been further hampered by the lack of information on market preferences abroad. Exporters have usually been caught unaware of the changes in the demand for specific varieties, and were often informed by their buyers only when the demand was already there. Unable to anticipate demand, they are limited by what they have produced and thus have missed business opportunities.

Expansion of the industry has also been hampered by other problems such as the low level of technology in packing, with fewer fish being packed in boxes compared with what is being done in Singapore. Inadequate airfreight facilities also constrain the industry. Direct flights out of Sri Lanka have been less frequent than those from Singapore and other major exporters of ornamental fish. In view of these drawbacks, promoters of the industry cited the need for greater collaboration between the private sector and government as well as stronger government support for the industry.

Because of these inadequacies, REDS was considering playing a stronger role in market research and product development and even in exporting ornamental fish. Whether REDS should carry out these activities themselves or by getting stronger public and private sector support should be discussed. Government agencies such as NARA are already in charge of research and development on the country's aquatic resources. Furthermore, the private sector has been active in the industry and has made its voice heard in policy and programme issues. The presence of both private and public institutions, which already enjoy a good relationship with REDS, may warrant a more facilitative role for REDS rather than a direct role in developing the industry.

Key issues in providing business development services

Market orientation

The importance of access to markets was obvious in this case study, where maximum use was made of training and financial and technical assistance because a market existed for the product – ornamental fish. The project sought to help people become effective suppliers to that market. As part of its market-oriented approach, REDS established market links and secured commitments from buyers before the project was launched. Once the market was assured, the project produced noticeable benefits.

Such market orientation is in contrast to production-oriented approaches in which beneficiaries are given credit and training but are left, with limited information, to look for markets on their own – when in some cases there might have been little potential market to begin with. Any increase in production will reach a bottleneck in the absence of strong buyers and dynamic markets that can absorb the additional production. Such a situation results in minimal improvement in incomes, low-quality produce and squandered resources.

Working within an established network

A factor that contributed to the favourable benefit/cost ratio was the nominal cost of services that the project incurred per beneficiary. Because SEEDS worked within an established network, the Sarvodaya Shramadana Society, it easily reached a large number of people. The presence of Sarvodaya and SEEDS in all districts throughout Sri Lanka allowed them to implement each new project at a nominal cost.

Because of the institutional reputation and networks of LJSSS, the central organization, SEEDS could tap into external expertise to the advantage of its members and at minimal cost to itself. In the case of the ornamental fish project, SEEDS was the catalyst that helped members to enter an industry, and it linked them with existing markets, resources and experts. Because of its minimal intervention, SEEDS could carry out this project at low cost.

Specialization versus diversification

The reasons why SEEDS preferred a diversified approach in this project are several. SEEDS promotes a whole range of products and services to society members, choosing different economic options for different target groups. Furthermore, since alleviating poverty is the priority of its economic empowerment programme, SEEDS attempts to reach large numbers of people through different economic opportunities. Either promoting single industries or graduating growth-oriented businesses would probably result in lower outreach. This diversified approach of SEEDS could also be the result of its own internal capability, insufficient workforce, and a broad socio-economic mandate, which prevents it from aggressively promoting a single industry, given the responsibilities and competencies needed for such an approach.

Increasingly, REDS finds that this general approach is less effective among growing enterprises, which have more complex needs. This is corroborated by the survey results, in which the two outstanding performers cited only the private sector as their future source of business help. It is further supported by extension officers, who felt inadequate in advising entrepreneurs and cited their need for further technical and business training. Thus, REDS hopes to develop its competency further. At this juncture, it can be debated whether more complex and specialized requirements of growing companies would be better addressed by developing the internal capability of a non-governmental organization, such as REDS, or by establishing stronger links with experts and the private sector, which might be in a better position to address the concerns of more mature businesses.

Role of an intermediary

The intermediary role is critical where markets do not work well. This occurred in the ornamental fish project. First, SEEDS was instrumental in linking Sarvodaya members with the ornamental fish business. Given the limited information available to the people the project was designed to help, and their general unwillingness to take economic risks, the role of SEEDS was obvious in identifying this business opportunity. It encouraged and motivated people to invest in the project. It also developed ways of helping that encouraged Sarvodaya members into the new business.

Likewise, SEEDS enlisted support from exporters, NARA, non-governmental organizations and academia, all of which were brought within the reach of project participants. The reverse is also true. The semi-rural communities of Sarvodaya were brought within the purview of exporters and other dealers, who were introduced to these rural households through SEEDS. Previously, they had dealt with, and had preferred to deal with, denser communities where they could operate more efficiently.

As most of the technical assistance was provided by exporters and local dealers, REDS felt it should work outside this framework, especially where needs were not met within these arrangements. For instance, some outgrowers wanted training in areas that exporters considered to be unnecessary, such as breeding varieties not assigned to them but for which local demand was good, such as discus. Given the limited resources and market information of low-income households, REDS constantly helped to find local buyers, which was especially beneficial during lean export seasons.

REDS considered taking a more active role in breeding and in market research and exporting, given the inadequacies in export market research and product development. To the extent that the role of the intermediary produced immediate payoffs in terms of greater efficiency, profitability and viability for its clients (both outgrowers and buyers), the intermediary might provide its services commercially.

Institutional capability building

REDS continuously develops its competence in supporting products and sub-sectors. It develops this competence by linking with existing institutions and by committing its own personnel in identifying and assessing the projects.

For instance, REDS personnel prepared feasibility and market studies themselves rather than hiring external consultants to collect and analyse information. REDS personnel found this beneficial in maintaining a close link between study findings and field realities. Through this process, several staff members within REDS became in-house experts in farming ornamental fish. The experts were the senior enterprise development manager and the district extension officer of Colombo.[4] They maintain links with their technical mentors, whom they regularly consult on ornamental fish farming, and their familiarity with the main institutions and resources within the industry is extensive.

This process, if continued and carried out consistently, can produce experts within the pool of extension officers within REDS. Extension officers would have technical expertise and at the same time would be generalists. REDS and its officers do not aspire to become specialists but prefer to remain generalists, tapping outside resources for technical needs, but at the same time developing relative expertise within the institution with respect to the enterprises being promoted.

Group approach

A group approach is helpful if microentrepreneurs hope to get into mainstream markets such as export markets. The export orientation of the ornamental fish farming project provided a relatively profitable opportunity for Sarvodaya's members. While this project has allowed project participants to earn a sizeable income, its export orientation limited its outreach to fewer people than in other sectors that cater for the domestic market, such as garment and dairy products. This project tended to reach those located near the urban centres, since participants needed to be near exporters.

To tap distant markets, one has to reduce costs. Those who have the motivation and capability to run larger operations can, by themselves, achieve scale economies and thus internalize the costs. The majority, however, who do not have the interest or skill to develop a large operation may form clusters in their neighbourhood. Through clusters they can organize transportation in getting fingerlings and in delivering grown fish. Additionally, they may organize breeding activities in their neighbourhood to cut transportation, and possibly fingerling costs. Such a cluster was organized experimentally by an exporter, Aqua Ceylan, which helped one group of 23 outgrowers, located some 48 km from its premises. The exporter trained three people in the cluster to breed fingerlings so that these three could supply the rest of the outgrowers. The cluster began in July 1998 and has so far worked well. The outgrowers have been able to save on transportation costs for fingerlings, since fingerlings were available from nearby breeders. With the large, combined volume of grown fish, outgrowers could share the cost of transport or pass it on to Aqua Ceylan, which would collect the fish as long as the harvest was large.

Clustering had not been a REDS strategy in promoting the ornamental fish project. But it took place spontaneously in the Kegalle District, where a number of producers operated as a cluster to share transportation costs and to help each other when additional hands were needed during the harvest period. Some REDS officers said they needed to consciously develop clusters of outgrowers among future participants.

Summary and conclusions

The ornamental fish project that REDS implemented was reasonably successful. REDS took a market-oriented approach, linking project participants with markets and helping participants to supply these markets effectively. With their markets assured, growers could make maximum use of the assistance that SEEDS provided. The fish were readily bought, and participants thus earned better incomes.

All this was done at minimal cost. REDS tapped into an institutional network within Sarvodaya, which allowed REDS to reach more people at the same time and thus reduce the cost per beneficiary. Furthermore, in this project, REDS played essentially a linking role in which it introduced project participants to the economic activity and to buyers, who subsequently supplied the market, technology and inputs. The main role REDS played was to act as a conduit of information and technical assistance as well as to mend relationships when problems cropped up. It continued to provide support through diverse business development services, including technical training, financial assistance and further market identification.

REDS played an important role in identifying this particular project, identifying markets and putting the support system in place. Once these systems were set up, REDS receded into a more catalytic and supportive role in helping people get started. Because its involvement was catalytic, it also implemented this project at a relatively low cost, yet reached many people at once. Cost per beneficiary and benefit/cost analyses made in this study showed favourable results.

Nonetheless, it was found that for this particular project the outreach was limited. Because of the export orientation of the project, participants were limited to the urban and semi-urban areas of Sri Lanka. The difficulty of transporting goods to exporters and to mostly urban buyers was a problem for many rural people. Because of this difficulty, REDS officials are now considering promoting the cluster system more strongly.

Because of the links and relationships forged, the sustainability of the project seemed to be quite favourable, as REDS could take a back seat after linking the two parties. However, REDS still played an active role in supplying inputs and in supplying information about additional markets when the information available to farmers was inadequate or was withheld by exporters. The need for greater inputs could be gleaned from the satisfaction of the project participants. While their satisfaction with the ornamental fish project was high overall, they expressed some dissatisfaction about specific inputs.

The financial sustainability of the project may gradually be strengthened by charging client fees for the services provided. Based on cost calculations, these amounts did not seem to be substantial; however, the crux is the degree to which the services were valued by those who can and have been asked to pay – the project participants and the exporters who received a valuable service from REDS through its coordinating role. REDS sought to strengthen its competency in providing such services to project participants, since the assisted enterprises were growing and were meeting more complex issues. This need was corroborated by extension officers, who also articulated their need for greater technical and management skills.

If REDS contributed to the profitability and viability of the exporters and dealers, then REDS could ask to be paid for its services. Exporters had mixed reactions to this.

The sustainability of the industry appears less positive as a number of problems confront the ornamental fish industry in Sri Lanka. Lack of a strong research and development programme on fish varieties, deteriorating water quality, lack of information on overseas demand, and inadequate transport and packaging facilities all hamper the growth of a promising industry and have caused opportunities to be lost. These losses have prompted REDS to consider a stronger role for itself in research and product development as well as in exporting direct. However, this role may be superfluous given the presence of public agencies and active private businesses that could be assisted instead to link up with small outgrowers and breeders.

A number of useful insights may be derived from this case study. First, since a market already existed for ornamental fish, REDS focused on linking clients with strong buyers at the outset of the project.

Second, SEEDS provided a whole range of support to project participants at a relatively minimal cost by tapping into the established network of Sarvodaya and using existing administrative structures. It assumed the role of a catalyst, then it took a back seat once it had helped participants enter the industry and linked them with existing markets, resources and experts.

Third, REDS saw itself as a generalist rather than a specialist, and this enabled REDS to respond to the needs of a wide range of clientele. REDS promoted many subsectors as well as providing a broad mix of inputs in helping its clients to operate effectively. While its diversified approach allowed REDS to reach more people, it was unable to serve the more specific and complex needs of a few growing businesses. Whether it should develop its competency in more specialized areas or simply link growing businesses with the private sector and other institutions is a matter for consideration.

Fourth, the role of an intermediary is crucial where markets are not currently working well. In this case, REDS, as an intermediary, introduced opportunities to poor rural households who had little access to market information. It also provided assistance, including credit and training, where these were unavailable to its clients, even within outgrowing arrangements. It would be useful to determine the extent to which REDS could charge fees to its clients, both project participants and exporters, if its services contributed to the profitability and viability of the businesses. It would be appropriate for REDS to take an active role in the absence of other such providers. However, it is debatable whether REDS should actively undertake market research and product development where others in the market are already doing this but only need greater support.

Finally, a group approach was appropriate for small producers who wished to tap mainstream and distant markets. In this case, those who were able to supply export markets efficiently were those whose operations had grown enough to cover such costs as transport and delivery expenses. Those who are content to remain micro in scale but nevertheless wish to tap distant markets or meet volume requirements need to combine their individual enterprises.

Notes

1 LKR – Sri Lanka rupee; conversion rate per US dollar: 83.50 (Jan 2001), 77.01 (2000), 70.64 (1999), 64.45 (1998), 58.99 (1997), 55.27 (1996), 20.0 (1981).
2 Computed by using the following assumptions:
   ○ average length of participation in project (among survey respondents) – 2.42 years
   ○ inflation rate for 1997, 9.6 per cent; 1998, 9.4 per cent; 1999, 9.0 per cent (source: *Asian Development Outlook Update* 2000).
3 Information from Anura Atapattu, deputy director of SEEDS.
4 The experts were V.N. Jayasinghe, senior enterprise development manager, and Vipule Dasanayake, former district extension officer of Colombo, now of Kalutara.

Further reading

[REDS] Sarvodaya Rural Enterprise Development Services (1995) 'Training report about the ornamental fish project', unpublished.
Weerakoon, D.E.M. (1998) 'The ornamental fish industry of Sri Lanka', *Aquaculture Asia* January–March, Bangkok.

7 Light engineering to generate employment in Zimbabwe

JONATHAN DAWSON

The problem

ZIMBABWE FACES A huge and growing unemployment problem. Official estimates, from government budget speeches in 1995 and 1996 and from the 1997 Zimbabwe Reserve Bank Annual Report, of the proportion of the working population without employment rose from 22 per cent in 1992 to 35 per cent in 1996 and to between 50 and 55 per cent in 1997. In addition, 300 000 secondary school leavers enter the job market every year in pursuit of the 10 000 to 16 000 formal sector jobs available. While these figures almost certainly do not fully reflect the absorption of 'unemployed' workers into the informal sector, they do give some indication of the growing unemployment problem facing the country.

An important source of new employment should undoubtedly be in small business. Indeed, diversification and growth in the informal sector are already evident throughout the country. However, a shortage of equipment that small enterprises require hampers their employment-generating capacity. Making more and better-quality equipment available to small entrepreneurs has been the aim of this project.

The project seeks to promote small-scale light engineering. It is a sector that can manufacture production equipment for small enterprises in Zimbabwe to use. It can help to generate employment; strengthen indigenous small manufacturers; decentralize manufacturing, maintenance and repair capabilities; and slow the rural-to-urban drift so evident in the country. The manufacturers are small-scale engineering businesses or capital goods producers. The equipment is used in small enterprises.

Throughout this case study, a distinction is made between *manufacturers* of production equipment and *users* of that equipment. The manufacturers are referred to as small-scale engineering enterprises or capital goods producers; the users are called end-users or simply small-scale enterprises.

The small-scale light-engineering sector has grown strongly in recent years. Contraction in formal manufacturing has led to an in-flow of skilled labour. However, several important constraints have inhibited this sector from playing a role in the national economy that is significant. Prominent among these has been poor access to modern machine tools. Sharp devaluations of the Zimbabwe dollar in recent years have pushed the price of imported equipment well beyond the means of all but a few small entrepreneurs. Commercial machine shops do take on jobs for businesses without machine tools. However, such shops are mainly geared towards large clients and they cannot offer affordable service suited to the flexible and smaller workloads of small clients. Where the small firms are able to use commercial machine shops, they usually find themselves at the end of the queue and consequently they suffer delays in delivery.

Additionally, large retail outlets dominate in distributing production equipment for small-scale enterprises. Consequently, small engineering firms seeking to manufacture production equipment have to use underdeveloped and less formal channels. The large retail outlets are poorly equipped to deal with much of the technology that the small entrepreneurs need. Previous attempts by ITDG-Zimbabwe projects to use large retail outlets to distribute light machinery have yielded little fruit. Turnover and margins are generally too low to encourage large retailers to undertake the necessary promotional work, compared with most of the equipment that these outlets stock.

There is, moreover, widespread suspicion in the country concerning the quality and reliability of goods produced by the small engineering enterprises. Investment in improving product design, quality control and promotion is required to address this problem. Finally, as a result of the relative dominance of the formal manufacturing and retail sector, there is little awareness among potential clients of what machinery small-scale engineering enterprises could produce.

Intermediate Technology Development Group (ITDG)

Founded in 1966, ITDG is an international NGO that works with people in poverty to promote the policies and practices that ensure the appropriate development and use of technology in developing countries to reduce poverty while safeguarding the environment. ITDG concentrates its efforts on technical change and small-scale production because it recognizes the importance of technology to poverty reduction and sustainable development. ITDG's head office is in the United Kingdom, and it has regional and country offices in Bangladesh, Kenya, Nepal, Peru, Sri Lanka, Sudan and Zimbabwe. It also has two business subsidiaries: IT Consultants spreads the group's influence and mission by selling expertise to other development organizations, and ITDG Publishing is the world's largest publisher and supplier of books and journals about appropriate technology.

ITDG promotes appropriate technology in the following sectors:

- manufacturing
- food production
- agro-processing
- energy

- building materials and shelter
- disaster prevention and mitigation
- transport
- mining.

ITDG-Southern Africa has all these programmes, except transport and disaster prevention and mitigation. The light-engineering project fell under the manufacturing programme.

Project business development services

The light-engineering project delivers services to both small engineering enterprises and the customers of the capital goods they produce to address the various constraints. These are summarized in Table 7.1.

Table 7.1 Business development services provided by the project

Business development services	Activities
Tool and equipment hire	• fixed equipment for hire-service centres • portable equipment rented out
Product development	• new or adapted technology
Training	• informal training provided to the producers of capital goods • business management training (initial phase only)
Hiring out workshop space	• workshop space at commercial rates to Harare service centre clients
Marketing: initial stage	• promotions to raise the project profile and link client engineers and larger businesses
Marketing: second stage	• business shops as retail outlets for production equipment
Information	• information on other service providers

The Department for International Development (DFID) and Comic Relief, both of the United Kingdom (UK), funded the project.

Methodology

The case study was prepared from project records and interviews with ITDG staff in the UK and in Zimbabwe by e-mail and telephone. The project manager was consulted during a visit he made to the UK.

Exchange rates

Precipitous devaluation of the Zimbabwe dollar in recent years (losing 80 per cent of its value between 1997 and 2000) and consequent high price inflation

(40 to 50 per cent per annum) make comparisons over time using this currency difficult and misleading. Consequently, financial and economic data are provided in US dollars. Project funding that was provided in pounds sterling has also been converted to US dollars at the prevailing rates.

The light-engineering project

Project strategy

The project emerged out of activities that ITDG-Southern Africa had already undertaken over several years with blacksmiths and carpenters. It became clear that availability of high-quality hand tools was a problem for these artisans and that local small-scale manufacturers had the potential to increase their production of tools for them and many other small entrepreneurs.

The light-engineering project's first year (1995/6) comprised field research into how the project could build on previous experience to develop a support programme for small manufacturers. This included working with artisans in their workshops, linking up with small producer associations and providing business training. In addition, Dr John Powell, the head of the Technology Consultancy Centre (TCC) in Kumasi, Ghana, was hired to carry out a study about support for small light-engineering enterprises in Zimbabwe. TCC developed the model of the intermediate technology transfer unit, a machine shop located at the heart of informal industrial areas, and undertook technology research, development and transfer activities with its small engineering clients.

Out of these steps emerged the concept of tool hire. Both the nature of the services to be provided and the scale of operation were significantly more modest than those in the Ghanaian model. It was believed that this modest approach was more appropriate to Zimbabwe and would help small engineering enterprises to expand, break into new markets and generate additional employment.

Two service centres providing a tool hire service were opened in Harare and Gweru in 1996. From this point, project staff devoted much energy to creating awareness among potential clients of the facilities available at the service centres and promoting subcontracting between client small-scale engineers and larger enterprises.

It soon became clear that the project's initial focus on relatively unsophisticated, small enterprises was not working. These workshops did not have the basic skills and training required to make the best use of the hire equipment at the service centres. Consequently, the project rapidly turned its attention to more highly skilled entrepreneurs, many of whom had been trained and employed in formal sector enterprises. This shift in focus was justified because relatively sophisticated engineering enterprises were better able to manufacture small-scale production equipment.

It also became clear that attempts to broker subcontracting were bearing little fruit. A number of the more highly trained entrepreneurs had already succeeded in winning subcontracts without any assistance from the project. With such links developing without project assistance, and having failed to define for itself an effective role, the project team devoted progressively fewer resources to this activity.

By the end of 1998, the service centres were both operating at a profit. However, project impact was disappointingly low. Few jobs had been created among those enterprises using the service centres. Moreover, while there were encouraging indications of enhanced productive capacity and links within the small-scale engineering sector and between small and large enterprises, developing and disseminating production equipment for other small enterprises had not been as successful as had been hoped.

Two insights gained during the initial years of the project provoked a radical shift in strategy. First, the benefits of the project would be felt not primarily among the manufacturers of production equipment (where project efforts had been concentrated) but rather among the users of that equipment. That is, while only a relatively small number of entrepreneurs could make use of the machines at the service centres, the potential for increasing income and generating employment was among those purchasing new and improved capital goods for small-scale economic activities.

Second, selling production equipment to small-scale enterprises was more difficult than had been foreseen. This was for three reasons: the domination by large retail outlets in distributing production equipment; widespread suspicion about the quality and reliability of the products made by the small-scale sector; and lack of exposure among potential customers to the capital goods that small manufacturers could produce.

A project review at the end of 1998 resulted in focusing project activities away from the manufacturers towards the users of production equipment. A new logframe was designed for the project's second phase (June 1999 to June 2004) with the revised purpose: 'to create sustainable mechanisms for the delivery of an improved quality and quantity of capital goods to end-users and to promote the model internationally'.

This new strategy involved important innovations. To address the marketing constraint, four 'business shops' were to be opened in various parts of the country to show and sell small-scale production equipment. Since the emphasis of the project was now shifted to providing production equipment to end-users, the business shops could purchase machinery from sources other than client small-scale engineering enterprises using the service centres. To increase the coverage and impact of the project, two service centres were to be opened in Mutare and Bulawayo. The service centres would increase the variety of production equipment for hire, reducing the risks for those seeking to test the profitability of new economic activities. And efforts to introduce new technologies for small enterprises that had begun towards the end of the initial phase would be continued and expanded.

Tool and equipment hire

Tools and equipment were available for hire at the service centres, which opened in Gweru and Harare in 1996. A third service centre opened in Mutare in August 1999, and there were plans for a fourth in Bulawayo. Two categories of equipment were available for hire: fixed machine tools used by small engineering enterprises in manufacturing and maintenance, and portable equipment used in small enterprises.

All the equipment was made in Zimbabwe, although the Harare service centre manager was investigating buying industrial sewing machines from South Africa. Around 60 per cent of the equipment was second-hand and, with the phasing out of donor funding for the Harare and Gweru service centres, this percentage was growing. Table 7.2 provides details of the fixed machine tools at the Harare and Gweru service centres.

Table 7.2   Fixed equipment for hire at Harare, Gweru and Mutare service centres

Harare	Gweru	Mutare
2.0 kW lathe	1.5 kW lathe	Planers – 2
1.5 kW lathe	1.2 kW lathe	Circular saws – 2
1.2 kW lathe	Compressor	Band saw
1.1 kW lathe	Welding machines – 3	Spindle moulder
1.0 kW lathe	Battery charger	Sander
Power saw	Drill	Radial arm saw
Milling machine	Grinder	Lathes – 3
Surface grinder		Compressors – 3
Bench grinder		Welding machines – 3
Mill drill		

Capacity use for the fixed equipment at the Harare service centre is given in Table 7.3. One hundred per cent use was based on continual use from 9 in the morning to 5 in the afternoon, Monday to Friday, plus five hours on Saturday morning. Some items were used more than this, accounting for some figures in excess of 100 per cent. Other fixed equipment at the service centre not listed in this table was charged per job performed. No data on capacity use were recorded.

All the machine tools, especially the lathes, were in high demand. The principal reason for lower use rates on some machinery was stoppages for maintenance and repair work. Several pieces, including the 1.5 kW lathe and the surface grinder, suffered significant problems with reliability and breakdowns. Where equipment was not in regular use, it was sold off. About 100 small engineering enterprises regularly used the fixed equipment at the two service centres. Of these, 42 (36 in Harare and six in Gweru) were 'core clients', using the service centre at least once a week.

150

Table 7.3   Capacity use of equipment at the Harare service centre (percentages)

Harare	Nov 1998– Jan 1999	Feb 1999– Apr 1999	May 1999– July 1999	Aug 1999– Oct 1999
2.0 kW lathe	88	120	84	68
1.5 kW lathe	32	62	49	35
1.2 kW lathe	64	104	122	109
1.1 kW lathe	NA	NA	NA	76
1.0 kW lathe	NA	NA	72	52
Surface grinder	16	10	22	under repair

Capacity use is figured on 45 hours per week – an amount exceeded at times, hence figures over 100 per cent.
NA – not applicable, as the equipment was not yet purchased.

Following is the list of portable equipment provided for hire at the Harare service centre. This service was discontinued in Gweru because of lack of demand. It was not clear whether sufficient demand existed in Mutare to justify the service. Brick moulders were in high demand, but many small businesses did not have the money to purchase the cement and pay the labour to operate them. The project is working on a new, smaller model that would be introduced over the next 12 months. It is expected to prove very popular. The freezit is an 'ice-pop', flavoured iced water in a sealed plastic tube.

Industrial sewing machines – 18
Brick moulders – 5
Welding machines – 3
Overlockers – 2
Freezit machines – 2
Peanut butter machines – 2
Compressors – 2
Maize mill – 1
Mill drill – 1
Pipe bender – 1
Flypress – 1
Angle grinder – 1
Hand drill – 1

Decisions on purchasing portable equipment for hire were made from feedback received from service centre clients. The rate of use had been high for portable equipment, with industrial sewing machines, in particular, in almost continual use. Use of portable equipment was carefully monitored and where it remained low over a long time equipment was sold off. Equipment sold by the Harare service centre, for example, included woodworking tools, for which there was limited demand, and hand grinders and drills, as a result of breakdowns and theft.

151

In an important sense, the tool hire business was independent of the business shops. That is, equipment was hired out to anyone prepared to pay for the service and not just to those supplying goods to the business shops. This permitted relatively high use of most equipment and allowed the service centre to keep hire prices relatively low. The hiring out of portable equipment at reasonable prices was a particularly important service in that it permitted those wishing to explore the profitability of a new small business to minimize both cost and risk. Core service centre staff included a manager, a maintenance technician and an office supervisor. Auxiliary staff were a driver, a cleaner and a watchman.

Product development

To date, nine products have been introduced by the project:

- electric peanut butter maker
- manual freezit machine
- brick moulder
- electric maize mill
- diesel maize mill
- oil expeller
- T-shirt printer
- concrete tile-making machine
- welding machine.

In some cases, these represented machinery entirely new to small enterprises in Zimbabwe. In others, design modifications rendered existing technology more appropriate to small enterprises and the needs and purses of their clients. In some cases – the brick and tile machines and the oil expelling and peanut butter making machines, for example – the designs arose out of work undertaken by other programmes within ITDG-Southern Africa. These programmes had struggled to find private sector partners in technology development and dissemination. Large companies had generally not been attracted by the prospect of manufacturing small-scale technologies, while smaller enterprises tended to experience problems with quality control. As a result of the light-engineering project, small engineering enterprises increased their capacity to achieve the quality required for commercial production.

In other cases, ideas for the technologies developed by the project arose out of collaboration and feedback between project staff and client engineering enterprises. Work at each stage in developing new technologies involved significant collaboration between project staff and client workshops. For example, clients, including women, often developed and tested prototypes. Only women were involved in the development of the peanut butter

152

machines, for instance. Women provided much feedback on modifications for machines they had purchased.

Since the business shop opened in Harare, users and potential users of production equipment were given a voice in influencing the technology development work undertaken by the project. The business shop provided them with a channel through which they could contribute ideas for new (or adaptations of existing) technology. Customers provided feedback on the performance of equipment already purchased. These proved to be important feedback loops.

As a general rule, formal market analysis and feasibility studies were not undertaken before work was begun on developing a new technology. Rather, requests from prospective clients through the business shops and the willingness of client engineering companies to devote their resources to developing prototypes were taken as sound indicators of a new product's likely viability. Among the products in development as a result of suggestions coming through the service centres and business shops were a bottle sealer, a candle mould and a small-capacity brick mould.

Training

Most of the training took place informally through the close working relationship between client engineering workshops and project staff. While unsustainably expensive in the long run, informal training involving small groups and one-on-one sessions was essential in developing trust and establishing a successful working relationship between the project team and its clients. Project staff also provided training for personnel at two national training institutes – the Institute of Agricultural Engineering (IAE) and Silveira House – to manufacture the welding machine introduced by the project. Both of these agencies added the technology for this machine to their training curricula for artisans. In its first training course in welding machine manufacture, IAE trained 39 artisans, 34 from Harare and five from Gweru. All made their own welding machine during the training course. Since the course, Silveira House has manufactured over 50 welding machines and sold them through hardware outlets in Harare.

Initially, the project aimed to provide general technical and business management training. Several courses were designed and delivered, but demand and willingness to pay for them proved low and they were quickly dropped.

Marketing

During the project's first phase, marketing efforts were dominated by promotions to increase the profile of the service centres and the products and services provided by client workshops. These included the following:

- eight short broadcasts on ZBC Radio 2
- regular advertisements in the classified section of the national *Herald* newspaper
- posters
- personal visits by service centre staff to potential clients, including large enterprises where there was believed to be potential for subcontracting links.

Despite these efforts, project impact continued to be somewhat limited. Consequently, following the review in late 1998, it was decided to devote considerably more resources to the marketing constraints facing client engineering workshops. Central to the new marketing strategy was the decision, following market surveys by independent consultants, to open four business shops to promote and disseminate small production equipment. The first of these opened in Harare in June 1999.

The business shop made production equipment available to the public through business kits that had several components:

- production equipment
- an instruction manual
- an ITDG-Southern Africa seal of approval
- a guarantee.

For an increased fee, business kits also included the following:

- spare parts as required
- consumables as required (for example, plastic tubing for the freezit machine)
- training in the use of the equipment.

The business shop also held spare parts and consumables in stock. Business kits for sale at the Harare business shop included the following:

- maize mills
- electric and manual peanut butter machines
- electric and manual freezit machines
- oil presses
- de-hullers
- beehives
- screen printers
- brick and block presses
- tile makers
- welding machines
- diesel engines.

Which business kits were stocked at the business shop was determined primarily by requests and feedback from prospective clients. Both to promote the profitability of the business shop and to stimulate growth as widely as possible throughout the small enterprise sector, the project team decided not to hold a tight sectoral focus but to disseminate many different business kits.

The seal of approval and guarantee were considered important innovations in overcoming the suspicion of clients of small enterprise products. Even though the guarantees were in the name of the business shop, effectively the manufacturers – who would have a vested interest in continuing to be commissioned by the business shops – were responsible for any repair work required (although they were likely on occasion to require assistance from project staff in correcting problems). Agreements to this effect were made between the project and manufacturers before the latter were commissioned. So far, two types of machines sold in the business shops – maize mills and brick presses – have been returned as defective under guarantee. Problems on both items are being resolved and project staff are confident that they will soon be back in production.

Eighty per cent of business shop stock was expected to be made by client small manufacturers during the project's second phase. While the project emphasized strengthening the local small engineering sector, its core goal was to generate employment by manufacturing and selling production equipment. To this end, it was expected that the business shops would also purchase equipment from sources other than its own client engineering enterprises, where appropriate. To date, such purchases have included manual peanut butter mills supplied by the Zimbabwe oil press project as well as Chinese-made oil mills and diesel engines. Business shops have also explored stocking solar panels.

It was hoped that the business shops would develop a reputation among entrepreneurs and agencies promoting small businesses as prominent suppliers of small-scale production technology in and outside Zimbabwe. In a number of neighbouring countries, particularly Mozambique, production equipment was in short supply. As the profile of the business shops grew, an increasing number of clients – individuals and development agencies – might place orders for business kits. The expected importance of Mozambique as a market was one reason for opening a business shop and a service centre in Mutare.

Hiring out workshop space

Of the 120 regular users of the service centres by late 1998, 17 (11 in Harare and six in Gweru) did not have separate premises but used the service centres as their base. This served a very useful function in that customers coming to the service centre for machining work had a ready supply of qualified labour to hire. Nonetheless, client enterprises in the Harare service centre (where congestion was a much greater problem than in Gweru) were served notice in 1998 that by the beginning of 1999 they would have to open independent workshops. It was expected that this would make them less dependent on the project and encourage them both to expand and to move from repair and maintenance into manufacturing. For these reasons, the project rented workshop space close to the service centre. The space was divided into seven workshops, which were rented out to client enterprises at commercial rates.

This served several purposes. First, space in the service centre was freed up to house more items of hire equipment and serve as 'office space' for client enterprises when they rented desks by the hour for discussions with customers. Second, it maintained the benefits of 'clustering' evident during the first phase of the project – mutual learning and specialization among client engineering enterprises. Third, it made skilled labour available for hire near the equipment in the service centre. And finally, clients occupying the workshop space served as a window for the new technologies and techniques that the project introduced. Had its client enterprises been able to hire workshop space near the Harare service centre, the project would not have taken this step. But suspicion on the part of proprietors towards small enterprises and their preference to rent space to one large client rather than many small ones made it necessary. The project sought to demonstrate that small engineering enterprises were viable and trustworthy, which would make it easier for them to find appropriate workshop space without outside assistance.

Providing information on other service providers

The project set out with the aim of being an information resource to its clients on the full range of services available in Zimbabwe for small-scale enterprises. Towards this aim, it developed a directory of small enterprise support agencies with the services they offered. This was used to refer clients to relevant agencies about services the project did not provide. The directory was not published.

Project management

Project employees were a manager, a part-time marketing officer, a technician and a part-time quality control engineer. The finance and communications departments of ITDG-Southern Africa also provided services and ITDG-Southern Africa's manufacturing sector programme manager provided overall management supervision. All staff were Zimbabwean nationals, except the project manager, who was an expatriate. Advice came from the UK-based ITDG senior specialist in manufacturing and enterprise development. All service centre staff were funded direct by income from the service centres.

The concept of the tool hire centre arose out of the field research done by project staff and artisans during 1995 and 1996. The project management team developed the project strategy, although they called on the services of an expatriate consultant to help with the review in late 1998.

The Zimbabwean managers of the service centres had a high degree of autonomy. Only two days per month of the project manager's time were allocated to supporting them. The managers of the business shops will have similar autonomy once these are up and running profitably.

The technology support and development work involved close collaboration. The choice of a new technology (or adapting an existing one) introduced by the project, for example, arose out of the ideas, expertise and experience of client engineering enterprises; the activities of other programmes within ITDG-Southern Africa; information available to the project team on technologies successfully disseminated elsewhere; and increasingly, feedback from clients of the business shops. Client engineers were involved in developing technology from the earliest stages of the process. They played a leading role in introducing new ideas and, with support from the project team, they were generally responsible for developing and testing prototypes.

Project performance

Impact

It should be remembered the project is still at an early stage. Little impact data have been generated. It has been less than a year since the change in strategy shifted the focus of the project towards the machine users. Although methodological challenges remain (see 'Challenges' section), this shift, together with the establishment of the business shops, should provide a simple and cheap method of measuring project impact. Formulae should be developed to track the income and employment generated by each item of equipment the project has promoted. Business shop records should provide information on equipment sold.

Impact assessment should be undertaken annually by a team of external consultants. However, during this first year of the new approach, efforts were concentrated on setting up the new business shop in Harare and establishing a third service centre in Mutare. The first impact study had not yet been commissioned.

During the first three years of the project, when the primary focus was on client manufacturers, few useful data were generated. This was due in part to the methodological difficulties inherent in measuring the impact of what the project was attempting. Four difficulties proved particularly troublesome. First, keeping track of the number of items of each machine introduced by the project and produced by its clients proved difficult. Many client entrepreneurs were initially suspicious of the project, fearing it constituted competition rather than assistance.

Second, among small manufacturers throughout Africa, product innovations spread rapidly through imitation. Manufacturers that had no contact with the project took up production of several of the pieces of equipment that the project introduced. Sales of such equipment were difficult to track, or even to estimate.

Third, a core aim of the project was to increase the productive capacity and technological self-confidence of small manufacturers. An important measure of success in this lay in project clients developing and introducing new machines independent of the project. This, too, was difficult to track.

Finally, the increased capacity among client workshops as a result of the project was manifested not just in discrete finished products, but also in parts and components. Many items of working equipment would not have been made, would not have been repaired, or would have been more expensive to make or repair without the project. Trying to calculate these benefits was a methodological minefield.

Failure of the project team to undertake a baseline survey exacerbated already substantial methodological difficulties in attempting to track project impact. Moreover, with the project's focus during the initial phase on capital goods producers, no data were gathered where, it became progressively clearer, the greatest impact would be felt – on the users of production equipment. As a result of all these factors, the impact of the project on income and employment has not been quantified.

Some data that were generated during the first phase of the project described an increase in productive activity that could be attributed to the project. Engineering enterprises using the service centres provided two types of goods and services:

- subcontracts for medium and large enterprises and state clients
- equipment and components for intermediary manufacturers who made production equipment for small enterprises.

Details of the performance of client engineering enterprises during the first phase are provided in Tables 7.4–7.6. Twenty-two engineering enterprises provided subcontracting services (Table 7.4). Some subcontracts listed did not represent new value-added activities. Several of the engineers using the service centres had used commercial machine shops, and brought their clients and contracts with them. In addition, some contracts were the result of large companies subcontracting to former employees.

Nonetheless, significant new subcontracting work was created. As in many countries, large companies and state bodies in Zimbabwe had narrowed their focus to their core business and were subcontracting ancillary services, such as catering, cleaning and engineering support. This opened up markets for small enterprises. Trained Zimbabwean engineers, with access to modern equipment as a result of the project, benefit from these trends.

Table 7.4   Client engineering enterprise subcontracts

Name of subcontractor	Nature of product or service subcontracted
BP Shell	maintenance and installations
Conte shoes	shoe moulds for soles
Cremos Engineering	equipment maintenance; parts manufacture
Dairy Board	milk homogenizer
Dulux Paints	equipment maintenance; manufacture of machine parts
Fine Foods Ltd	vibrators and conveyors
Furniture makers	springs
Grainthorpe Ltd	injection moulds for plastic goods; manufacture and maintenance of various machine parts
Gweru City Council	wheel studs; couplings and pneumatic fittings; bore-hole pistons and shafts; diesel engine cylinder sleeves
Harare City Council	wheel studs; couplings and pneumatic fittings; bore-hole pistons and shafts; diesel engine cylinder sleeves
Imperial Plastics	moulds for plastic bottles
JATI Millers	equipment maintenance; manufacture of machine parts
Metal Box	injection moulds for plastic goods; manufacture and maintenance of various machine parts
N&B Bakery	repairs to dough mixer
Ocean Breeze	shafts and repairs to meat cutters
Plastic Version Ltd	equipment maintenance; manufacture of machine parts
Private transporters	wheel studs; couplings and pneumatic fittings; various parts
Santana Transformers	punch tools for laminations
Steam and Mechanical Services	press tools and shafts
Uniframe Design	press tools and a wire straightener used for making mattress springs
WRS Ltd	gate rollers
ZIMALLOYS	parts for crushing equipment
Zimbabwe Electricity Supply Authority	components for electricity meters
Various schools	repair and maintenance of boreholes; school furniture; playground equipment

Table 7.5 lists capital goods produced by client engineering enterprises for intermediary capital goods enterprises during the initial phase. Engineering enterprises recently moved into producing new capital goods, including wood-turning lathes, circular saws, metal rollers and metal-spinning moulds. This machinery could have a significant long-term impact on Zimbabwean manufacturing.

In addition to the items listed in Tables 7.4 and 7.5, client engineering enterprises manufactured thousands of smaller items, including nuts and

Table 7.5 Capital goods and components produced by engineering enterprises for intermediary capital goods producing enterprises

Item	Quantity sold
Axles for trailers and carts	2000*
Hammer mill parts	50
Welding machines	38
Parts for food-packing equipment	30
Punching tools	25
Punch tools for window and door components	16
Moulds for plastic buckets and bottles	8
Roller-mill shafts	5
Circular saws	4
Cut-off machines	2
Metal rollers	2
Metal-spinning moulds	2
Punch tools for electric transformers	2
Wood-turning lathes	2

*This is such a widespread activity among client small-scale engineering enterprises that it is very difficult to estimate the total number with any degree of accuracy. This is a conservative estimate.

bolts, window hinges and latches, and all manner of one-off machine parts during the project's first phase. This enabled manufacturers to increase the range and quality of the equipment they provided.

As well as subcontracting and providing engineering services to intermediary manufacturers, many engineering enterprises also manufactured equipment for end-users (Table 7.6). Technologies introduced by the project were prominent, although it may not have adequately monitored its manufacture of production equipment. Client engineering workshops have been able to move into producing new products without direct assistance from the project, except for improved access to equipment. This indicates increased technological capacity and self-confidence. Estimates of the quantities of each item produced by engineering workshops cannot be made:

- mixers for animal feeders and for chemical and paint companies
- replicas of other commercially available oil mills
- metal-benders for scotchcarts and window and door frames
- tobacco rollers
- irrigation pumps
- presses for maintenance work
- dies
- solar dryers
- sliding gates.

While the distinction between client engineering enterprises and intermediary manufacturers is useful for conceptual purposes, in practical terms the line dividing the two is somewhat blurred. Many of the items of equipment produced for end-users were manufactured by both engineering workshops and intermediary manufacturers. Engineering workshops made components, such as axles, shafts and machine parts. They provided some parts to intermediary producers for manufacturing equipment; some they used themselves in their own manufacturing. Where both engineers and intermediary producers made the same types of equipment, they are categorized under which class of entrepreneur produced most of it: intermediaries, Table 7.5; engineers, Table 7.6.

Table 7.6   Production equipment produced by client engineers for end-users during project phase

Item	Quantity sold
Manual freezit machine	254
Electric maize mill	44
Diesel maize mill	32
De-huller	17
Concrete tile machine	8
Brick moulder	5
Peanut butter machine	4
T-shirt printer	2

Another case study project, the Zimbabwe oil press project (see Chapter 8), also promotes the manufacture and dissemination of peanut butter mills.

Business kits sold by the Harare business shop during the second phase are listed in Table 7.7.

Table 7.7   Business kits sold by the project in 1999

Business kit	Quantity sold
Maize mills	64
Brick and block presses	56
Electric peanut butter machines	37
Manual freezit machines	33
Manual peanut butter machines	25
Welding machines	21
Oil presses	18
Beehives	14
Screen printers	6
Tile makers	6
Automatic freezit machines	5
Diesel engines	5
De-hullers	4

Several of these machines were used primarily by women, including peanut butter machines, maize mills, freezit machines and bag sealers. The ability to hire rather than purchase machines outright was important in giving relatively poor entrepreneurs – men and women alike – access to improved technology.

The project sought to benefit the relatively poor by developing manual as well as powered equipment. Manual machines were often cheaper than powered ones, required less capital and were more appropriate for a small enterprise.

Cost effectiveness

It was difficult to make a judgement on the cost effectiveness of the project because of the lack of data and because the project was engaged mostly in field research. Without doubt, the costs of the project to date have far exceeded its benefits. Indeed, it was this realization that led to the change in strategy at the beginning of 1999. No authoritative conclusion can be drawn until the service centre and business shop models have had several more years. Costs incurred by the project to date:

1995/6	US$79 000
1996/7	225 100
1997/8	235 700
1998/9	235 670
Total	775 470

Many of the costs involved represent investment in activities that have yet to bear fruit – the Harare business shop, the Mutare service centre and the groundwork for opening the remaining business shops and service centres. The Gweru tool hire centre was a very small operation. Despite various efforts to stimulate demand for its services, it remained small, with running costs, income and turnover of around 15 per cent of the Harare service centre.

One unit established by the project performed strongly – the Harare service centre. It ran at a profit with minimal help from the project. Figure 7.1 compares the project expenses and income associated with the Harare service centre. Table 7.8 provides gross income, running costs and net income of the centre itself.

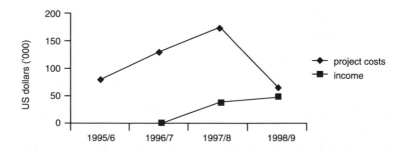

Figure 7.1   *Expenses and income from the Harare service centre*

Table 7.8   Harare service centre gross income, running costs and net income (US$)

	1997/8	1998/9	Total
Service centre income	40 982	49 150	90 132
Service centre running costs	44 982	46 530	91 512
Net service centre income	(4000)	2620	(1380)

No records were kept of service centre running costs in 1996/7. Income during that year was negligible.

Costs at the Harare service centre were modest for the first year of the project, during field research, and then rose sharply in 1996/7 and 1997/8, before falling in 1998/9. In 1999/2000, project expenses for the service centre dropped to almost zero, only two days per month of the project manager's time. The two high-expenditure years resulted from intense contact between project staff and client enterprises. Project staff experimented in providing business training and promoting subcontracting links, which have since been abandoned.

With the opening of new service centres in Mutare and Bulawayo and three new business shops, project costs were expected to rise again, but not as much as in 1997/8. Around 20 per cent of the expenses associated with the Harare service centre were spent on capital assets. Most project spending paid ITDG-Southern Africa staff and overheads (including inputs from UK-based staff) associated with designing and developing the project and experimenting with different approaches. Now that the model has been developed, costs associated with the new service centres and business shops should fall.

Both the Harare and the Gweru service centres have now recorded one year of profit. Income from equipment hire covered all staff, premises rental and equipment replacement costs. However, because of the high currency devaluation rates, project management decided to use the equipment replacement budget (funds raised from service centre business) to purchase new equipment rather than set money aside to replace worn-out machines. This raises the question of how large and expensive machines will be replaced when they come to the end of their natural lives. The project has not had to face this problem. But it does place a significant question mark over the claim of financial self-sustainability for the service centres. The only remaining direct subsidy is two days per month of the project manager's time, which the project pays for. A more definitive judgement on the cost effectiveness of the project should count the hidden subsidy represented by the expertise and expense involved in developing the machinery introduced into the project by ITDG-Southern Africa's building materials and food processing programmes – the brick and tile machines and the oil expelling and peanut butter making machines.

Sustainability

Formidable challenges face the project team as it attempts to prove that the model can be cost effective and sustainable. If they were not profitable, the

163

service centres and business shops would simply cease to exist. Working on the assumption that the service centres and the business shops will be commercially viable, three options present themselves: sell to an entrepreneur, franchise an entrepreneur, or establish a private company with a high level of operational autonomy but ultimately answerable to ITDG-Southern Africa for policy decisions.

The first option has the merit of removing project staff from interfering in the business (good for efficient business) but has no guarantee that the purchaser will continue to provide a developmentally valuable service. Just because tool hire and selling production equipment is viable (albeit following substantial initial investment on the part of the project) does not mean that they would necessarily be profit-maximizing activities for a private entrepreneur. Without some continuing role for ITDG-Southern Africa, there would be nothing to prevent the new owner from cashing in the assets or switching to some more lucrative market niche. Both of the other options present interesting approaches to the dilemma of promoting business efficiency while maintaining a developmental dimension to commercial activities. Both will be explored as the project develops.

Lessons learned

The project is too young to have generated more than provisional lessons or conclusions. It has been mostly experimentation, its strategy representing a radical reorientation. For most of its life, the project has been feeling its way towards an effective approach. This has been justifiable – indeed, it may even be considered to some extent inevitable in an initiative pioneering a new model for supporting small enterprises. However, it is not the stuff that solid, transferable lessons are made of. The model that the project sought to demonstrate has not yet proved itself.

Several lessons can nonetheless be drawn. Tool hire can be a valuable service to small enterprises. Despite the paucity of data generated, there is little doubt that the tool hire service that the project provides has been valuable to its clients. Most of the equipment operated at high capacity, small enterprises developed subcontracting links with larger clients that otherwise would not have been possible, and the quality and range of small-scale production has improved.

Hiring production equipment has allowed would-be entrepreneurs to explore the viability of new business at low cost and low risk. This has been especially valuable in a country like Zimbabwe where the formal sector is strong and small-scale self-employment is a new concept for many.

Project experience has suggested that service centres could be viable businesses within two years of opening, even if the problem of how to replace large and expensive machines when they wear out has not yet been resolved.

However, on their own, without complementary interventions, they cannot be considered to be a cost-effective use of donor funding. Complementary interventions, to a significant degree, should be context-specific. In the case of Zimbabwe, with its history of formal sector dominance in both production and marketing, the project has developed two complementary services that hold promise of high impact and cost effectiveness – introducing new technology, and opening market outlets. In other places, appropriate complementary interventions are likely to differ.

New approaches require substantial field research before being launched. Much of the expenditure incurred in the project's early years represented research and development costs. These included commissioning studies by consultants, experimenting with different approaches and services, and identifying the target group. It is legitimate to question whether such costs should, at least in part, have been financed out of general research and development funds rather than allocated to a project. Certainly, the expenses incurred during the light-engineering project's early years, when it was clearly feeling its way towards an appropriate approach, made achieving a positive benefit/cost ratio over the lifetime of the project all but impossible.

One lesson to emerge from the case study is that if donors wish to see new and innovative approaches to business development, more untied research and development funding will be required. During this preparatory phase, capital investment should be limited. It appears probable that the pressure to demonstrate results and justify project expenses pushed the project team into a premature and over-ambitious capital investment programme. Had this initial period been conceived as preparatory field research, the pressure on the team would have eased and investment would have been more coherent and gradual.

With innovative projects, there is a need for flexibility in developing project strategy. The orientation of the project changed radically over the course of its short life. Beginning as a technology support project targeted towards small engineering enterprises, the core thrust of the project today could more accurately be described as a marketing push aimed at the users of small-scale equipment. Such a radical restatement of project objectives and strategy is a tribute to the flexibility of both the project's management and its donor sponsor.

With innovative approaches, some learning by doing is inevitable. Nor can it be assumed that this learning will be either smooth or rapid. Patience, flexibility and a willingness to question what the project seeks to achieve, and how it does so, are necessary.

Poverty can be addressed through assisting relatively sophisticated modern enterprises. An important change in strategy early in the life of the project shifted the focus from unsophisticated microenterprises to more modern small firms. The microenterprises could not use the equipment provided by the project to manufacture equipment to an acceptable standard. This step in the evolution of project strategy reached completion with the launch of the project's second phase in mid-1999. It shifted the focus from the manufacturers to the users of production machinery. What is clear in retrospect is that the shift to small enterprises permitted the manufacture of a quality and range of production equipment that would otherwise not have been possible. This permitted the project to enjoy significantly greater impact than if it had retained its initial focus. It improved availability of inexpensive, manual production equipment for relatively poor producers.

Product guarantees may be important in overcoming the widespread suspicion about the quality of goods produced by small-scale enterprises. Clients purchasing goods and services from small enterprises generally have little recourse to the law with faulty or substandard service. Indeed, this is one of the attributes of 'informality'. The resulting vulnerability has inhibited the development of stronger links between large and small businesses, perhaps especially so in countries with strong formal sectors. Effective guarantee schemes have proved important elsewhere; they may have the same effect in Zimbabwe. This feature of project design appears crucial to interesting 'institutional' clients – aid agencies, local government, large retailers and so on – in the production equipment sold in the business shops.

Simple, affordable monitoring needs to be built into project design. Impact monitoring is not just to prove to one's donor that value for money is being provided; it is also a key management tool. Project staff, convinced of the legitimacy of the model they are attempting to prove, can be tempted to plough on even though methodological problems with monitoring have not been resolved. This is a mistake to be avoided. Without clear systems feeding information to management on project performance, project staff can become confused and demoralized and projects can lose their way.

Nonetheless, methodological difficulties exist when measuring the effect that interventions have on enhancing the technological capacity of small engineering enterprises. Initiatives that seek to increase the technological self-confidence and capacity of small engineering enterprises present particular difficulties. Benefits accrue not just to direct beneficiaries but also to those supplied with production equipment, those supplied with components and parts, and those imitating the innovations introduced. Even measuring project impact on direct beneficiaries is not simple, since the beneficiaries use their enhanced capacity to introduce new products and techniques independently. Problems of attribution and data collection abound.

In the face of these difficulties, donors may be tempted to abandon funding of 'capacity-building' initiatives in favour of those targeted at helping to introduce specific products, although there would be no possibility of innovation, since the impact is easier to measure. This would be unfortunate, as enhanced capacity within the small engineering sector in developing countries is a prerequisite to sustainable development of indigenous technology. Rather, greater resources should be devoted to developing an affordable impact assessment for such initiatives.

No decision was made about the long-term status of the organizations created by the project. However, the option of simple transfer to a private entrepreneur offers no guarantee that the developmental benefits of the project will be retained. Two options present themselves as interesting approaches to reconciling independent business management while retaining development focus. Franchising or establishing a private company under the aegis of ITDG-Southern Africa are interesting possibilities that should be explored as the project develops.

Challenges

Formidable challenges lie ahead for the project team as it seeks to demonstrate the viability of the service centres and business shops. The project team must develop cost-effective ways to help small engineering enterprises achieve the quality standards that the market requires. This will not be easy. The project has attempted to work with many clients engaged in producing a wide range of equipment. All experience in this area has taught that successfully upgrading small enterprise products to consistent standards is expensive and time consuming. Already, two of the machines introduced by the project have had problems and a number have been returned under guarantee as defective. Such problems appear bound to be repeated as the project promotes new machines entering the market.

To achieve high impact, the project will need to find ways of transferring products and production methods that will not require extensive follow-up on the part of its staff. Only thus will they be able to devote time to developing new production equipment and new client enterprises. The project team postulated that since many of its clients had trained and worked in the formal sector and understood well the need for quality control, this should not be a major problem. Only time will tell whether this optimism has been well placed.

The ability of project client engineering enterprises to compete successfully in manufacturing small-scale production equipment has not been proved. Competition has come from two sources. First, the formal engineering sector produces a range of machines used by small producers, including some agricultural and food processing equipment, block-making machinery, and so on. Second, already a number of donor-funded initiatives in this field have sought to improve the efficiency and increase the market share of their client enterprises. Prominent among these has been the Zimbabwe oil press project (see Chapter 8 in this volume), which is diversifying away from its original focus on the oil press. It helped to establish a private company, RAM

Ltd, which produces small production equipment in bulk for sale in Zimbabwe and for wide export in Africa. RAM Ltd already competes with clients of the light-engineering project. Both produce peanut butter mills that are similar. As RAM Ltd looks around for other products that it can profitably manufacture, competition appears set to grow.

The core issue here is the scale on which the equipment in question can most efficiently and profitably be produced. International experience suggests that small enterprises have advantages over larger ones in markets not suited to production and distribution in bulk, those characterized by relatively low and dispersed demand and high distribution costs. Yet it must be assumed that low demand will often not be true for those businesses the project is interested in. That is, if the business shops are to be profitable, they will need to achieve a relatively high turnover of goods.

It may not be easy for project client engineering enterprises to compete successfully. It is, for example, not difficult to imagine that project clients may open market niches only to have them invaded by larger competitors once their profitability has been demonstrated. Many client engineering companies had already found profitable niches as subcontractors of larger companies. They might abandon subcontracting in favour of manufacturing small production equipment if they could be sure of increasing their profits. Helping to bring this about would be a major challenge for the project.

A third challenge has been to demonstrate that there exists a sufficient unmet demand for small machinery to warrant establishing business shops. A concerted marketing drive, including attending agricultural shows, trade fairs and other fora would be required. This represents yet another potentially significant drain on staff time and project resources.

To date, the project has collected little baseline and impact data. By switching the focus to the technology users, tracing impact should be considerably easier through the simple recording of equipment sales in the business shops. This, however, will not record the full impact of the project. It is probable that client engineering workshops will sell through channels other than the business shops. But it does represent a simple and affordable way to capture the bulk that can be attributed to the project, providing clients do, in fact, supply most of their output to the business shops. While the new monitoring system focuses heavily on recording the business kits supplied to users, some attention will be required to measure the impact of project activities that enhance the technological capacity of client small engineering enterprises.

The challenge lies in the way in which the effectiveness of each of the business kits is calculated. There are two key issues. The first concerns attribution and displacement. It is not sufficient to calculate the financial and employment gains that a technology is capable of generating and equate that with impact. Reasonable assumptions about likely utilization rates must be made. First, account needs to be taken of the value of activities previously undertaken by entrepreneurs and their employees that are displaced by the new activity. Second, the manner in which the calculations are made will have to be adjusted, as employment and income for most technologies are likely to vary according to weather, input supply and other factors.

Should the businesses created by the project prove viable, transferring them to the private sector lies some distance down the road. That transfer will be a further challenge for the project staff, and finding the right balance between business efficiency and continued development will call for sound judgement.

A final challenge over which the project has little control is how to operate in spite of political and economic instability. Devaluation, high inflation and periodic rioting are not conducive to business growth.

8 Building Zimbabwe's edible oil industry

JONATHAN DAWSON

The problem

INSUFFICIENT CONSUMPTION OF dietary fat, an important source of calories, is a common health problem in most developing countries (Hyman 1993). Although the Food and Agriculture Organization of the United Nations (FAO) recommends an annual per capita intake of 9.6 litres of edible oil (an important source of dietary fat), studies have shown consumption to be as low as 5.9 litres per year in Zimbabwe, 2.3 litres in rural Zambia and 1.5 litres in some rural areas of Kenya. In much of the region, young children subsist mainly on maize meal porridge with sugar and milk. Adding edible oil would be nutritionally desirable (Lobulu 1990).

Until the mid-1980s, most edible oil in the region was produced by large-scale private and state-owned processing plants. Their product was often too expensive for the poor. Distribution costs further exacerbated problems of affordability for those in the rural areas, where 70 per cent of the population lives and where poverty is greatest. Moreover, from the early 1980s onwards the quantity supplied was less than the quantity demanded, and oil was simply unavailable in many rural areas.

Yet land suitable for growing oilseeds is relatively plentiful and conditions for processing them at village level by small-scale producers have long been favourable, but appropriate processing technologies were not available in Zimbabwe before this project. With unemployment rising and rural–urban migration a progressively more serious problem, new higher-value agricultural and processing activities are desperately needed.

Two key elements, however, have been missing: a regular supply of high-yielding oilseeds and an affordable technology for small-scale manual oilseed extraction that could be used in villages far from the nearest repair workshop and electricity supply. Small-scale screw presses have been available in the region for some time. However, they are relatively expensive, and to press soft-shelled seeds such as sunflower and sesame, a decorticator is also required, which is a separate piece of equipment. Consequently, the screw press has never been widely used in the rural areas of sub-Saharan Africa.

EnterpriseWorks Worldwide (then known as Appropriate Technology International, or ATI) commenced project activities to address these problems in 1984 when it launched an oilseeds project in Tanzania. In 1989, the Zimbabwe Oil Press Project was launched as a replication and refinement of the Tanzanian project; and subsequently EnterpriseWorks and the other NGOs it assisted also launched oil press projects in the Gambia, Kenya, Mali, Mozambique, Uganda and Zambia.

In the early years, the World University Service of Canada (WUSC) implemented the Zimbabwe project since EnterpriseWorks did not have an office in that country. From the outset, however, EnterpriseWorks had primary responsibility for project strategy, funding and all major management decisions. EnterpriseWorks formally took over the project from WUSC in 1996.

The Zimbabwe Oil Press Project promotes the oil press as a business opportunity with the potential to create widespread benefits in the community, as it

- produces affordable oil
- improves nutritional standards
- by virtue of its low investment cost, creates widely accessible opportunities for processing to add value to agricultural crops, generating additional income and employment in rural areas
- produces seedcake – a nutritious animal feed – as a by-product
- stimulates the production of economically high-value crops like sunflower, groundnut and sesame.

EnterpriseWorks Worldwide

EnterpriseWorks Worldwide is an NGO with a head office in the United States, which designs and implements business development services for small-scale producers in developing countries.[1] In 1999, it had programmes in 11 countries in Africa, five in Asia and five in Latin America. Between 1993 and 1998, EnterpriseWorks assisted over 38 200 enterprises, benefiting nearly 241 000 people and generating monetary benefits of US$48.95 million. About 47 per cent of the producer participants were women (Hyman, pers. comm. 2001).

Business development services provided by the Zimbabwe Oil Press Project

In effect, the Zimbabwe Oil Press Project needed to create a new rural industry. To do so, it needed to take a number of steps in the production and marketing chain, listed in Table 8.1.

When EnterpriseWorks took over the activities of WUSC by implementing the Zimbabwe Oil Press Project through its own new local office, it continued to train press manufacturers, demonstrate and promote the ram press and oil filters, promote expanded cultivation of oilseeds, and market and distribute the press and filters to buyers. It covered some of the costs of the activities through a price margin on the oilseed processing equipment sold, and gradually increased the margins to pave the way for commercialization. In 1998, EnterpriseWorks developed a plan to spin off the

171

Table 8.1 Business development services provided by the Zimbabwe Oil Press Project

Business development service	Specific activities in Zimbabwe
Technology development and adaptation[a]	
Initial stages	• develop four different sizes of ram press for different market niches • train artisans
Later stages	• develop new press (a fifth size) suitable for mass production • identify mass production facility and establish manufacturing company
Technology dissemination	• improve access to processing technologies
Planting seed multiplication and distribution	• identify and multiply improved seed varieties • promote multiplication of planting seed • facilitate market development for planting seeds in rural areas
Pressing seed production and distribution	• improve farmers' access to inputs • promote improved farm management practices • facilitate small farmer access to better markets
Primary product marketing (oil)	• disseminate information on edible oil marketing
Secondary product marketing (seedcake)	• disseminate information to end-users on seedcake utilization • promote market for and provide information on seedcake

Source: Data submitted by EnterpriseWorks-Zimbabwe for EnterpriseWorks WorldWide's annual impact tracking system
[a]Development of the various models of ram press occurred through the Zimbabwe project, its predecessor Tanzania project and EnterpriseWorks' regional programme funding.

commercial press production and marketing activities to two separate private companies, while retaining the not-for-profit development activities.

Today three key organizations are involved in implementing the Zimbabwe Oil Press Project:

Appropriate Technology Zimbabwe (ATZ) is a not-for-profit non-governmental organization, established in 1996. It is registered in Zimbabwe as a trust with its own board but is affiliated with EnterpriseWorks Worldwide. Its function is to undertake research and development activities for which commercialization cannot be achieved. This NGO was created to undertake research and development, pilot and promotional activities. It is an outgrowth of earlier NGO activities of EnterpriseWorks in Zimbabwe.

Rural Associated Manufacturers (RAM) Pvt. Ltd is a for-profit company established in 1997 that manufactures oil presses and associated accessories. It is a joint venture between EnterpriseWorks and a private Zimbabwean entrepreneur.

ZOPP Pvt. Ltd is a for-profit commercial company that started trading in 1997. It distributes and markets ram presses, peanut mills and planting seed. ZOPP, as used here, refers exclusively to the private marketing company; the project is referred to as the Zimbabwe Oil Press Project or simply 'the project'.

Over the lifetime of the project, the following donor agencies have provided funding:

- USAID – Africa Bureau and the Microenterprise Innovation Project (MIP – USAID funded)
- Africa Now (UK)
- Food Industry Campaign against Hunger (USA)
- Canadian International Development Agency
- Kellogg Foundation
- Japanese Embassy to Zimbabwe.

Exchange rates

Sharp devaluation of the Zimbabwe dollar in recent years and associated price inflation make comparisons over time using this currency difficult and misleading. Using the US dollar also distorts the picture, since the low-income sector does not immediately or fully see devalued incomes adjusted by the new rates, but the scale of distortion is not as great.

End-of-year exchange rates for the Zimbabwe dollar against the US dollar were as follows:

1993	US$1 = Z$3.89	1997	US$1 = Z$9.29
1994	US$1 = Z$4.97	1998	US$1 = Z$10.82
1995	US$1 = Z$6.20	1999	US$1 = Z$18.51
1996	US$1 = Z$8.36	2000	US$1 = Z$55.20

Technology development

Commercial production of a small-scale manual ram press began in Tanzania in mid-1986. This was a small, continuous-flow press with automatic loading and unloading. Invented by Carl Bielenberg, it was considerably more versatile than other available presses, having the capacity to process edible oil from sesame, shelled groundnut, canola, mustard seed, niger nut, copra, safflower, cucurbit seeds, de-hulled oil palm kernels, avocados and de-hulled almonds. Importantly, it could process sesame and soft-shelled sunflower seed without decorticating them before pressing. It could also be used to produce castor bean oil for industrial use or jatropha seed oil as a diesel fuel substitute.[2]

The press, however, was large and heavy with a piston diameter of 50 mm. Two women or one man, who attached a large rock to the handle, generally operated it.

After numerous design modifications, the project developed four more ram press sizes, each smaller than the original.[3] The smaller models are less costly, and a woman working alone can easily operate one. The oil extraction rate is similar in all models, and the throughput rates of the smaller models make them much more appropriate for operation by smaller-scale entrepreneurs and farmers.

The Zimbabwe Oil Press Project began in 1989. The initial intention of the project had been to work with one or two large-scale firms to produce the ram presses. However, the large firms contacted were either not interested or quoted very high prices. Consequently, it was decided to work through a number of small-scale producers, and over time the project trained the 11 producers selected. As orders for presses came to the project, these producers were invited to submit their tenders for making them, to encourage them to compete with each other.

However, production at this scale presented a range of problems. Quality control was often poor and the technical performance of the presses suffered. Training, supervision and back-up support that the project provided to numerous, disparate small-scale workshops was expensive and time consuming. Impact and outreach were restricted by the limited production capacity of the small-scale manufacturers. This was a particular concern in view of the growing demand for presses, both in Zimbabwe and from other countries in the region.

EnterpriseWorks concluded that the scale of manufacture had to be stepped up by mass producing the presses in one factory, which would export throughout eastern and southern Africa and beyond. In 1997, the United States Agency for International Development's (USAID) Microenterprise Innovation Project funded the shift to commercialization with a grant of US$595 000.

EnterpriseWorks opted to enter into a joint venture with Shamen Engineering – one of the eight small-scale manufacturers it had trained. Rural Associated Manufacturers (RAM) Ltd was established in April 1997 with 56 per cent shareholding by EnterpriseWorks and 44 per cent by Shamen Engineering. RAM Ltd has a sales agreement with EnterpriseWorks projects in Zimbabwe, Uganda and Tanzania. It also supplies presses to ZOPP Ltd, which distributes them within Zimbabwe and to programmes in several other African countries.

The model developed for mass production was the RAM-32, which was superior to previous models in wear, reliability, appearance and ease of service. Smaller and lighter than previous models, it was also more appropriate for export. The project was able to increase its profit margin on the RAM-32 and still retail it for 10 per cent less than any of the other models available.

It had been expected that when the RAM-32 was introduced, previous models would fall in popularity. However, sales of two of the earlier models, BP-30 and BP-40, have remained high, and two-thirds of the ram presses sold in 1997 were BP-30s.

The BP-30 dominates the market for two reasons: 1) the importance of familiarity in dictating choice – sales of the RAM-32 did not begin until 1997, and 2) the second and third batches of RAM-32s to be distributed in the first year had a technical shortcoming, which adversely affected the model's reputation. This shortcoming stemmed from a design change made to keep the seedcake from clogging up the press so that it had to be removed manually rather than automatically. This design change inadvertently reduced the expected lifetime of the press. Because of the lack of sufficient field testing, the project recalled 350 of the first 843 presses for retrofitting, at no expense to the press owners. The RAM-32 presses produced after that did not have this problem. But it cost the young company three weeks of production time and substantial financial loss.

The project also developed several models of filters for the edible oil as well as other technologies for small-scale farmers and microentrepreneurs. In other countries in the region in which EnterpriseWorks has oil projects, the oil is refined by boiling it with water and skimming off the oil. In Zimbabwe, however, fuelwood is relatively scarce, so clarifying the oil through boiling to remove the suspended small particles of seedcake and other foreign matter presents more of a problem. The method introduced to undertake this process initially consisted of a wooden filter stand with a filter made of brown wrapping paper. Later, a bucket filter was introduced to save labour in filtration and to keep the oil more sanitary. The bucket filters are sold together with the press as an option.

To increase the scope of the project and to promote the commercial viability of RAM Ltd and ZOPP Ltd, EnterpriseWorks and RAM Ltd also developed and introduced a number of other machines that have potential for mass production and marketing, as listed in Box 8.1.

In mid-1999, production of two new technologies – the motorized peanut blender and the peanut roaster – began. The peanut sheller should also soon be in production. Several other technologies will be introduced after RAM Ltd purchases additional equipment. ATZ decided to promote the treadle pump designs that Carl Bielenberg had developed for Senegal and that were being promoted by EnterpriseWorks Worldwide there and in Benin, Burkina Faso, Côte d'Ivoire, Mali and Niger.

Promotion and sales

In the early stages of the project, project staff undertook all promotion and sales activities for the ram presses. The price that press purchasers were charged covered the full costs of manufacturing. However, a wide range of project services in these early years was subsidized. These services took various forms. After producers were trained in press manufacture, supervision visits were required to ensure quality control and to screen out those not able to achieve acceptable quality standards. Meanwhile, the project undertook an active promotional campaign involving field demonstrations, participation at agricultural fairs, newspaper and radio coverage and advertising. Free training was given to press purchasers on maintenance and simple repairs, and ATZ provided more extensive training on repairs to local artisans in the areas where ram press activities were concentrated. The project produced manuals to accompany the presses and provided guarantees against technical failure. It published a newsletter in English and Shona, and it gave a free 5-kg bag of hybrid sunflower seed to each press purchaser.

During the initial years of the project, it also offered credit to purchasers of most presses. This was both because early models were relatively expensive and because the technology was unfamiliar to the potential market. In 1996, however, the project decided that it could now stop providing this service direct, and it referred clients to specialist credit agencies.

The multifaceted nature of the project's activities during this period was of critical importance in inspiring confidence among press manufacturers and prospective purchasers alike. However, with a limited project budget, the sheer burden of work falling on project staff imposed strict limitations on the potential scale of impact. More widespread dissemination of the press was also inhibited by the need for the project to increase the price margin to recoup more of the costs of the services it provided. Consequently, press sales were heavily concentrated in the two eastern provinces – Manicaland and Mashonaland East – where the project had begun, and where it appeared that it would be difficult to achieve wider impact.

This scenario lay at the root of the decision in 1995 to adopt a more commercial approach to press sales. The distribution and marketing company ZOPP Ltd was established and the project decided to try to

- abolish all subsidies
- significantly increase both production and sale of presses and widen their geographical spread
- identify other rural technologies that could be sold, thus increasing the impact of the project and the financial viability of the distribution company, ZOPP Ltd.

From the beginning of 1995, the gross margin was increased to 35 per cent above the ex-factory price. By decreasing the production cost of the press, mass manufacturing, introduced in 1997, permitted a further increase in the margin received by the private companies spun off by the project and freed NGO staff time – previously devoted to quality control and supervision of the trained workshops – to work on other development activities.

In parallel, several innovative market distribution channels were explored. These included advertising on the radio, direct mail promotion, promotion through the medium of theatre and retailing through large-scale farm equipment distributors.

In 1996, the presses were sold through just ten shops; by 1998 they were being retailed by six sales agents and 93 retail stores. In Zimbabwe, and in neighbouring countries, partner NGOs also act as distributors of the presses produced by RAM Ltd through their own project initiatives. These include AFRICARE (in Zambia); and CARE International, Food for the Hungry and World Vision (in Mozambique).

In addition to ram presses, ZOPP Ltd sells a number of other products and accessories from sources other than RAM Ltd, mostly manufactured by other Zimbabwean companies:

- sunflower planting and pressing seed
- manual maize sheller
- electric maize grinder and sheller
- foot-powered treadle pump for small-scale irrigation
- bucket filters and filter stands
- peanut butter mill stands.

Despite the increases in turnover of oil presses and other technologies that have been achieved through this marketing strategy, sales remain below target and a significant portion of the profit margin is taken by the wholesalers and retailers. Consequently, the project has recently launched a new marketing tactic, which focuses on RAM Ltd and ZOPP Ltd selling direct rather than through wholesalers. Several elements are key to the new strategy:

- identifying zones throughout Zimbabwe that have high potential for large sales volumes
- developing a network of retailers and commissioned agents that sell the technologies
- placing all ZOPP Ltd staff on commission, reducing basic salaries by 50 per cent and setting commissions on turnover at such a level that a 10 per cent increase in sales yields salaries at the same level as at present
- establishing permanent urban-based demonstration units
- finding donor funding to develop stronger sales in neighbouring countries.

Identification, multiplication and dissemination of seeds

The oil content of most sunflower varieties conventionally grown in eastern and southern Africa is relatively low because the varieties were originally selected to yield bird seed for export. Consequently, they yield less oil than do hybrid varieties, and so are less profitable. Also, the hard shell of locally grown varieties is abrasive and can reduce the life of the ram press if the seed is not decorticated or heated to soften it before processing. The advantage of hybrids is higher potential yield – not improved oil content or shell softness. However, farmers can plant their own seed from their open-pollinated varieties rather than buy the hybrid seed. In Tanzania, where farmer incomes are lower and the agro-input distribution system is less developed, EnterpriseWorks has promoted an open-pollinated variety of sunflower that has a soft shell and high oil content.

Good hybrid varieties of various crops were already available in Zimbabwe's relatively well-developed system for supplying agricultural inputs, and farmers had higher average incomes than in most neighbouring countries and so were more likely already to be planting hybrid maize. Still, when the Zimbabwe Oil Press Project was launched, it had to buy hybrid sunflower planting seed from private producers and distribute it to most of the areas in which the project was active. However, once the potential market had been demonstrated, a private company (Pannar Ltd) decided to open 60 rural depots. Another major oilseed company, Cargill, then followed suit.

ATZ continued to help ten village stockists of planting seeds to become established in parts of the country where Pannar Ltd did not operate. These fully autonomous private enterprises received training from the project in business management and in helping farmers to address technical aspects of oilseed production. Thus the project was able to limit its sales operation to those few areas where no other source of hybrid seeds was available. Between 1989 and 1996, the project distributed over 60 tonnes of hybrid sunflower seed.

Nonetheless, lack of an adequate supply of high-quality hybrid seed continued to hamper small-scale oil processing in Zimbabwe, particularly during years in which weather conditions were unfavourable. To address this problem, ATZ produced educational material on sunflower to promote the production and saving of seed. Although this material was originally available only in English, it was translated into the Shona language, and similar material on groundnut was prepared.

ATZ worked closely with government extension officers of the Agricultural Technical and Extension Services (AGRITEX) to persuade small-scale farmers to grow hybrid sunflower pressing seed. It commissioned lead farmers to grow pressing seed, which it collected and distributed. It tested different varieties of seeds in collaboration with the Department of Research and Specialist Service's Sunflower Breeding Unit.

ATZ worked with the Development Technology Centre (DTC) of the University of Zimbabwe, which produces hybrid pressing seeds at its experimental farms throughout the country. ATZ provided seed while DTC contributed land, inputs and expertise. ATZ and other NGOs working in the poorer areas of the country purchased and distributed the seed produced on DTC farms.

The project cooperated with other organizations, including AFRICARE and DTC, to persuade the state Agricultural Finance Corporation (AFC) to provide loans for the purchase of pressing seeds. To date, AFC has provided loans totalling US$13 850 to ten entrepreneurs.

These initiatives have borne fruit, and Zimbabwe is producing much more hybrid sunflower seed than before. Smallholders grow around 90 per cent of the seed today. Nonetheless, lack of pressing seed continues to hamper increased oil production, particularly during years of bad weather. With a significant increase in demand for pressing seeds expected, this represents an important ongoing challenge for the project.

Marketing of oil and seedcake

Because of the relative sophistication of the Zimbabwean economy, the project has not needed to devote as much effort to marketing oil and seedcake as in other countries with oil press projects. Nonetheless, product marketing, including costing, record-keeping and labelling, was an important element of the management courses run for oil processing enterprises.

EnterpriseWorks also supported a study of the nutritional value of sunflower seedcake as animal feed in another project (Zimbabwe Livestock

Project). Once the best feed formulae for particular types of animals have been determined, ATZ plans to create links between livestock farmers and oilseed processors and to develop and sell small mixing machines for formulating the feed.

Project management

Responsibility in the project for strategic and management decisions has been diversified and indigenized. EnterpriseWorks undertook initial project design and led the decision to shift to a more commercial approach. Pivotal to this shift was its regional perspective that mass production of technologies for export to the various countries in which it had projects (and beyond) would be more economical and have greater impact than the earlier strategy of production by multiple small-scale producers.

The shift to a more commercial strategy has given RAM Ltd and ZOPP Ltd progressively greater levels of autonomy for day-to-day decision-making. Through mid-2000, responsibility for strategic decisions for all of EnterpriseWorks' projects in eastern and southern Africa remained with the director of EnterpriseWorks' Regional Oilseeds and Staple Foods Programme. However, EnterpriseWorks helps partner organizations to develop their own capability and promotes a team approach.

EnterpriseWorks also continues to play an active role in identifying technologies that can be mass-produced for the eastern and southern Africa region and beyond. Here, the international relationships that EnterpriseWorks has with other technology development agencies in the region is an important source of information and ideas.

Project performance

Impact

The project's impact tracking system measures project performance against various indicators:[4]

- sales of presses and other technologies
- number of producer participants:
  - press owners and their workers
  - press sales outlets
  - repair artisans
  - filter manufacturers
  - peanut butter processors
  - press and seed sales agents
  - farmers growing oilseeds for sale to processors
- number of economic participants:

- ○ all the producer participants listed above
- ○ households saving money on edible oil
- monetary benefits:[5]
  - ○ sales value of oil, peanut butter and seedcake produced
  - ○ consumer savings from lower-priced oil[6].

Sales of presses and other technologies

Data on ram press sales in Zimbabwe are only for presses sold in the project (Figure 8.1); they totalled at least 1932.

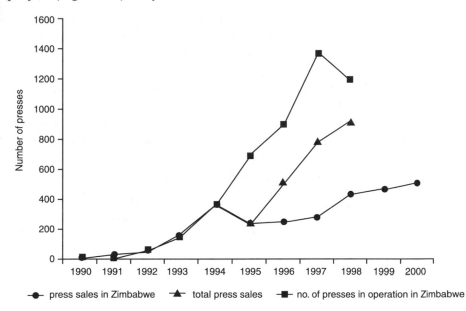

Figure 8.1 *Ram press sales in Zimbabwe, estimated number of ram presses in operation, and total ram press sales, in Zimbabwe and exported, 1989–2000*

Estimates of the number of presses in operation for each year of the project (Figure 8.1) are based on the number of presses sold less the number over five years old, which is conservatively estimated as the active life of a ram press,[7] and those temporarily out of operation – that is, those processing less than 20 litres of oil a year.

Press sales increased steadily for the first five years of the project but then fell back between 1995 and 1997 before recovering in 1998. The number of presses in operation increased in every year of the project before 1998.

A sharp increase in ram press sales might have been expected as a result of the shift to mass production in 1997. However, two key reasons prevented this. First, the most important variable determining the level of press sales is weather conditions; in years of unusual or unsettled weather, the entire agricultural economy suffers. The 1990s saw a number of years of low rainfall in Zimbabwe, with particularly serious droughts in 1992 and 1996, and adverse El Niño weather conditions in 1998. Such conditions limit the farmer's willingness and ability to invest in technology whose profitable operation is dependent on good seed harvests.

Second was the technical problems with some of the RAM-32s produced in the first year, already mentioned, which both eroded confidence in the new model and diverted the energies of RAM Ltd from producing new stock to retrofitting returned pieces.

The number of presses in operation fell in 1998, despite the fact that significantly more were sold in that year (447) than were counted as falling out of operation after their five-year life (the 193 sold in 1993). However, a large number of presses (493) were classified as temporarily out of operation in 1998 because of the unfavourable El Niño-related weather conditions. Press sales in Zimbabwe increased by about 10 per cent in 1999.

RAM Ltd has also produced a significant number of presses for export to other countries in the region (Table 8.2). While these sales have not been included in a benefit/cost analysis of the Zimbabwe project, they are crucial for appraising the strategy of centralized mass production.

Table 8.2   Ram presses exported from Zimbabwe to other countries

	1994	1995	1996	1997	1998	Total
Angola	–	–	2	27	4	33
Lesotho	–	–	50	–	–	50
Malawi	–	–	19	–	–	19
Mozambique	–	9	154	227	232	622
Namibia	–	–	4	–	–	4
South Africa	–	–	12	–	–	12
Swaziland	1	3	–	–	–	4
Sudan	–	–	–	–	1	1
Tanzania	–	–	–	250	–	250
Uganda	–	–	4	–	250	254
Venezuela	–	–	–	1	–	1
Total	1	12	245	505	487	1250

In addition to those exported from Zimbabwe, including 95 in 1999 and 2000, a sizeable number have been manufactured by small enterprises in other African countries under the aegis of EnterpriseWorks' regional oils programme and projects: Benin 2, the Gambia 40, Kenya 802, Mali 172, Mozambique 360, Senegal 44, Tanzania 2848, Uganda 702, Zambia 3052.

Adding together sales of ram presses in Zimbabwe and in other countries, Figure 8.1 shows total project sales of presses manufactured in Zimbabwe (excluding those sold independently of the project after 1994).

If sales to other countries are added in, the rate of sales growth increases sharply. So, while project oil press sales in Zimbabwe were only 23 per cent higher in 1998 than in 1994, total sales of presses manufactured in Zimbabwe during the same period rose by over 250 per cent. Moreover, the period

1995–98 included two years of unfavourable weather conditions throughout the eastern and southern Africa regions, where most exported presses are sold. But sales held up in Zimbabwe and increased sharply elsewhere during this period, suggesting that, given favourable weather conditions, press sales are likely to grow strongly for some time to come.

The Zimbabwe project discovered that a small manual mill designed for grinding paprika and other spices had been imported from the Czech Republic into Zimbabwe as a peanut butter grinder. ZOPP promoted the use of the device and sales increased rapidly, as it proved to be hugely popular for household and microenterprise use. ZOPP Ltd sold 2185 mills in 1997, 1890 in 1998, 442 in 1999, and 1355 in 2000, totalling 5872 peanut butter mills. In addition, 20 motorized peanut mills and 29 peanut shellers were sold in 2000. If the figures for presses and mills are added (482 in 1999 and 519 in 2000) the project sold 8854 equipment items in Zimbabwe – 7905 to processing enterprises. Assuming 1.12 items of equipment per enterprise, the project contributed to establishing 8854 processing enterprises in Zimbabwe.[8, 9]

Producer and economic participants
The number of producer participants and economic participants benefiting from the project is shown in Figure 8.2. Only producers earning at least US$20 per annum because of the project are included.

Although the number of oil presses in operation almost doubled between 1995 and 1997, the number of estimated producer and economic participants per operable press dropped sharply during the same period. Three key reasons for this are 1) the poor weather in 1996 and 1998 caused operating mills to work at low capacity and many people who were previously counted as participants were omitted since they earned less than US$20 per annum through the project; 2) most of the presses now in operation are smaller and process fewer seeds than in the project's early years; and 3) the number of consumer households benefiting also fell when oilseed availability problems

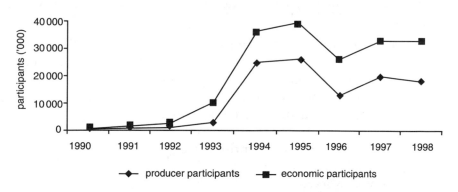

Figure 8.2   *Number of producer and economic participants*

limited oil production. The breakdown of producer participants for 1998 is shown in Figure 8.3. With 1182 presses and 4153 oilseed processors active in 1998, each ram press generated employment for an average of 3.5 people.

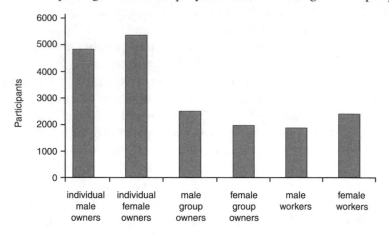

Figure 8.3   *Producer participants by gender and employment category.*

A number of assumptions are used from the impact surveys:

- All of the numbers refer to individual economic actors (manufacturers, processors, retailers and farmers).
- Each branch of a chain store is counted as one enterprise.
- One man and one woman from each household growing sunflower and sesame are cultivating these crops.
- All eight of the independent workshops trained by the project that are still producing ram presses are included as producer participants, even though it has not proved possible to keep track of the number of presses they are producing.
- The categories male and female group owners do not refer to the number of single-gender groups; rather, the number of male and female participants within mixed or single-gender groups is extrapolated from the impact survey data.

More women than men own ram presses and peanut butter mills, and more work in peanut butter-making enterprises. Men constitute a majority of the workers who operate the ram presses, whether they are owned by men or by women. Women usually operate the peanut mill. A few women are employed as workers in press manufacturing firms. Women make up:

- 52 per cent of all individual enterprise owners
- 45 per cent of all group owners
- 56 per cent of all workers
- 51 per cent of all producer participants.

184

Some 14866 households were estimated to have benefited from cheaper oil in Zimbabwe in 1998.[10] Counting one beneficiary per consumer household saving money – the person who provides the primary financial support for the household – and adding this figure to the number of producer participants (owners, workers and raw material suppliers) gives a total of 33287 economic participants for 1998.

Monetary benefits

The economic impact of the project is calculated by adding the increased income deriving from greater production of oil and seedcake with the savings accruing from cheaper oil (see Table 8.3 for impact in 1998).[11] In the same year, the 14 866 consumer households saved US$135 582 through price reductions. Monetary benefits accruing to project participants in Zimbabwe alone totalled US$639 927 in 1998 and US$2 063 813 in 1999.

Figure 8.4 provides year-by-year estimates of the total monetary benefits that the project generated in Zimbabwe; Figure 8.5 describes the cumulative benefits.

Table 8.3   Increases in production, sales and income as a result of the project in 1998

	Unit of measure	Increase in production	Increase in sales	Increase in income (US$)
Oil	litres	423 693	423 693	351 665
Seedcake	tonnes	1441	1296	43 374
Peanut butter	tonnes	1366	1366	109 306
Total				504 345

Prevailing prices in Zimbabwe in 1998 are used as the basis for the estimates. The estimated increase in income from seedcake includes a valuation of that retained by households for their own livestock.

Year-on-year benefits have increased only slightly since 1995, despite the greater number of presses in operation. In addition to the two causative factors already discussed – poor weather and the smaller size of the presses now in operation – this can be explained by the fact that monetary benefits are converted into US dollars and the Zimbabwe dollar was greatly devalued during this period.

Cost effectiveness

Three measures are used to consider the cost effectiveness of the project:

- its benefit/cost ratio
- whether the strategy chosen represented the least expensive way in which the project's objectives could have been achieved
- the profitability of oil-pressing enterprises using the technologies sold by the project.

185

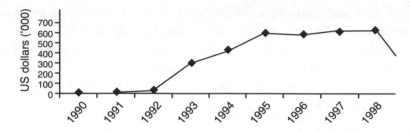

Figure 8.4 *Annual monetary benefits generated by the project*

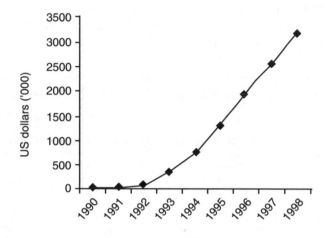

Figure 8.5 *Cumulative monetary benefits generated by the project*

Benefit/cost ratio of the project

By the end of 1998, cumulative project expenditures stood at US$1 573 145. Total monetary benefits in Zimbabwe as a result of the project by the end of 1998 totalled US$3 227 149. This represents a benefit/cost ratio of 2.05:1. Even if no further sales were to take place, benefits would continue to flow for the operating life of ram presses in the field.

Capacity now exists for considerably greater project impact than has been experienced to date in Zimbabwe. The current output capacity of RAM Ltd is around 2000 presses per year – over double the highest amount of annual sales recorded to date: 934 in 1998 – and the new equipment that it is scheduled to add will expand its capacity further. Given favourable weather conditions, strong growth in ram press sales can be expected.[12]

Analysis of the project strategy

Project strategy evolved in two distinct but overlapping phases. The first, until around 1997, was the foundation-building phase. Establishing this new rural industry involved heavy project investment in building capacity and establishing operating structures and mechanisms. Interventions were made on many fronts, incurring heavy expenditures in the early years of the project. To ensure that quality standards were maintained, project efforts were focused on a relatively small part of the country. Consequently, impact in both number of presses in operation and total monetary benefits were somewhat restricted.

The decision in 1995 to adopt a more commercial strategy, thus opening the way for significantly increased project impact, could not have been taken without the earlier capacity-building efforts. By 1995, the project had demonstrated a technology that had proved both popular and dependable, an effective training package for press operators, a network for the distribution of high-yielding seeds, and distribution channels for oil and seedcake. Only on the basis of these achievements was the move to more widespread sales possible.

Further capacity-building investments were necessary to move towards commercialization:

- development of a new press model suitable for mass production
- investment in equipment and establishment of a mass production plant
- development of a nationwide network of retail outlets for the sale of ram presses and other technologies
- implementation of strategies to improve the supply of oilseeds to processors.

The trends in year-on-year project expenditures and monetary benefits (Figure 8.6) vindicate the strategy adopted and demonstrate the importance of both the early foundation-building activities of the project and the later capacity building undertaken in preparation for the shift to commercialization.

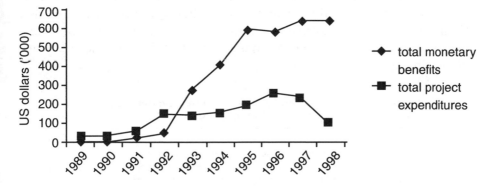

Figure 8.6   *Total project expenditures and monetary benefits. Expenditure data include all costs incurred in Zimbabwe and the costs of Washington-based staff. For the years 1996–98, timesheets of Washington staff were coded by project and this figure is accurate. Calculations for the years before 1996 are made on the basis of an indirect cost rate of 23.5 per cent for Washington staff*

187

The manufacturing and marketing channels that the project has established appear to be able to support production and sales of other machines. The commercialization strategy now being followed means that project-related expenditure will continue to fall over the next few years. RAM Ltd and ZOPP Ltd are already financially viable companies. ATZ will continue to develop technologies and promote the supply of oilseeds through mid-2001.

Weather and the political climate permitting, project impact in Zimbabwe and beyond looks set to grow, and costs should fall to relatively low levels.

Analysis of the profitability of oil processing enterprises

A 1997 study on performance and profitability of the ram presses indicated that the two key variables in determining press profitability were throughput rate and extent of service pressing. The study concluded, unsurprisingly, that the greater the throughput, the greater the profitability.

Service pressing is the system in which farmers pay the press owner to have their seeds processed, either for cash or for a share of the oil and seedcake produced, and the farmers retain the products. It was found both to increase throughput, since generally processing entrepreneurs were themselves unable to purchase enough seeds to keep the press at full capacity, and to broaden the benefits, since farmers who do not own a press can make substantially more money this way than by selling unprocessed seed. A 1994 EnterpriseWorks survey found that only around 30 per cent of press owners offered service pressing, the lowest in any of the countries in Africa where EnterpriseWorks has projects. Reasons for the lower rate of service pressing in Zimbabwe were that 1) entrepreneurs knew they could earn more if they purchased the seed outright instead of service pressing it, and 2) they did not want to risk the increased wear on the press that would result if customers brought in abrasive, hard-shelled sunflower seed. The benefits to owners, workers, service pressers and customers as identified by the study are included in Table 8.4.

Table 8.4   Present value of net benefits of oilseed pressing per press (in 1996 US dollars at a 15 per cent real discount rate)

Scenario	Net present value for press owners and workers	Net present value for service pressers and customers	Total present value of benefits per press
Low throughput	92	363	455
Medium throughput	286	534	820
Medium high throughput	479	696	1175
High throughput	559	643	1202
Very high throughput	757	783	1540

This analysis preceded the large drop in the value of the Zimbabwe dollar in 1997 and 1998.

188

Project institutions

Three entities evolved out of the Zimbabwe Oil Press Project of EnterpriseWorks Worldwide: the NGO ATZ, the manufacturing company RAM Ltd, and the distribution company ZOPP Ltd.

The long-term sustainability of ATZ is dependent on its ability to attract continued donor funding. It is currently seeking additional funding from a variety of US, European and multinational donors; its resources at the end of 1998 were a balance of US$145 000, from the USAID/MIP funding and a grant of US$312 000 from the Kellogg Foundation.

When the donor funding for ATZ ran out in 2000, EnterpriseWorks continued supporting it for another year. However, in mid-2001 this support ended and ATZ suspended operations. The two private companies, RAM and ZOPP, continued operating. *This shows the critical importance of for-profit spin-offs in ensuring sustainability because NGOs eventually exit from project activities.* It is becoming progressively more difficult to persuade donor agencies to fund activities where no exit strategy is evident, and securing long-term funding for ATZ will be a challenge for its staff. The survival of RAM Ltd and ZOPP Ltd lies in their realizing financial viability, which seems possible, at least in the short to medium term.

Both companies recorded healthy operating profits in 1998. On a turnover of Z$92 066 ZOPP Ltd made a profit on trading of Z$22 226. However, when the costs of ATZ promotional activities on behalf of ZOPP Ltd. are taken into account, ZOPP Ltd's income for 1998 represented only 65.7 per cent total cost recovery (just above its target of 64 per cent). The cost-recovery target of 96 per cent for 1999 was exceeded during the first six months of the year when ZOPP achieved a cost-recovery rate of 109 per cent. Effectively, then, from the year 2000 (when indirect subsidies from the project ended), ZOPP Ltd would be a fully profitable, stand-alone company.

RAM Ltd exceeded its revenue targets in both 1997 and 1998. Despite losses totalling US$24 975 because of the early technical problems with the RAM-32, RAM Ltd recorded operating profits of US$634 in 1997 and US$89 025 in 1998.

Now that the technical problems with the RAM-32 have been resolved, and if the weather is more favourable than in recent years, conditions are conducive for a growth in sales. Moreover, future trends in Zimbabwe are expected to increase demand further. Land reform and redistribution, which are bound to continue for some years to come, may promote the trend towards greater small-scale mechanization in agriculture. But there are factors that threaten the long-term sustainability of RAM Ltd and ZOPP Ltd. Perhaps the most serious is the need for continual product innovation. The market for oil presses in Zimbabwe does not yet appear to be nearing saturation, and saturation is probably even more distant in many of the other countries to which presses are currently exported. Nonetheless, a ceiling necessarily exists on the number of presses that the market will support.

The peanut butter mill offers substantial promise as the next high-volume product on which the continued financial success of the two companies can be based. The continued, long-term viability of these companies is dependent on their being able to identify, in collaboration with ATZ, a stream of new technologies that can be produced and distributed on a large scale.

While competition is limited at present, there are signs that it may increase. The light-engineering project of ITDG-Southern Africa, for example, is setting up two 'business shops', which will wholesale and retail a wide range of technologies manufactured by small-scale enterprises, including a model of the peanut butter mill. Moreover, while the presses that RAM Ltd currently produces are much less expensive than those made in Kenya and Mozambique, this may change.

This points to a more general issue and potential threat: those demonstrating the profitability of a new product line are vulnerable to competition from new market entrants. It may be that RAM Ltd and ZOPP Ltd have already achieved sufficient market supremacy to be able to withstand such competition, and the sales agreements that ZOPP Ltd has already negotiated in other African countries will stand it in particularly good stead in this respect. However, this cannot be taken for granted and, despite the lack of serious competition at present, they need to maintain rigorous commercial standards to ensure that they continue to dominate the market.

The political and economic instability that has afflicted Zimbabwe in recent years also threatens company sustainability. Put simply, Zimbabwe is an increasingly difficult place in which to do business; devaluation has driven the cost of imported inputs sharply upwards; and high rates of inflation (32 per cent in 1998, 58 per cent in 1999, and 56 per cent in 2000, according to IMF statistics) erode the value of cash holdings.

Newly introduced legislation has exacerbated the situation. Since November 1997, companies are no longer allowed to run foreign exchange accounts and all incoming funds must be converted into local currency. Thus, they are no longer protected against currency devaluation.

A further related problem is that, despite the attractive discounts that ZOPP Ltd offers to distributors to purchase stock, they generally wait to buy until they receive orders. This strains working capital resources.

A final, critical challenge to their sustainability lies in the transition from aid-supported to fully independent for-profit companies. Both firms have enjoyed special privileges by virtue of their relationship with the Zimbabwe Oil Press Project. ZOPP Ltd is largely staffed by former ATZ employees. ATZ has provided, free of charge, substantial promotional and market development activities. And two EnterpriseWorks staff members based in Zimbabwe provide advice and assistance to the project.

Meanwhile, RAM Ltd has benefited from generous equity participation from EnterpriseWorks: the stake of US dollars that EnterpriseWorks injected gave it the capital it required to move into mass production.

In short, while RAM Ltd and ZOPP Ltd have performed strongly in the commercial world, both have continued to enjoy benefits from their relationship with the project. And indeed, it appears likely that they will continue to enjoy some level of ongoing, long-term project support in terms of 'development activities', such as identifying technological possibilities and developing and promoting cultivation of pressing seeds.

Project services

The project has from its outset built alliances with partner organizations, and this should be an important factor in sustaining the services it provides (see Table 8.5).

Table 8.5 The project's key partner organizations

Category of partner	Organization	Nature of collaboration
Government	AGRITEX, Department of Research and Specialist Services	Training, extension services, monitoring farmer activities
NGOs	CARE, Zimbabwe Institute of Religious Research and Ecological Conservation, Association of Zimbabwe Traditional Environmental Conservationists, AFRICARE, Citizens' Network for Foreign Affairs	Sharing of experience in technologies, training, joint ventures in programme implementation
Donor agencies	WK Kellogg Foundation, USAID/MIP	Funding, assistance to private sector in technology dissemination
Private sector	ZOPP, RAM, Pannar Ltd, distributors, Seed Cooperative	Manufacture and distribution of technologies and seed
Information disseminators	Development Technology Centre of the University of Zimbabwe	Sources of information on technologies, enterprise development
Farmers' groups	Zimbabwe Farmers Union, Commercial Farmers Union, Resettlement and Indigenous Commercial Farmers Union	Farmer mobilization, training and extension

The capacity building that has taken place, often informally, as project organizations and their partners collaborate, should ensure that non-project agencies will continue to deliver at least some services. Pannar, for example, will continue distributing high-yielding seeds. DTC will continue its field tests in identifying appropriate seed varieties. Partner NGOs such as AFRICARE will continue to promote the presses and other technologies. And AGRITEX extension staff will promote good seed-farming practices.

191

Lessons learned

NGOs are vitally important in helping to develop and promote new income-generating activities in the rural community. Perhaps this is the single most important lesson that the project has demonstrated. This is not to downplay in any way the role of the private sector. Indeed, the project has sought to involve private sector operators at every stage of the project and, where possible, to transfer project functions to them after their potential viability has been demonstrated.

Without the intervention of the NGO EnterpriseWorks, the private sector would probably not have achieved the kind of progress its oil press projects have achieved over the past decade in Africa. There are three reasons for this. First, the domestic private sector in sub-Saharan Africa does not usually have access to critical information on, for example, successful project interventions elsewhere or the availability of potentially appropriate technologies. Second, private companies are generally unwilling to invest in the overhead and development costs of small-scale technologies since they find it difficult to protect their products from imitation by others. And third, few private operators have either the expertise or the capital to undertake parallel interventions in various different fields, as is often required when promoting new rural activities. It is in conditions such as these that NGOs can play a decisive catalytic role.

EnterpriseWorks and ATZ continued to provide support through mid-2001. However, it was never intended that they would continue this role for the long term, since NGOs are supposed to exit after they have played their market-facilitating role. The problems associated with an adequate supply of pressing seed can be successfully addressed in the medium term, and long-term support in this field will not be necessary. However, as already noted, the continued competitiveness and profitability of RAM Ltd and ZOPP Ltd does appear to be dependent on their continuing to identify and develop new - technologies.

This raises the question as to whether complete transfer of the initiative to the private sector is possible – or indeed desirable. The prospect of EnterpriseWorks generating sufficient revenue from its shareholding in RAM Ltd to cover the full costs of technology development activities appears unrealistic.

Moreover, even if RAM Ltd is able to generate sufficient revenue to fund its own technology development work, can it do so effectively? One of the strengths of NGOs relative to private companies is their connection to international networks, which provide them with a wealth of information on new small-scale technologies and how to sell them successfully.

EnterpriseWorks has become an international centre of excellence, an important resource for partner organizations with ongoing activities in the oilseeds sector in many other African countries. It will naturally continue to be an important source of information for RAM Ltd and ZOPP Ltd. Although the companies would probably not fold in the foreseeable future without such support, their performance would not be as good without it.

It is also worthwhile to explore the future involvement of EnterpriseWorks in the oilseed subsector in Zimbabwe from a developmental perspective. Serving the needs of small-scale and predominantly rural markets is rarely, if ever, the most profitable strategy open to a manufacturing company. In the face of falling sales or loss of the vision that inspired the founders of the company, there is little reason why an entrepreneur would not choose to abandon the current focus in favour of a more profitable (but less developmentally oriented) one.

In short, to demonstrate that the production and dissemination of small-scale technologies may be profitable is not to guarantee that this is the *most* profitable strategy for a manufacturing enterprise. Long-term equity participation by EnterpriseWorks may be the only way to guarantee that RAM Ltd maintains its current focus.

The long view in promoting new economic activities

The commercial, mass-production strategy that the project adopted has proved to be essential for sustaining the manufacturing and distribution companies. However, it could not have occurred without the seven-year foundation-building phase from 1989 to 1996. This early phase permitted experimentation and learning, and it established trust on which later success was built.

All this has required an important investment by EnterpriseWorks and its donors. The willingness of EnterpriseWorks to invest equity capital in an unproven venture that would be unlikely to generate significant returns for a private manufacturer in the country in the short term has been particularly important. A manufacturer would not be concerned with the broader economic and social benefits that oilseed processing has had for rural microentrepreneurs, farmers and rural consumers.

Separation of for-profit and not-for-profit project activities for commercial sustainability

Creating an institutional distinction between project activities that can be commercialized and those that cannot appears to be at the core of the project's success. NGOs have a poor record of economic proficiency in the marketplace. By creating for-profit companies, the project has created the conditions in which its manufacturing and distribution elements can adopt fully commercial working methods, thus promoting their long-term sustainability.

193

Although no attempt has been made to measure the level of subsidy the project afforded to either the two private companies it established or the purchasers of ram presses and other technologies, it is clear that the level has fallen steadily. With commercialization, the project took a greater margin on each press and recovered more for its services.

EnterpriseWorks invested in RAM Ltd and ZOPP Ltd on conditions that would have attracted few private entrepreneurs. Substantial donor funding has been required to create the infrastructure on which their success depends. While all of the costs of production and marketing the press are currently being covered and the manufacturing and distribution companies have earned profits, the costs that EnterpriseWorks and ATZ have incurred in developing the technology and marketing the machines have not been recovered – nor should their recovery be expected, as these are 'public good' functions.

Such subsidy, however, is inherent in all development projects. If no external support had been necessary, the private sector would have already filled the market niche. But as the level of subsidy decreases, the prospect for the long-term viability of these two companies looks bright. The decision to separate for-profit and not-for-profit elements of the project have contributed to this in no small measure.

Enterprise promotion and cost recovery through innovative NGO funding arrangements

Investment by EnterpriseWorks of equity capital in RAM Ltd represented a most unusual and innovative step for an NGO. Two obvious advantages are inherent. First, it allowed the newly established company to operate in the private sector from the outset, thus obviating the generally difficult transition from NGO to private company status. Second, it gives EnterpriseWorks the option of long-term holding in a profitable business, thus giving it a potential source of income for ongoing development activities. With donor funding falling, this may prove of great value and may be a model of interest to other NGOs.

Appropriateness of scaling up to mass production

With certain agricultural technologies, scaling up may require a mass production strategy. With the ram press, both the quality control inputs required from project staff and the productive capacity of trained small-scale manufacturers imposed a low ceiling on the amount of impact that could be achieved in the early years.

The project team's decision to change production strategy away from the use of multiple small-scale manufacturers to mass production by a single larger-scale company reflects the fact that the core focus of the project is on end-users – oil processors – rather than press producers. It may at times be appropriate that the natural inclination of many support agencies to work with small-scale producers be sacrificed to the greater good of mass dissemination of the technology in question.

This does not, however, mean that mass production by a relatively sophisticated manufacturer is always – or even generally – the most appropriate means for delivering capital equipment to end-users. Two observations are in order.

First, the larger the market, the more standard the product and the easier the transport, the more will mass production be favoured. In product markets not sharing these characteristics, mass production may not be practicable.

Second, while the Zimbabwe Oil Press Project has recorded considerable success in marketing new processing technologies, it has had less effect on enhancing the productive capacity of the local manufacturing sector. Since the shift to mass production, the project has encouraged one manufacturer to produce the technologies, many of which were designed by outside, expatriate engineers. However, the mass manufacturing company is headed by a Zimbabwean citizen whose demonstrated capacity to adapt other rural technologies has been improved by the project. For example, he has developed a whole set of equipment for peanut processing.

This is not to criticize the project. There are, however, cases where helping the local, small-scale sector to respond in a creative and innovative way to the various and changing market demands may be the most appropriate way to deliver production technologies to end-users. Then encouraging small-scale producers would be appropriate.

The value of product guarantees

Introducing a new technology is seldom easy. Risk-averse as the poor are, they are particularly resistant to purchasing new equipment before its reliability is thoroughly proven. Centrally important to the ram press's rapid sales was the guaranteed replacement of equipment that was operational but that did not meet the project's quality standards.

The importance of continued technology development work

The importance of continuing to develop technology after the first approved prototype is delivered is demonstrated by the five sizes of ram press that the project introduced, each of which filled a different niche. Three of the models remain popular in Zimbabwe. ATZ has worked on developing a motorized oil press together with a number of other technologies to serve other identified niches.

The importance of adequate field testing of new technologies

The RAM-32 was introduced too fast. The field-testing protocol was not adhered to and little testing was done outside the workshop in Zimbabwe and Tanzania (and none at all in Uganda). This led to around 350 of the second and third batches (which totalled 843) being recalled and retrofitted, at an expense of US$24 975 and a damaged reputation for a young company.

The value of untied and regional funding

Important in the success of EnterpriseWorks' oilseeds projects in Africa has been the generous funding it has received from donors for activities not restricted to use within a single country. This regional type of funding is relatively difficult to obtain since many donors programme their budgets by country. The regional funding that EnterpriseWorks received has permitted it to host conferences, prepare newsletters and manuals, develop and test new models of the ram press, conduct market and feasibility studies, evaluate, and provide backup and assistance in developing and implementing new strategies. The fact that this funding was not country specific has helped in developing an Africa-wide strategy, with mass production in Zimbabwe at its core.

The importance of developing strategic alliances

Finally, the project has demonstrated that it is important to build alliances with other organizations to localize and sustain project activities. The project has effectively built capacity and transferred expertise to a range of other agencies in Zimbabwe. Developing the capability of small-scale workshops in manufacturing and quality control in the early phase of the project and of the larger-scale mass manufacturer in the current phase contributes to their ability to produce these and other products in the future.

Challenges for the future

The need for continued technical and product innovation

While the market for ram presses and peanut butter processing equipment appears buoyant in Zimbabwe and beyond, at some point a ceiling exists on the number that can be sold before the market is saturated. Also limited is the number of rural technologies that can be produced on a large scale and for which there exists extensive demand. However, the market saturation point for the ram press, peanut mills and other rural technologies is still far from being reached.

Other appropriate technology agencies active in the region are also seeking to help their client producers gain an increased share of the market for rural technologies. The task facing ATZ and the two commercial companies is to develop a stream of products that will justify the long-term existence of a mass producer and distributor of rural technologies.

Establishing RAM Ltd and ZOPP Ltd on a firmer commercial footing

The greatest short-term challenge facing the project is for the two for-profit companies to become truly autonomous, commercial operations. While both have achieved operating profits, they have continued to receive various forms of project support and subsidy. With reduced support from EnterpriseWorks and ATZ, the next two years will be critical in their transition to genuine autonomy. The way in which the transition is managed will have a strong bearing on the ability of these new companies to survive in the open market.

A longer-term issue for EnterpriseWorks in this context is what to do with its equity shareholding. EnterpriseWorks currently holds 54 per cent of RAM Ltd. It could be argued that for the model that the project developed to prove entirely sustainable, it needs to be completely localized. Large devaluations of the country's currency over the past few years makes this extremely difficult.

Imaginative approaches to transfer shares to company employees may need to be considered. Alternatively, should employees prove unable to absorb the remaining shares, it may be appropriate to offer them for sale to the public. A further interesting approach in this era of donor funding cutbacks would be for EnterpriseWorks to retain ownership of the shares and use the profits to continue other not-for-profit NGO activities in Zimbabwe and elsewhere. NGOs like EnterpriseWorks have to seek new funding arrangements like the private sector to survive and thrive while traditional donors (especially government agencies) continue to cut their development assistance budgets.

Effective implementation of the new marketing strategy

The new marketing strategy that the project recently launched marks a bold departure from its previous approach. If RAM Ltd and ZOPP Ltd succeed in increasing sales while cutting out the large distributors they have been using, the rewards will be great indeed. Linking income to sales should guarantee staff commitment to the new direction. However, identifying and servicing new networks of commissioned agents and retailers is no small task. The previous experience of other NGOs with technology promotion mandates, such as International Development Enterprises and ApproTEC, in developing such networks for distributing small-scale technologies will be of great value. It is, nonetheless, a significant challenge.

Addressing the shortage of seed for pressing in years of poor weather

A recurring problem is the shortage of seed for pressing when the weather is poor. The number of working presses in the field can press many more seeds than have been available in recent years. The demand for new presses may well grow; given favourable weather, demand for oilseeds is likely to rise sharply.

The project has already invested much effort in improving the distribution of seed to small-scale processing enterprises. A top priority of the project over the coming years is to ensure that these efforts are translated into solid achievements.

New developments and ongoing problems

Two new developments should be mentioned. In mid-2000, the funding for the two EnterpriseWorks regional representatives stationed in Zimbabwe ended, but ATZ continued its activities. ATZ was suspending activities in mid-2001 because it lacked new donor funding. Such funding has been greatly reduced as a result of the political problems in the country. The two businesses, RAM Ltd and ZOPP Ltd, will continue their activities, although they too have been hurt by the high inflation rates and continued loss of value of the domestic currency. The final challenge for the project, over which it has no control, is the present political and economic instability in Zimbabwe. Devaluation, high inflation and periodic rioting are not conducive to business growth.

Notes

1 Henceforth the organization is referred to as EnterpriseWorks, even when describing its activities before it changed its name.
2 Oil processing enterprises in Zimbabwe have used the presses sold by the project primarily for processing sunflower and sesame seeds, since these are the most profitable in the country. In other countries, however, presses have been used for processing the crops listed in the text.
3 The smallest of these, with a 20-mm piston diameter, was produced commercially only in Tanzania. The smaller presses in common use in Zimbabwe have piston diameters of 30–40 mm.
4 The assumptions on which estimates of project impact provided in this section are based are derived from project records, secondary data and periodic surveys. In all cases, these assumptions constitute a conservative estimate of impact. It has not been possible to conduct impact surveys every year, but four surveys have been undertaken in Zimbabwe since 1993. These have permitted the project to adjust coefficients according to key variables regularly during the project rather than assume constant relationships of impact.
5 For a discussion of the methodological issues involved in estimating the monetary benefits deriving from the project, see note 11.
6 Estimated consumer savings indicate the total monetary benefit resulting from the project. This, however, introduces two methodological difficulties when attempting to equate project benefits with impact on gross national product (GNP). First, the inclusion of consumer savings does not take into account the displacement effect on the producers of (previously consumed) higher-value products. However, as EnterpriseWorks' mandate is to assist small-scale producers, it is not concerned about effects on large-scale oil manufacturers or producers in major edible-oil-producing countries. Second, among households consuming edible oil (and assumed for the calculation of benefits to be enjoying the benefits of a cheaper product) are a number that did not consume at the higher previous price. They are not saving money as compared with before, but they are now able to afford the oil and are receiving nutritional benefits from it.
7 Given the capacity of Zimbabwean artisans for improvisation, some oil presses undoubtedly remain in operation for more than five years. However, impact survey findings suggest that this is a fair, if conservative, estimate of average press life.
8 The impact survey undertaken in Zimbabwe in 1997 found that 12 per cent of purchasers were repeat buyers; thus the average number of presses per enterprise was 1.12. A similar pattern is assumed for peanut butter processing enterprises.

9 A little under half of peanut butter mills (48 per cent according to a 1998 survey) are used in processing businesses. The remainder are domestic appliances.

10 This was calculated by dividing the estimated ram press oil production resulting from the project of 423 693 litres by the average annual consumption per rural household of 28.5 litres per year (derived from the Nutrition Department of the Zimbabwean Ministry of Health). It is assumed that one person per household (the principal bill payer) benefits from access to cheaper oil.

11 Monetary benefits in this project include the gross value of producer income gains from the sale of final goods and services (oil and seedcake: in this context, ram presses and other technologies are considered intermediate goods) and consumer savings. The gross sales value of the oil and seedcake captures the profit to the oilseed producers, the income their hired workers receive, and the profit of the press manufacturers, their hired workers and input suppliers.

Since part of the steel used in producing ram presses and other technologies is imported, this represents a third methodological problem (in addition to those referred to in note 6) in relating the project's monetary benefits to its contribution to the gross domestic product. However, the value of oil and seedcake is a useful and easily obtained proxy measure using survey data. Furthermore imported steel is a small part of the cost of the ram press. The retail price and import content value of the RAM-32 and BP-30 oil presses are given below:

Product	Retail price (US$)	Value accounted for by imported materials (US$)
RAM-32	163.80	21
BP-30	187.50	14

12 This press production capacity assumes that the oil press is the only item of equipment manufactured by RAM Ltd. As other products are introduced, so the capacity to produce presses drops.

Bibliography

Appropriate Technology Zimbabwe (1999) *Strategy Document,* ATZ, Harare.

Hyman, E. (1993) 'Production of edible oils for the masses and by the masses: the impact of the ram press in Tanzania', *World Development* 21(3).

Hyman, E. (1997) 'How NGOs can accelerate the commercialization of agricultural technology in Africa', EnterpriseWorks Worldwide, Washington, DC.

Hyman, E. (1998) 'Strengthening the roles of public and private sector research in technology research and dissemination for the rural non-farm economy', in *Proceedings of the IFPRI Workshop on Strategies for Stimulating the Growth of the Rural Non-farm Economy in Developing Countries, 17–21 May 1998.* International Food Policy Research Institute, Washington, DC.

Hyman, E. and S. Johnson (1995) 'Evaluation of the strategy and impacts of the Zimbabwe Oil Processors Project (ZOPP)', EnterpriseWorks Worldwide, Washington, DC.

Lobulu, W. (1990) 'Village Sunflower Project, Arusha, Tanzania: Project implementation and spread of benefits'. PACT Oilseeds in Africa Network, New York.

Silva-Barbeau, I., S.G. Hull, M. Prehm, W.E Barbeau and K. Samba-Ndjure (forthcoming), 'The consumption smoothing effects of a sesame ram press on children during the pre-harvest lean season in the Gambia', *Journal of Nutrition.*

Zulberti, C., O. Schmidt and L. Navarro (1990) 'Generation of an oil/protein generation strategy for countries with low dietary fat intake', in *The Bielenberg Ram Press and Small-Scale Oil Processing: Proceedings of a Conference,* Appropriate Technology International, Harare.

9 Overview and conclusions

SUNITA KAPILA, DONALD MEAD, JONATHAN DAWSON, ERIC L. HYMAN[1]

THIS FINAL CHAPTER distils from the comparative study of the documented projects some good practice principles for the design and delivery of business development services. It comments on current issues in BDS for the rural and urban poor, and summarizes concerns around the assessment of BDS performance through an overview of the case study experience.

BDS design and delivery success factors

The comparative analysis of the seven projects suggests that the following factors are critical to the success of BDS support to small producers:

- the scale of intervention
- diversification in the delivery of services
- the key role of the implementing agencies.

Scale of intervention

The most striking feature of the seven case studies is the sheer scale of their ambition. These were not short-term, minimalist interventions aimed at addressing imperfections in generally well-functioning markets. These projects were all attempting to bring about basic, structural change. To do this, they introduced new economic activities. They helped poor and generally rural people, whose activities were previously limited to the production of primary crops, gain access to commercial activities; they addressed traditionally unequal power relationships between poor producers and other actors further up the value chain.

This set them somewhat apart from the types of intervention that have featured so prominently in recent discussions at the various fora hosted by the Committee of Donor Agencies for Small Enterprise Development. These latter initiatives have been primarily urban in nature and minimalist in orientation, providing short-term, highly focused inputs to correct specific market malfunctions. The target of these mainstream interventions has tended to be growth enterprises – that is, those individual businesses that are perceived as having strong potential for development. The aim has been to improve the quality of BDS available and to enhance the capacity of such enterprises to make informed choices about which services will best serve their needs.

Those interventions are quite a different scenario from that of the case studies described in this book. Here, the focus is systemic in nature. The success of the projects lies not in identifying *growth enterprises*, but rather *subsectors with growth potential* and the bottlenecks that constrain the many small producers within them.

Given the systemic nature of the problems addressed in each of these projects, it is not surprising that tightly focused, minimalist interventions were rejected in favour of more comprehensive approaches. To create a local market for edible oils in Zimbabwe, for example, meant attention to a number of activities and support for them: a supply of oilseed (by encouraging growers), a seed-pressing technology, a distribution network for presses, and entrepreneurs trained in press operation. Failure to address any one of these elements would have threatened the viability of the whole initiative.

Similarly, the capacity of SEEDS clients to supply ornamental fish to higher-value markets was dependent on the whole range of services (technical training, extension, credit and market mediation) that the project provided. Removing any one of these building blocks would have threatened the viability of the entire edifice. The same principle holds true, to a greater or lesser degree, for each of the other case studies.

Diversified delivery of services

It is notable that, as a general rule, the implementers of the case study projects chose to deliver the range of required services in-house, rather than enter into relationships with other specialist agencies. There are exceptions: ITDG-Bangladesh has partnered with other local agencies to deliver important complementary services and provided them with training; SEEDS drew on government and private sector specialists for some of its training sessions; and several of the projects facilitated credit access for their clients, rather than providing it themselves. Nonetheless, the point is generally valid and three of the projects (SEEDS, the Zimbabwe Oil Press Project and the El Salvador coffee initiative) even provided the credit themselves.

This is an important finding, contradicting the widely accepted principle that implementing agencies are most effective when they focus relatively narrowly on their core area of specialization. The reality, however, is that collaboration between different agencies is difficult where various bottlenecks need to be unblocked in a coordinated manner. The lead agency risks losing control of the process and becomes dependent on the capacity of project partners to deliver. This, for example, was the experience of TechnoServe in its efforts to identify local partners to whom it could transfer its capacity in group mobilization and organization. None of the several candidates identified proved able to undertake the activities concerned with the thoroughness or at the speed required for the other project components to be implemented successfully.

The key role of the implementing agency

A further distinctive feature of all the case study projects is the leading role that the implementing agency played in most phases of project design and execution. In all cases, both identifying the economic opportunity that the project would exploit and designing the project were almost exclusively the responsibility of the lead NGO. Similarly, most of the key strategic decisions made later – for example, the shift from small-scale to large-scale production of oil presses in Zimbabwe; the fundamental refocusing of marketing activities in the Zimbabwe light-engineering project; the decision to scale up the El Salvador coffee marketing project by including other countries in the region – were strongly driven by the implementing agencies themselves.

This is not to say that other stakeholders played no active role: the small-scale engineers working with ITDG's project in Zimbabwe, for example, worked closely with the project team in identifying and developing capital goods; and farmers' groups were involved both in identifying the need for an umbrella organization to take over many of the functions that TechnoServe played in Ghana, and in deciding what form the organization should take.

Nonetheless, the level of participation of stakeholders (and particularly project clients) was relatively low in most of these projects. There are good reasons for this. The initiatives are often complex and multifaceted and are meant to assist relatively poor people who may have limited education and who live in areas that are often remote, with generally poor infrastructure. These types of producers are generally unable either to spot potential economic opportunities or to identify or mobilize the various interventions required to exploit them. The NGOs, with their range of expertise and experience and their connections to international networks of information, were able to play these roles.

There is, of course, an attendant danger here that NGOs run the risk of being sucked into the role of market players – a role they have traditionally played poorly. However, the case study projects suggest that this lesson has been learned and that lead NGOs tend to recognize that their forte lies in identifying and exploring the profitability of market opportunities, building the capacity of their clients to exploit them, and then linking them up to private sector partners (input providers, equipment manufacturers, marketing companies and so on). The growing number of employees among the case study NGOs with a private sector background appears to be important here – both in permitting the NGOs to spot and develop income-generating opportunities and in restraining their involvement in business activities.

The case studies suggest that there may on occasion be an important ongoing role for the lead agency even after the project (or project phase) has formally ended. This is generally the case where further external inputs are required in identifying new economic opportunities. For example, EnterpriseWorks has an important long-term role to play in identifying and developing new technologies for RAM Ltd to manufacture and ZOPP Ltd to disseminate – the two companies that the oil press project in Zimbabwe established. The long-term profitability of both companies is likely to depend to a significant degree on the success of these ongoing research and development efforts.

Similarly, in Ghana, TechnoServe will continue to search out new market niches on behalf of its smallholder clients and work to develop them. These efforts will become progressively more important as the profitability of the inventory credit scheme falls. This ongoing role for support organizations appears to be a common feature of systems-based projects, where successfully removing one bottleneck frequently reveals the existence of others that need to be addressed. This is a common feature of all of the case studies in this volume.

Developing commercial BDS

Each of the projects reviewed in this book attempted – some quite successfully – to link up with the private sector to help sustain the effectiveness of the BDS interventions after the NGOs and donor support were gone. Several challenges qualify the market-based and demand-driven approach to BDS espoused in the guidelines for donor intervention in BDS for micro- and small enterprises; two of them are outlined here.

Difficulties in drawing a clear distinction between BDS 'facilitators' and 'providers'

The central role of the lead NGO in these case study projects, and the difficulties experienced in finding project partners with whom to collaborate, raise important implications in the distinction that the Donor Committee guidelines insist be made between BDS 'facilitators' and 'providers'. The former, it is argued, should create, through donor-funded initiatives, the conditions under which the latter, private sector concerns, can provide business development services for a profit. The case studies suggest that with these projects of multifaceted initiatives working with poor producers, this may not be possible.

There are two reasons for this. First is the dearth of service providers in the form of either for-profit enterprises or not-for-profit organizations. Second, real problems of cost recovery exist for service providers when working with poor, rural producers. While there are, in the case studies, incidents of financially viable companies being established to provide BDS on an ongoing basis, there are nonetheless many other important project services that it appears cannot be transferred to the private sector. Here, the economic justification of the project lies in the fact that benefits can be quantified as exceeding costs – even where many of the individual services may not recover their costs.

Synergies between credit and BDS

The Donor Committee guidelines do not consider the BDS credit complementarity that entrepreneurs often require. Several of the case studies in this book show strong synergies between credit and BDS. Several different patterns are evident. In the case of the inventory credit scheme in Ghana, various BDS were required (building group capacity, introducing improved storage and treatment facilities, and so on) for it to be possible to deliver credit against stored grains. In Bangladesh, the food processing activities that poor people adopted as a result of the training provided for them were essential to enable them to repay loans received (many of which were used for other productive activities).

In the Sri Lanka ornamental fish project, as in each of the other sectors in which SEEDS is active, BDS and credit are both seen as necessary elements of the package of assistance required to permit small producers to move into new areas of activity. Indeed, a core reason for creating a BDS unit within SEEDS was as a way to increase the outreach and repayment rates of its credit programme.

In sum, the projects documented in this book suggest that many new market opportunities cannot be exploited without access to the financial resources required to purchase equipment and raw materials. Credit is made available to enable client small enterprises to take advantage of these identified market opportunities. On the other hand, achieving the mass outreach required for credit-providing organizations to cover their costs when working with poor producers generally requires some mix of BDS to enhance clients' productive capacity. If BDS are to be promoted as distinct commercial products, it would be useful to consider ways of complementing them with access to credit.

Evolution of project services

The evolutionary nature of the business development process

Most of the projects presented in the case studies undertook important strategic reorientations at some point in the project's life. The Zimbabwe Oil Press Project, for example, shifted production of presses from small- to large-scale units as a result of quality-control problems and a need to scale up and reduce costs. ITDG-Southern Africa introduced a major new marketing component into its light-engineering project design as it shifted its focus from manufacturers to end-users of capital goods. TechnoServe's initial engagement in the maize sector in Ghana was in promoting green revolution technologies; only after the storage and marketing bottlenecks became obvious did it develop its inventory credit initiative.

Most of the projects have also expanded their range of activities or the number of products with which they work. In addition to beans, ASOMEX now markets several other crops and has moved into marketing furniture. It is looking to diversify further. The manufacturing company that the Zimbabwe Oil Press Project created, RAM Ltd, is now also producing peanut butter mills and several other items of equipment. Once again, the search for new products continues.

Each of the projects first started with only one product, enabling the developers to capture the benefits that come from focused specialization. In each case, the impetus for diversification came from a desire to increase turnover, generally with a view to increasing the cost effectiveness and promoting the prospects for financial sustainability of the bodies that the project created. The commercial viability of ASOMEX, RAM and ZOPP all appear to various extents to be dependent on this broadening in the scale of their activities.

As pioneering projects, there is clearly a strong element of action–research in most of the case study initiatives. Moreover, given the relative complexity of what it is they are trying to achieve, with interventions on various fronts, it is perhaps not surprising that projects of this type periodically find a need to reorient themselves. The obvious question this poses for commercial delivery of BDS is whether and how such delivery can incorporate action–research and evolutionary design, which have been so important in the success of the projects reviewed in this book.

The emergence of innovative forms of development assistance

The case studies illustrate several innovative approaches to small enterprise support that borrow direct from conventional commercial business activity. On the one hand, these relate to the way in which the initiatives were set up. EnterpriseWorks, for example, provided equity investment for establishing RAM Ltd, the company manufacturing the oil presses and other technologies that the project disseminated. In the Ghana inventory credit project (as in all its other projects), TechnoServe based its assistance on a management agreement drawn up between the NGO and its client producers, which required that client producers invest equity in enterprises that the project established.

Innovative developments oriented to the private sector are also evident in the routes to sustainability that several of the case study projects pursued. They involved transfer to the private sector of profitable service-providing enterprises that the projects created. This is true of the manufacturing and distribution companies that the Zimbabwe Oil Press Project established, the ASOMEX marketing company, and the tool hire centres and retail outlets the light-engineering project created in Zimbabwe. The Zimbabwe Oil Press Project deliberately created a conceptual and institutional distinction between the services that could be provided profitably and those that could not. The former were transferred to private enterprises that the project created, and the latter have remained with an indigenous development NGO dependent on ongoing donor funding.

Harmonizing commercial and development objectives of BDS

Transfer of services to the private sector has, in each of the case studies, involved a process of transition from subsidy support to fully commercial operation. In none of the projects has this been achieved without attendant problems. With ASOMEX, for example, significant confusion exists between developmental and commercial interests, with the marketing company needing to serve the interests of its parent NGO (ASOPROF) at the same time as it plays an independent market role. This confusion of roles has been identified as a key factor in explaining the suboptimal performance of the company to date. Similar issues arose in the ZOPP project, as functions first performed by the NGO were shifted to commercial organizations.

Additional problems exist with the bodies created by the two projects in Zimbabwe. Here, the dilemma resides in finding a way of giving the new enterprises full commercial autonomy while also ensuring that they continue to perform the developmental function for which they were created. That is, while the projects may have demonstrated that equipment hire and the manufacture and dissemination of small-scale equipment may be profitable, this does not mean that these are necessarily the most profitable activities that the new enterprises could be undertaking. In short, if full control is handed over to the private sector, can the new owners be prevented from diversifying into more profitable but less developmentally favourable activities?

EnterpriseWorks is considering holding on to its stake in the press manufacturing company for some time as a way of ensuring that it continues to perform a developmental function. The equipment hire and retail outlets that the light-engineering project created will become private companies owned by ITDG-Southern Africa, thus ensuring its continued voice in policy. It is yet to be seen how successful these arrangements will prove to be in reconciling commercial and developmental requirements. They should be seen as first steps in a process of exploration in an area that is likely to grow in importance as similar initiatives develop.

Assessing successful performance: the case study experience

These considerations raise a number of issues about the assessment of projects against measurement criteria for impact, cost effectiveness and sustainability.

It was obvious from the outset of this study that it would be problematic to apply a common standardized set of indicators to the case studies. The BDS approaches have been diverse. The NGOs involved used different definitions of the term 'project' and different methods for assessing costs and benefits. In the comparative analysis of the seven projects, setting numerical standards or benchmarks for performance was particularly problematic because of the diverse client groups and participating NGOs. In several cases, the lack of rigorous data made even simple benefit/cost calculations impossible. Nonetheless, the case studies were able to trace some achievements resulting from project interventions and to note the process that led to these outcomes. A major concern in attempting to assess performance was how to mark the start or end of any particular BDS activity.

Impact

Difficulties in defining a project

All of the case study projects have, to some extent, built on previous activities that the lead development agency had undertaken. ASOMEX was established to exploit the potential for export marketing of the beans already promoted by a previous MEDA project. ITDG-Southern Africa's work in the light-engineering sector in Zimbabwe grew out of previous project activities with informal sector carpenters and blacksmiths. The oil press project in Zimbabwe was able to draw on substantial work in technology development already undertaken by EnterpriseWorks in Tanzania. The foundations of the inventory credit project in Ghana were built on previous work by TechnoServe in promoting green revolution technologies in that country. SEEDS drew on a network of community-based offices throughout the country. Their linking method, evolved over a number of years, is used to promote activities in various sectors of the economy. It reduces the marginal cost of undertaking new activities such as raising ornamental fish, but makes it difficult to demarcate the boundaries of that activity as a separate project.

In the same vein, systemic interventions will often evolve into new forms. Having promoted a model for the storage of crops, for example, TechnoServe is now promoting processing activities, including mechanical grain drying. The manufacturing and distribution capacities that the Zimbabwe Oil Press Project created are being used to produce other small-scale technologies. Moreover, the switch to mass manufacture in one central location permits the dissemination of these technologies to many countries outside Zimbabwe.

This analysis reveals the unsatisfactory nature of the concept of 'the project' as a tool for isolating interventions of a systemic nature and for measuring their impact, cost effectiveness and sustainability. Where does one begin to count the costs of interventions that build on previous initiatives, and where does one finish calculating benefits in situations where other related interventions emerge? How does one make a judgement on sustainability, when, as in the case of the TechnoServe initiative in Ghana, inventory credit and the group strengthening that goes with it can be seen as one element of an ongoing process of assistance and development? How to isolate the benefits to be counted when, as in most of the case studies, producers having no direct contact with the project adopt its innovations through imitation? Or when client producers use the enhanced capacity they have acquired for purposes other than those directly relating to the project goals? These are all important methodological questions to which we do not yet have satisfactory answers. Yet until we develop more appropriate impact assessment techniques, we are likely to continue to miscalculate – generally to underestimate – the true impact of systemic, capacity-building projects such as those described in the case studies.

Project achievements

As a result of the El Salvador Small-scale Coffee Producers' Project, 1568 small-scale coffee farm owners and workers each earned at least US$20 in additional income in the 1998/9 production year. The project's total monetary benefits (in gross income gains of the cooperatives and producer cost savings for the cooperatives and farmers) are almost identical with project costs (from January 1995 to December 1998) at around US$1.7 million. However, the capacity that the project created among the cooperatives, including a profitable coffee marketing company, means that benefits will continue to accrue while costs progressively decline. The project is currently being replicated in a regional initiative covering El Salvador, Honduras and Nicaragua.

The Zimbabwe Oil Press Project is generating employment for 4150 people in oil press enterprises and permitting 6000 farmers to increase their production of sunflowers. In 1998, the project delivered benefits to 18421 producer participants in Zimbabwe (categorized as press owners and their workers, press sales outlets, repair artisans, filter manufacturers, oilseed and peanut butter processors, press and seed sales agents and farmers growing oilseeds for sale to processors). Some 51 per cent of all producer participants were women. An additional 14 866 households benefited from access to cheaper oil, giving a total of 33 287 beneficiaries. The project has succeeded in constructing the infrastructure for a new rural industry in Zimbabwe – small-scale oil pressing – which is now largely self-sustaining. By the end of 1998, monetary benefits in Zimbabwe (US$5.3 million) exceeded project costs (US$1.6 million) by a benefit/cost ratio of 3.36:1. Once again, benefits will continue to flow while costs, already at a relatively low level, are phased out over the next few years.

Of the approximately 8700 people trained in food processing by the agro-processing programme in Bangladesh, which started in 1990, around 1300 have established new enterprises. These are generally very poor, landless people. Incomes of beneficiaries starting their own enterprises were found to have increased by 82 to 140 per cent. Evaluation exercises undertaken in 1996 and 1998 calculated benefit/cost ratios to be 12.5:1 and 7:1 respectively. Sustainability of project achievements is being promoted by transferring skills to trainers of various other indigenous Bangladeshi organizations and by establishing an organization, the Forum for Food Processing Enterprise Development, to take on the roles played by the project to date.

The first three years of the light-engineering project in Zimbabwe, from its launch in 1995, can be seen as a period of action–research, as it felt its way towards an appropriate approach to developing and disseminating small-scale production equipment. Significant progress has been made towards achieving the project's core aims: the creation of financially self-sustaining equipment hire service centres and small equipment retail shops. Little in the way of impact data has yet been gathered.

The crop marketing company established in 1993 by the ASOMEX project in Bolivia serves the marketing needs of over 2000 small producers per year. Many of these farmers, having achieved their first exports through ASOMEX, have almost doubled their previous incomes.

Started in 1995, the ornamental fish project in Sri Lanka generated a 13 per cent real increase in incomes for participating farmers. Receiving training in the technologies of this innovative activity were 345 farmers, of whom 115 actually used the training and improved their incomes and range of skills. Benefit/cost ratio was calculated as 5.6 to 1.

Beneficiaries of the cereal storage, processing and marketing project in Ghana include 1800 direct participants and a substantial number of other farmers who have adopted the techniques introduced by the project. Participating farmers accessed around US$117 500 of inventory credit as a result of the project in 1998/9 and have seen their annual incomes rise by up to 29 per cent. Total project costs between 1992 and the present (US$1 754 708) have exceeded benefits (US$1 238 445) by a factor of 1:1.42.

In addition to these direct, quantifiable benefits, each of the projects has generated other significant benefits. Several of the projects, for example, have been replicated or extended into other areas. The private manufacturing company established by the Zimbabwe Oil Press Project supplies oil presses to ten other African countries and is diversifying into the production of several other small-scale technologies for sale both in Zimbabwe and abroad. Several banks and other development agencies have adopted the inventory credit model that TechnoServe introduced in Ghana. The coffee promotion project has now been extended to two other countries in Central America.

The projects have also created various qualitative and ripple or down-stream benefits that have not been included in the benefit/cost calculations. These include improved food security, enhanced capacity among client pro-ducers that has been used in ways and for purposes other than those directly relating to the project goals, and enhanced capacity among institutions and producers not directly connected to the projects but adopting the new techniques and technologies they have introduced. Difficulties of factoring these benefits into impact assessment calculations have dogged all of the case study projects and constitute a major challenge in gauging the true impact of projects.

Cost effectiveness

The various definitions of 'project' and what it means affected the scope and meaning of the cost-effectiveness calculations. Some case studies included only costs incurred by the NGO itself (ITDG-Bangladesh and TechnoServe), while EnterpriseWorks included the costs of all the partner organizations and clients. Cost-effectiveness calculations for the ITDG food processing project were affected by the fact that ITDG was a BDS facilitator and not a provider. It trained fieldworkers of other agencies but did not work directly with end-users. Cost-effectiveness analysis for indirect service providers would need to take into account the costs of other field-based agencies providing training or technical and business management assistance.

Other reasons also made it hard to compare the relationship between costs and benefits across the case studies. The organizations did not all treat historical costs for direct predecessor projects in the same way. While EnterpriseWorks counted historical costs of predecessor projects in the same country, it did not count those in other countries. TechnoServe did not count costs incurred by organizations other than itself, on the grounds that it was concerned with the cost effectiveness of its own resources. The costs per beneficiary could be estimated for many of the case studies, although many of the differences between projects reflected differing inclusions and treatment of costs. Furthermore, this is a less useful measure than the relationship between costs and benefits.

Monetary benefit measures also differed between projects. In many cases, the value of the benefits was not converted from local currency to US dollars, although many of the projects spanned a time of major devaluations of the local currency. Reported income gains were often not adjusted for inflation or discounted to reflect the time value of money. There can also be non-monetary benefits, which are difficult to include in such calculations.

Both benefits and costs can be defined at various levels: clients, communities, a subsector or system, or countries. Some of the case studies used proxy measures to estimate the impact on the GDP of the country. Because of the complexity of changing production systems and markets, attribution of benefits (association between the services and the impact) required difficult judgements.

Cost-effectiveness analysis also illustrated the context specificity of interpreting some performance indicators. The ASOMEX case study commented as follows on the challenge of estimating the level of cost effectiveness: 'a major factor in making the financial records of limited value in providing cost-effectiveness indicators is Bolivia's tax incentive and export bonus structure, which seem to promote some rather non-conventional accounting practices. The quantity of export bonus received is determined by the amount of expenses incurred in the export. This is an incentive to overstate costs of export, and weakens the incentive to minimise costs.' The ASOMEX example also underlines the finding that where multiple services are offered by the same provider, separate records of costs and revenues are not usually kept for each of the services offered.

The relationship between cost recovery and the role of the NGO is a question that runs across all the projects. Where an NGO has primarily played the role of facilitator rather than provider of BDS, the project beneficiaries are not direct clients of the NGO. In the case study of the food processors in Bangladesh, for example, ITDG-Bangladesh trained local agencies, which in turn gave the training to the entrepreneurs. In such cases, it is difficult to expect client enterprises to pay fees that would help the BDS facililitator recover its costs.

Sustainability

The case studies differed in how sustainability was defined and measured. Some projects emphasized the sustainability of the enterprises being supported, either the client MSEs or those providing the BDS; others focused on the sustainability of impact. In our study, these issues were handled mainly through an explanation of the projects' strategies for achieving sustainability as they defined them.

To promote sustainability of services introduced during the project period, some NGOs turned the services over to private providers after the demand for them and successful approaches to supply had been demonstrated. Most of the projects succeeded in establishing market linkages so that the various players might be expected to continue to interact in profitable ways after the project support ended. For example, in the case of ASOMEX, the development of the marketing service stimulated other commercial service providers to deliver the same service. In the Zimbabwe Oil Press Project, the replication of the ram press by private sector manufacturers strengthened the demand for the capital goods and raw materials that were the principal focus of the project. While BDS delivery through NGOs was often subsidized, the example was then set for commercial providers to adopt. One of the projects transferred service delivery from the NGO to a government agency that will continue to subsidize it; the NGO considered this a sustainable pattern.

All of the projects involved subsidization of the BDS, although in many cases the degree of subsidy was deliberately reduced over time. Since not all subsidies were quantified, it was not possible to make numerical comparisons of this measure of sustainability across the projects. In some of the cases, certain services were cross-subsidized by other activities that generated a profit, sometimes involving commercial transactions downstream in marketing a final product. Sunk costs for technology R&D and the start-up of other types of BDS were not generally recovered. In several cases, the full costs of purchased inputs were charged to the client enterprises, but the full distribution costs were not charged during an initial period and promotional and demonstration activity costs were not recovered. In all of the cases where private businesses had been established by the NGOs, the companies continued to operate despite several years of initial losses that were absorbed by the NGOs, or paper losses for their staff members who had taken an equity share.

To put this in perspective, private businesses in industrialized countries also absorb losses for extended launch periods. Transnational corporations that have contract farming arrangements with suppliers often cross-subsidize the costs of input supply or extension services with profits from processing the commodities. Subsidies are a practical business tool during a start-up/launch phase and can play a role in a profitable, ongoing business strategy.

All of the projects paid considerable attention to the development of indigenous human resources and institutional capacity to sustain the impact of their interventions. Some invested considerable effort in building the capacity of groups such as cooperatives and farmers or processors groups. Working with these groups often resulted in lower service delivery costs through economies of scale and easier access. This principle was borne out in the case study of ASOMEX (Bolivia), where MEDA brought this in as a lesson from previous experience, and in projects in Ghana and El Salvador, where cooperatives received facilitative services and were the BDS providers for small-scale producers. In Bangladesh, ITDG trained local partners in food processing technologies in order that the skills transfer would continue after the project ended. In the Ghana Inventory Credit Project, farmers' groups were trained in crop treatment and storage as well as in accessing credit and markets.

Each of the case study projects is following strategies for the sustainability of specific benefits that they have generated. In five of the seven case studies, sustainability is being pursued primarily through market mechanisms. The various approaches to sustainability exhibit a high degree of innovation and, in several cases, mark new departures for NGOs. Equity participation by EnterpriseWorks in the manufacturing and distribution companies in Zimbabwe and by MEDA in ASOMEX constitute important new dimensions in risk-sharing and partnership between support agencies and their clients. ITDG-Southern Africa's exploration of the potential for franchising out the operation of the business shops and the service centres represents another exciting new direction.

In only two of the case study projects is a long-term role for the market not being explored. The main reason is that in neither of these cases would the market be able to sustain the services. In the case of small-scale food processors in Bangladesh, full cost recovery is not possible for the training, networking and advocacy. In future, it is expected that training will be provided by two organizations – one governmental, one an NGO – while advocacy will be undertaken by the newly formed Forum for Food Processing Enterprise Development. Similarly, the group animation services that TechnoServe provides in Ghana cannot be handled on a commercial basis. Newly created farmers' organizations are seen as the best mechanism for meeting the ongoing need for these services.

Absent from each of these sustainability strategies is an element that has been central to discussions at the various recent Donor Committee forums: namely, the payment by small enterprises of fees that cover the costs of the BDS provided. In exploring why this is so, we return to the distinction raised above between initiatives that promote the growth of individual enterprises (that, it is hoped, will be able to pay fees for services) and those that promote growth at the subsectoral level. With subsectoral interventions, many of the beneficiaries may have little or no direct contact with the lead NGO. This was the case with the end-users of the technologies disseminated by the ITDG-Southern Africa light-engineering project; the food processors trained by the agencies that ITDG-Bangladesh had initially trained; and the non-project farmers who adopted cereal storage and treatment techniques introduced in Ghana by the inventory credit project.

This calls into question the core justification commonly made for insisting on payment of fees to cover the full cost of BDS: that BDS are private rather than public goods. Many of the benefits accruing from the case study projects appear to be distinctly public in nature.

Building BDS markets for the rural and urban poor

While there are a number of differences between these projects in terms of both approach and performance, they share a number of important characteristics. As subsectoral initiatives using BDS to increase the clout of primarily rural producers, they represent interventions that involve a long-term commitment on the part of both NGOs and donors, that are multifaceted in nature and that are relatively expensive to implement.

This is in marked contrast to the Donor Committee guidelines, which give priority to BDS interventions that are tightly focused, relatively short-term and capable of rapid cost recovery. As noted above, such projects tend to be appropriate primarily in addressing localized market failures, often in urban settings. In such cases, demand for BDS services may be relatively easily stimulated and short-term support effectively delivered to BDS providers.

However, there are important segments of the economy where the problem could be described not so much as localised market failure but rather as an inadequacy – in some cases, an almost total absence – of appropriate market structures of any sort. This is particularly true for the rural poor, who are often far removed from market opportunities, both geographically and culturally. For this group, more comprehensive and longer-term interventions are often required if effective and appropriate BDS markets are to be developed.

It is clear that interventions attempting to engage in building of such markets pose formidable challenges. As we have seen, these interventions tend to be relatively expensive and time consuming and to involve coordinated activities on several fronts.

BDS design and delivery principles derived from the projects profiled in this volume have concentrated on interventions focused on subsectors with growth potential. The analysis presented here suggests that such interventions can result in substantial outreach and impact. The pioneering nature of the BDS in these case studies points to the significant role of research and development. NGO-initiated and donor-subsidized BDS activities can result in the development of markets that did not previously exist, while also considering the need to balance developmental and business goals of BDS. Above all, the case studies underscore the need for flexible and responsive approaches. They establish that BDS 'good practice' is a relative concept, dependent on context. Finally, they describe how difficult it is to try to assess BDS performance across sectors and regions using common core indicators of success.

Note

1 Although the authors jointly wrote this chapter, the comparative analysis presented in it draws from discussions with and contributions by Anura Atapattu, Pamela Fehr, Steve Londner, Julie Redfern, Andrew Scott and Sandra Yu.